AF352234

PHOTOGRAPHY BETWEEN COVERS

PHOTOGRAPHY BETWEEN COVERS

INTERVIEWS WITH PHOTO-BOOKMAKERS

Thomas Dugan

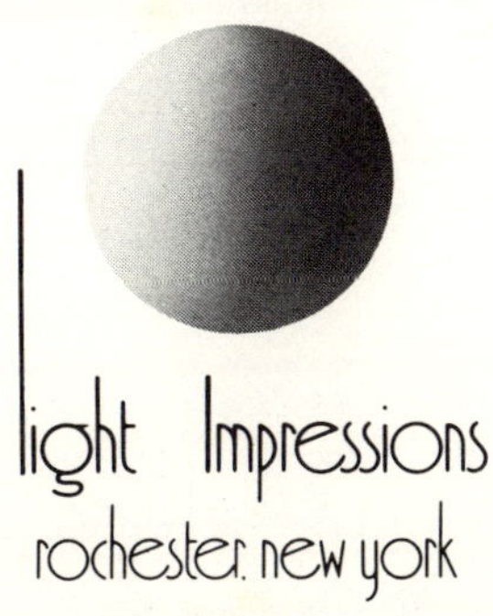

light Impressions

rochester, new york

Published by
LIGHT IMPRESSIONS CORPORATION
Box 3012, Rochester, New York 14614
Printed in the United States of America
Jacket design by Marcia Smith
First printing, 1979

Library of Congress Cataloging in Publication Data

Dugan, Thomas, 1938-
  Photography between covers.

  Includes bibliographical references.
  1. Photographers—Interviews. 2. Publishers
and publishing—Interviews. I. Title.
TR147.D83   770'.92'2   79-9260
ISBN 0-87992-012-2

Table of Contents

Introduction

These interviews are a direct result of my passion for and interest in the photographic picture book. As an artist I believe that the book is the viable form for the presentation of work. Lee Friedlander tersely summed it up in a conversation with Nathan Lyons: "I do books because it's a nice way to look at my pictures." A simple, albeit profound statement.

A book is tactile; it can be viewed again and again, under any number of conditions, in all states of mind and mood. Compared to original prints, books are inexpensive, durable, portable, available, and easy to store. Many artists work naturally in a sequential fashion, so the book presents itself as a ready solution for the dissemination of work. The printing process lends itself admirably to the reproduction of the photograph. In fact, photographs are sometimes noticeably improved via the printing process. "If your prints are just fair," states George Tice, "then reproduction can be to your advantage. For instance, with Brassai, you look at his monograph (**Brassai**. New York: The Museum of Modern Art, 1968), which is printed in gravure and they're clean; you look at his prints and they are crassy by comparison. They're ferrotyped glossy, they need spotting. Same with Cartier-Bresson; his prints come off better in reproduction."

Once published, a book, generally, is an archive in multiple of an artist's work. More and more artists are being challenged by the inherent possibilities of the book. Keith Smith, a maker of unique books, is obsessed with the urge to experiment with ways to exploit the book to its limits. "A book is more than the sum of its parts," he says, "that's the most important thing in a book."

In its brief history, the photographic picture book has not been consistently exploited in that sense on too many occasions. Beginning with the first book illustrated from photographs, Charles Philipon's **Paris et ses environs reproduits par le Daguerreotype,** (Paris: Aubert & Cie, 1840) which was not conceptual, but more a random collection of images, we have to wait a number of years before seminal works begin to appear in little clusters of activity. Mostly, however, books were albums of photographs on a single theme, rather than a concept dealt with in a complex, sequential, sophisticated fashion. Photographers such as Francis Frith, Maxime Du Camp, Henri Le Secq, Roger Fenton, Desire Charnay, John Thomson, Peter Henry Emerson, Thomas Annan, Carleton E. Watkins, Alvin Langdon Coburn, Arnold Genthe, Edward S. Curtis, and E.O. Hoppe presented their work in a variety of ways, but mostly in a conventional linear form.

In 1938, with the publication of Walker Evans' **American Photographs** (New York: The Museum of Modern Art, 1938), the photographic picture book came of age. Over the years a whole range of people approached the picture book as an outlet for work, and the activity, in recent history, has intensified. Many artists—for example: Ralph Gibson, Lee Friedlander, George Tice, Eikoh Hosoe, Keith Smith, and Joan Lyons are now committed to the picture book as the primary medium for their work. More seminal works have appeared in the last 40 years than collectively in the 100 years preceding **American Photographs.** Robert Frank's **The Americans,** Ralph

Gibson's trilogy, Syl Labrot's **Pleasure Beach**, Nathan Lyons' **Notations in Passing,** Lee Friedlander's **Self Portrait** and **American Monuments,** and Gaylord Herron's **Vagabond.** The bibliography is a lengthy, but impressive one.

Whenever I'm deeply moved by a book I have an urge to sit down with its creator and discuss the evolution of the concept. That, in essence, is why this series of interviews happened. I've talked to some of the artists who were available, but there are many I hope to interview, at some juncture, in the forseeable future. For certain: Robert Frank, John Szarkowski, Lee Friedlander, Ed Ruscha, Robert Delford Brown, Michael Snow, and Kishin Shinoyama. Additionally I intend to conduct a second interview with certain artists from the first series. Several have completed a book or books since the initial interview. Keith Smith, as an exceptional case, has produced twenty unique and two offset multiple books in two years. We are experiencing one of the most prolific periods in the history of the photographic picture book.

Photography Between Covers
is dedicated to:

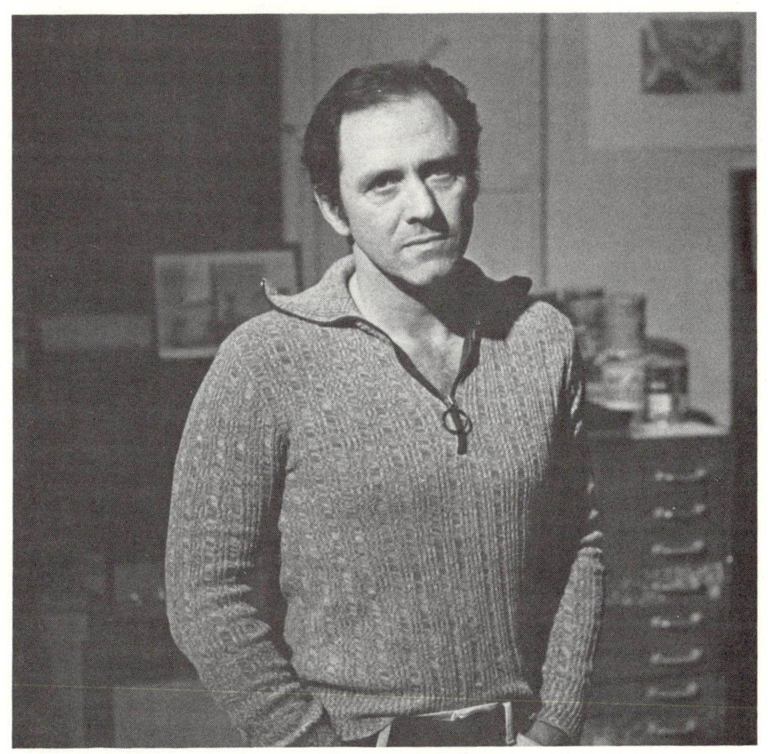

Syl Labrot
1929–1977

''As the history of photography begins
to cement itself publicly, my impulse
is to flee.''

Syl Labrot
November 12, 1975
Forward to **Pleasure Beach**

Syl Labrot

Interview: What got you into writing?

Syl Labrot: I'd written articles, but I'd never attempted anything creative, so to speak, but I have written a lot, written a lot of letters. I've written articles for the Encyclopedia of Photography. I've decided a lot of things I wanted to say about photography, in a round about way, the writing is about photography, what it is and how it relates to me and the whole idea of making up a place with all these pictures, constructing a scenario of a place, like **Pleasure Beach** is a whole idea about photography, of what the stuff is, what film is, and what life is in relation to film. That's sort of philosophical and thrills me. I'd say once the writing got going, the photography stylistically started coming together, but stylistically, it's a print maker's way with pictures, with the writing making it a book. That's really what I want to continue doing. I enjoy writing very much, and I think that's what I have to develop better now. The actual quality of the pictures doesn't seem as important to me as the way in which they're presented, the context in which they're presented, and that context is formed by the writing. So take the **Wisconsin Death Trip.** Michael Lesy sets those pictures up in a certain way. So you see them in a certain way. The writing about what those pictures are, makes those pictures mean something; whether they are, or not, is another question. I think a good picture is a good picture, and it's always a great thing to have. It's not so important, to me, to have bells ringing, picture after picture, as it is to adjust their context to the writing. In fact, in the last part, The Archeological Way, the pictures get pretty shitty at times. That's not really good camera work, but it still seems to work. That section was quite experimental. I had never done anything quite that casually. I've always had much more control, and the fact that I feel that I got away with it, and it works, that's very gratifying and liberating. I think the stronger the writing gets, the more that liberation works visually, for me. Of course, I don't want to get into being a professional writer either, which is another thing, because then you have to do a whole other type of writing. My whole bit as a writer is that I'm really a photographer, and as a photographer, I'm really a writer.

Syl Labrot was the first person with whom I discussed the concept of this book. It was February, 1974, at a point when I was somewhat unsure of its viability. Syl strongly urged me to do it. He thought it a very worthwhile and exciting project to undertake. I remember sitting with him, drinking wine, outlining the series of interviews I intended to do and, in turn, listening while Syl discussed his plans for **Pleasure Beach,** which was then at an early stage of development.

Pleasure Beach was published in January, 1976. He was beaming as he handed me a copy. I was staggered. I had seen individual pages from it as it was printed, but I was not prepared for the impact the book had on me. Very simply, it was beautiful. The most imposing presence a book ever had for me. I couldn't wait to get home, to be alone with it. For weeks thereafter I carried it around with me, showing it to any of my friends and acquaintances I could corner. Ritualistically, from time to time, I take the book and pore over it again, feasting my eyes, touching it, a total sensual experience.

On March 29, 1976, I interviewed Syl in his loft in New York City. He was surprisingly nervous, asking if he could have time to think before responding to each question. Naturally I agreed, and smiled at his stage fright. Always before he spoke with such ease, so articulately, eagerly, thoroughly enjoying discussions on a variety of topics. Once we began, he noticeably relaxed, his bout with stage fright over. Midway through, Barbara Wilson Labrot called us, and we had a wonderful, leisurely dinner, not returning to the interview until we finished what was left of a bottle of fine French red wine. It appears much as it was tape recorded.

Syl Labrot was a gentle, considerate, profoundly serious artist of the first rank. With the achievement of **Pleasure Beach** behind him, I believe Syl would have continued, indeed had one planned, working on books based, as **Pleasure Beach** is, on fantasy and autobiography. Before he could involve himself in such a commitment, he became ill, and learned he had terminal cancer. Syl Labrot passed away in July, 1977.

Born: New Orleans, Louisiana. November 12, 1929.
Attended: University of Colorado, Boulder, Colorado. 1947-51.
Books:
> **Under the Sun.** with Nathan Lyons and Walter Chappell. George Braziller, Inc. New York, 1960.
> **Pleasure Beach.** Eclipse (privately published). New York, 1976.

Tom Dugan: How did you get involved in photography?
Syl Labrot: I was at the University of Colorado, studying Political Science, in my junior year. I had been going to school steadily, through summer school, and I was really sick of it. I got sent a camera for Christmas, a Brownie Hawkeye, a cheap camera, read the manual through, started taking pictures, got very interested, and started doing nothing else for the next three, four, five, six weeks. I quickly traded in that camera on a Kodak Tourist, a 2¼ x 3¼ roll film camera, quite a nice camera, took really good pictures, good sharp lens. Within a month I had a darkroom set up in a closet, where I would asphyxiate myself with fixer. Every night I'd develop pictures that I'd shot that day, and my school work started going totally to hell. I dropped out of that semester and spent the whole quarter photographing. My school work was already a loss, and I figured if I dropped out I would not get F's on my record. I just thought of almost nothing else, got involved in photographing every day, developing the pictures, and printing them at night. I'd shoot about two rolls a day, and print them, small contacts, or 4 x 5's, at most. There was a friendly druggist selling me the camera equipment, who was a member of the Boulder Camera Club, his name was Jones. They had quite a good camera club, a few museum people, university people, and thought themselves quite aesthetic in their attitutde about photography. He got me into that, and there were weekly print competitions. I started making mounted prints, pictorial scenes of trees, with pathways. How far do you want me to trace this?
TD: To where you got involved seriously.
SL: Well, I considered myself seriously involved almost from the very beginning. I read a great deal about it, drowned myself in it, that's my habit with things I get interested in. I just dive in and bury myself, get everything I can and surround myself with all the information I can get. Within a month I considered myself an expert, fully professional. I started shooting color, developing my own Ansco color in this same

closet. I bought a Speed Graphic in about six months. At this time I was also taking a New York Institute of Photography correspondence course, and reading Ansel Adams' books on technique. I started shooting, very carefully, a little bit of 4 x 5 color, with the idea of selling to the freelance market, developing it myself, this was Ektachrome, E-1 in those days. After about nine months, I'd sold my first picture; the second picture I sold I got $500 for; a billboard for Atlantic Gas, which was used up and down the East Coast. It wasn't a particularly good picture, but fit their layout and their style. So I considered myself, at the end of a year, a total success, a real hotshot. From there, it was slower, but I stayed in the freelance field, and did as much local work as I could. My school career was staggering to a halt, by this time; I never did graduate. I lacked two hours of freshman sociology for graduation, and supposedly was going to take that by correspondence, at some point. Every now and then I have a nightmare about not having taken it. I always told my children, of course, that I graduated, up until they were old enough to realize that I was the head of the house. I continued my involvement with the camera club, and was President for the next year. The professional work continued; I didn't have that much luck in sales, but I had a fair amount of sales, plus I did local work such as weddings and architecture work. I worked for several architects in Boulder; there's a lot of good architecture in Boulder, a lot of young architects. I did a lot of work for Empire Magazine, the Sunday roto for the *Denver Post*, which was published independently and ran four-color covers and four-color inside of sometimes incredibly bad quality. But the art director liked me and used a lot of my stuff. The pay wasn't too good, but it was very steady and very good support. At about that time I got interested in creative photography, Weston, and started doing some Weston-like photographs, challenging the local camera club with these types of pictures of textured surfaces, rather than three dimensional pictorial scenes, which they were very much into still, and created great aesthetic debates. I was considered the young upstart. But they were a good club, very intelligent people, and once a week there would be at least twelve or fifteen prints that people had done during the week to discuss. So, it was quite an active situation.

TD: Do you think Weston was the one who got you moving in the creative field?

SL: Weston seemed like the great purist. I was, of course, taking in all the Pop Photo scene, the Pop Photo magazine articles. These people were all magazine photographers, or fashion photographers, in New York, and were glamour figures in the field. Weston was never mentioned; you'd never see anything about him, and yet when I found out that somebody had worked all their lives seriously in photography, as a creative media, with very little apparent public response, and developed a whole body of work, in the same way that a painter would, say Cezanne, it was extremely impressive as an idea, a very radical idea. Everything that I was getting was all about how this guy was doing these flashy pictures, and somebody else was doing those flashy pictures, and how hot everybody was about the new contacts. Here was this seemingly futile, feeble old man going on making these prints, quite in isolation, it seemed. I later found out that there was support. There was a museum community, even at that time, the new halls, that were aware of him, and did support him. Yeah, as a model, as an idealist, as an example, he seemed like the equivalent of Frank Lloyd Wright, a person who took his own direction, and took a stance.

TD: At what point did you decide that you would be an artist rather than a commercial photographer?

SL: I was very moved by the model of Weston, and gradually became aware that

Weston wasn't alone. He wasn't the only person who had taken that position. He was perhaps the most extreme, the purist of the group, but it wasn't quite that black and white a situation. I had been working in color pretty much all along, commercially, because there was much more money in color. You have to remember, this wasn't too long after World War II, the middle to late 50s, and there wasn't the stockpile of color pictures that there are today. The service had taken all the color film during the war; it wasn't invented that much before the war. It was still possible to shoot stock pictures of the Grand Canyon, and sell them, which you couldn't do today because there must be 30,000 pictures from every spot of the Grand Canyon. I moved into that market, which was really a stereotyped, hack market, but still I was doing color. I started shooting "creative color pictures," because in driving around shooting things, I'd often see things, and started fooling around, in color, with a smaller camera, primarily because of the expense. But occasionally I'd take a larger 4 x 5. The Denver Post, my friendly editor there, ran a few in a gallery section. They had never done color. It seemed I might have possibilities, in color, particularly. It seemed very wide open to new ideas and new developments. It did take a different position in that. I started doing dye transfer prints. About three or four years had gone by, I had a friend in Colorado named Reilly, who ran a place called "Color by Reilly," whose one giant account was Samsonite Luggage. He made about $15,000,-$20,000 a year making dye transfers for Samsonite. That was about all he did, as far as I could tell. He worked one month a year, the life of Reilly. He was a very friendly person. I showed my color transparencies, and talked to him about the possibility of making dye transfers. He said he didn't want to do it, but would show me how. He said, "Write down everything I say exactly, and do it exactly my way, and don't ask me why." He told me the filters, developing times, the whole thing, how to make separations, and said, "OK, go make your separations and bring them back." I followed exactly what he was doing without any real understanding of the principles involved, but he did not want to give me lectures in color theory, didn't have time. I made a whole bunch of separations and he looked at them, and said, "Fine, now we'll go ahead and make dye transfer prints." He made the first one for me up at his place, and it came out really beautiful. There was something about the way I was shooting things, the abstract way of shooting color. I hit upon something at a rather early point, I think. The color on the surface of the paper of a print has a great deal to do with what your spatial sense is in the picture, and once the subject was taken out of context, and more abstract, the nature of color, in color photography, would look different, because it would look almost flat on the paper. It's very much the same idea as the cubist painters, or modern art in general, was developing, the abstract expressionist art, in New York, at the time, all of which I was aware of, being an avid reader, and having a pretty good antenna for picking up what's available in the field. He liked this print very much; I liked it, too, and started making prints over the next several years, on my own, following his method of separations. I had about ten prints done and showed them to a guy in Denver, an art director, in charge of arranging exhibitions at a town mall, in the Mile High Center. He said, "Let's have an exhibition of these," and I said, "There're only ten." He said, "It doesn't matter, we'll still put them up." So, I had an exhibition in Denver, just on the basis of these, and it got pretty well noticed and I sold several prints for about $75 each. I went back East, stopped in Rochester, and went to Eastman House. Minor White was there at the time. He looked at them, liked them, gave me comments, showed me what he didn't like about some, what he did like about others. We had dinner. He was very encouraging, very friendly. Nothing happened, though. He said to keep working, this is just the start. About a year later, I had done about twenty prints, and showed them once again, this time to Beaumont Newhall, Nathan (Lyons) had just started at Eastman House as curator, and also Walter Chappell had just started. They were in their first year there. They did not have much power in the situation; Beaumont was the one who called the shots. Nathan and Walter were both very excited about them, and pushed them on Beaumont, and they gave me a show. And so, I had a one-man show at Eastman House. This was fairly early in my career; I was about 25 or 26.

TD: Where were you living during this time?

SL: I was living in Colorado. I was heavily into my commercial career by now, which was moving along at a pretty good rate. Primarily I was making a lot of money in calendar pictures, I would do red-shirt fishermen in trout streams with fish that I froze the day before into a leaping position, with the mouth wide open. I'd freeze them with a coat hanger stuck up their ass, and then anchor the coat hanger under a rock in the stream, so they were three-quarters out of the water, leaping in this wild motion. They'd quiver a little bit from the motion of the stream, so it would blur slightly. I'd use a self timer on the view camera and I would be the fisherman also, red shirt, waders, with flies on the side of the hat. The rod would be set up so that the line went into the water, weighted by a rock about a foot away from the fish. I'd start the camera going, run back and pick up the rod, bend it so it looked like there was great tension on it, like I was playing the fish. There would be this fish quivering on the coat hanger. The whole thing would come out pretty nice, most of the time. Every now and then a real fisherman would round the stream, working, and he'd see the sight of this giant fish leaping out of the water. It just blew their minds. They didn't know what to think, because if a fisherman hasn't caught anything all day fishing those streams and sees a big trout, he wants that trout. It was incredible. I'd carry the fish around in the station wagon with dry ice to try to keep it fresh, and sometimes, after shooting several locations, the fish would be so rotten, limp and falling apart, really a mess. The other big seller I did was pheasant hunting, where the pheasant was hung by nylon threads from a tree limb. It was a stuffed pheasant that I bought at a taxidermy store. The bird would be hanging there from a tree limb, and the tree limb would be either out of sight of the picture, or there would be enough blur on the nylon fishing wire holding it that it wouldn't show up. I would be the hunter posed, gun upraised, firing away at this bird, who'd also be blurred a little from the breeze. Those sold very well. I used to get $300 - $500 a piece for them from calendar companies. Nobody else was doing really action shots; everybody else was doing just the red-shirt fisherman fishing in the trout stream, no fish, or the hunter with his dog. But me, I had fish and birds, I sort of had a corner on this market. There were a couple of other photographers in Florida doing this kind of thing, but they used live fish, and would set it up, release the fish, and try to get them to break in the water. They were much better pictures frankly, much more authentic looking.

TD: They were the Cartier-Bressons of the calendar business, right?

SL: That's right. They were my main competition, and were better than me, but I wasn't going to go to that much trouble. I was living in Colorado, still trying to complete my freshman sociology correspondence course.

TD: How did you get out of the calendar business? I know at some point that you got into fine art.

SL: Well, both sides developed along the way. I had an agent in New York, and one in Chicago, and they didn't know anything about my show at Eastman House, and the people at Eastman House didn't know anything about my calendar pictures, so I had this double life going on.

TD: And you got into painting and gave up photography?

SL: No, that was later. I came to New York. I moved from Colorado to the East Coast, and settled in Connecticut, to try to unify the split. My idea, at the time, was to do color work that was more creative, to use what I was doing artistically, in a commercial way. Ernst Haas had done some color essays in *Life* magazine that were quite exciting, and it appeared that there were going to be some openings for more creative photography in the commercial magazines. My idea was to try to create a new image based on the action I was getting, to try to see if my reputation in the fine arts would blend over into the commercial field. I went around to the New York people, *Fortune* magazine, and Wolf, the art director for *Harper's,* I think at the time, and different people, that people suggested, who had more creative outlooks. In general, they liked my dye-transfer prints a lot, but really couldn't figure out any way to fit them in. I had a number of near-ideas that got dropped as projects. I got a few jobs. I got a job from *Fortune* (magazine) to do a study of concrete, to take that concept and to go with it. I got some pictures that were pretty good, and got paid for it. The art director, Leo Leone, was encouraging, and liked the whole idea, but it just never seemed to quite work out or materialize into any successful venture that ran. I think, in looking back on it, that it wasn't destined to. I don't know of anybody who has ever been able to blend these two things that well. And the magazine field was, of course, not expanding. It was beginning to shrink a little at that point, so, it wasn't the ideal time. I did get some play. Pop Photo ran some of my things. But again, the two audiences seemed very different. The serious photography museum audience, just beginning to develop, and the Pop Photo commercial audience, just didn't know each other. A lot of people hadn't even heard of Weston. A lot of people who should know better were totally unaware of Weston, not to mention people like Minor (White), who was fairly well known within the circle of serious photography, but not outside. I also had some work shown at the Modern (Museum of Art) around this time, 1959. Steichen was very flattering and liked the work a lot. He bought four prints, and allowed me to pick them out. He said, "You know much more about what you're doing than I know." I think at that moment I was a young pet at the Modern. Wait, let me tell you a good story. The first pictures I had shown at the Modern, they showed recent acquisitions or accessions. And these four pictures that Steichen had bought were in the show. One of them was hung upside down, another one had been cropped and bled, and, actually, a little bit of the picture had been cut off in the process, and was very important compositionally to the whole picture. I went to the opening. I was 26 or 27 years old, and it was like my big arrival. I had made it to the big time. New York City, the Museum of Modern Art, here I am. So, I go in there and see my prints, a disaster. Not only that, there was a whole bunch of color hung together, some of Eliot Elisofon, and all kinds of stuff that was really horrible, I thought, and my stuff was smashed right in amongst all this, upside down, bled, and I was just furious. I saw Steichen at the opening. He said, "Well, young man, how do you like having your work on the walls of the Museum of Modern Art?" And I said, "Well, it's terrible, one of them is upside down, another one is cropped incorrectly, it's really horrible" And he said, "Well, we can always take them down, you know." I said, "Please, I wish you would, I can't stand the way it is." And so I assumed they would be taken down. He said, "Well, all right," sort of gruffly, offended. I went in a week later to check. They were still up, still upside down. I was insane with anger, this whole thing was working up into a fit anyway. I went upstairs and demanded that they take them down, or else I'd take them down. What's the point of doing a picture if they're going to hang it upside down? So, they said they'd take them down, but they'd leave blanks on the walls. I said, "Blanks on the walls, what difference does that make? My picture's upside down." And so they said, "OK, OK." They took them down, and word got out in the photo community about my situation. Minor asked if I wanted to write a piece in *Aperture* about the shoddy treatment and the whole incident. And I said "No." I didn't want publicity from this situation. In retrospect, I wish I had. In fact, in retrospect, the thing to have done would have been to snatch them off the wall at the opening, and dive into the water at the pool, or something like that, and have my picture all over the *Daily News*. That would be the way to do things. But it's very idealistic, and I didn't realize what an opportunity I'd missed. So, the whole thing went very quietly. But, about six months later, they had a show called " A Sense of Abstraction," which was a major, large downstairs show, and dealt with the movement of abstract photography that had been going on during the fifties. It was a very important show for all of us involved in doing that kind of work. I half expected not to be shown at all, because of the incident, but, in fact, I was treated extremely nicely, and had four color prints in the show, plus five black and whites. I had practically a room to myself. I had more pictures in the show than anybody else, which was really disproportionate, because my role in the whole thing wasn't that big. But they really liked my attitude about the pictures. They felt here's somebody who really believes in what he does.

TD: A real artist.

SL: A real artist, right. And they gave me a beautiful hang, a really good spot, really good wall space. They came up to me at the opening, Steichen, and a girl who was in charge of designing shows at the time, and said, "Are you satisfied this time?" I said, "Yes." I was delighted, so we were old friends. Also they started having print sales at the Modern, and there was a certain black and white print that they'd used in that show that they'd blown up and made a huge entry piece out of, which in the small, fine-print version they sold nine of at the Modern print sale, and that was by far more than any other print they sold. They sold, I think, four Atget's and one or two of other things. I was, you might say, the new rising star of the field. The funny thing was, that show was very premature. Again, there was not the artistic interest, or the audience for the show. The Family of Man, a couple of years before, had been a great success, both as box office and as a book; the paperback book sold tons. That was really where the audience was at, at that period.

TD: Who was in "A Sense of Abstraction?"

SL: Well, just about everybody; it traced the history of abstract photography, Man Ray, you might think of those early people on up to Minor. There was a great deal that was miscellaneous. There was a guy who did smell photographs; I can't think of his name, traced the odor, smells, he related odors to film. A lot of experimental abstract, micro photography, a little bit of everything. Walter Chappell and Nathan Lyons were in it, certainly Weston, Adams, everybody that had done an abstract photograph, I guess. It was quite a beautiful show, but it didn't go anywhere at all. There was very little critical response to it. The New York art critics didn't notice it. Aaron Siskind certainly was a large part of the show, Callahan. But there was no feedback. I never heard a thing from anybody about the show, almost nothing got reproduced from it. *The (N.Y.) Times* did reproduce a couple of my things from the show, but there wasn't a good review. There was no Hilton Kramer or anything like that. I think it just confused everybody, because photography was supposed to be this great media of documentation, and here's this show that's just screwing up your mind; are these really photos? That's what most people felt, is this right for photography? So, in a round about way, that marked the end of that period in photography, I think, rather than the beginning. We all hoped that it would be the beginning of the development for photography in that sense. It was really the end, I think, the end of that sewerage, you might say; there wasn't another surge for serious creative photography for another five or six years. New people started coming along, like Jerry Uelsman, and then the thing picked up, and it did take off, but this time it didn't. It was stillborn.

TD: Did Under the Sun **come out of this?**

SL: Yeah, that was done about a year later. Walter Chappell and Nathan Lyons and I worked, collaborating, on a book. In one sense, **Under the Sun** was three photographers trying to get their work published. In another sense, it was a book of the type of photography that wasn't being published at all. That style of photography, in book form, really had not been published. We set out with a determination to somehow get this done. We found a man named J.J. Augustine, a printer with a plant in Germany, doing letter press. George Wittenborn put us on to him. He was willing and interested in printing the book and put us in touch with George Braziller, the publisher, who, in the end, published the book. We were paid for our work in books. Braziller did very little to promote the book, as far as I can tell, and remaindered it within about a year at Marlboro. It sold out, in its remaindered state, pretty quickly, but commercially was not a success. The books I was given, we each got 500 books out of the 5,000 production, all burned up. I had a house fire that totally gutted my house. Walter's books all burned up; he had a house fire that totally gutted his house, and Nathan sold his through the George Eastman House, and to workshop students.

TD: And Nathan got rich.

SL: And Nathan's the only one who made out. Walter and I got insurance money for them, which was really not so bad. Also there were about 1,000 unbound sheets in Germany, which *Aperture* bound and reissued in paperback, two or three years ago, and it sold pretty well.

TD: Did you get money out of that?

SL: Yeah, we each got a little bit of royalty. We had an exhibition also at the Poindexter Gallery. Mrs. Poindexter lived in Connecticut, down the road from me, and she had a pretty good gallery in New York that had originally been the Egan Gallery, and one of the first places that De Kooning, Kline and all those people were shown. And so, she had said, "Well Syl, I don't know about photography, is it art, or isn't it?" I said, "Well look, why don't you just let us have a show at the end of the season. You're going to close the middle of May, close the middle of June instead." And so she said, "Well, OK, since you live down the road." It was about like that. She had very little enthusiasm for the whole thing. But we put on as good a show as we could. I think it was a well hung show at one of the better galleries in New York. Photography, at that time, was not shown in art galleries, hardly ever. And for us to have a show in a New York art gallery was a breakthrough. Again, premature, I've since talked to people that saw that show and I'd say, "Well, what did you think of it?" And they'd say, "Well, we didn't know what to think of it, nobody knew where it came from, and what it was, or who it was; it just appeared, then disappeared, and that was it." So, of course, we had all our friends and relatives there, and some of the art community showed up to look at a De Kooning drape that had been used in *Sweet Bird of Youth* (Tennessee Williams) and there was quite a bit of haggling and talking about how much that ought to bring. They hardly glanced at the photography. But we had a big opening, liquor, the whole works, big deal. And that came and went, quite as the show at the Modern had come and gone. Nathan sold a couple of prints, and the rest of us didn't sell anything. In my own life, about this time, several things were happening. I was still getting income from my file pictures, but hadn't been doing any new photography for my calendar career. That income continued for awhile, because I, by this time, had about 6,000 transparencies with agents, one in Chicago, one in New York, and some I'd sell directly. I'd get some income, but over the years, it gradually was declining. My mother was very ill at this time, dying of cancer; she died in New York at the Drake Hotel. She was buried in Brooklyn, and my father, during the funeral, said, "Now you know exactly what to do if I should die. You do exactly the way I've done with your mother." And two weeks later he died, of undertermined causes really. He had an intestinal problem, blockage, lesion of the intestines, but that wasn't what killed him. He was operated on quite successfully; it's not that serious a thing. They just snip out that part, but his fever shot up after the operation. He really had very little desire to live; he'd been very close to my mother, and he'd been nursing her for the last year and a half. It must have been really a very strange situation for him. He came up to Connecticut and stayed with me during those two weeks, but I had young kids and young kids freaked him. He didn't like that so much, so he stayed at a place called the Halling Manor Inn down the road. He had hired a chauffeur and limousine from New York, and the chauffeur was deaf, a very odd quiet man. So, here was my father, his nerves really in a bad state, visiting me during the daytime; he'd take his meals with my wife and me, then go back with this deaf chauffeur to his room. One night, he got sick, was taken to the hospital, and died. About six months later, my house burned totally. I lost a lot of color prints. I'd been doing carbro as well as dye transfer. Carbro was more permanent, and my idea was to sell them as art pieces. I'd been interested in art generally, had gotten pretty well self-educated in art, especially since coming back east, and it seemed like a perfect time for a break, a change in my life, if I was going to make certain changes. I decided I would try painting. My financial situation was eased because my parents had been fairly wealthy, and I inherited some money. It seemed like the perfect time, if I was ever going to try painting; this was as though fate had set things that way. I started painting, self-taught primarily, took drawing classes at the Silver Mine Guild in New Canaan, and began working, first doing abstract expressionist paintings, like everybody else, seeing how nervy I could slush the paint around. Within a year, I started doing realistic painting, much more related to my color photography than to anything else, and I began developing a style of dry acrylic, not very painterly, realism. This was before photo realism had hit the scene, by the way, and it had a heavy abstract quality. There would be details and textures of very realistic looking things, a piece of pipe, or the edge of a building, but overall they were not logically realistic scenes. I really started just painting. I'd do a little photography, almost as a break, a relaxation, get in my car, drive around, take a few pictures, but both the lack of response in the art world, and the desire to try painting pretty much turned me off photography. Painting is slow and hard. I quickly found out that I wasn't going to do any great work in a couple of years, or in a year. Although, of course, as soon as you do a painting, you think it's great, at least for a few days. I did maybe a hundred or so fairly good-sized paintings that were quite worked over, and I began to have a little success. I had a painting hung in a show locally. One of the big events in New England is the Silver Mine annual painting show to which all New England people submit paintings. It used to be very good; I don't know how it is now. There's good prize money in it, and I got second prize, $500. It was really quite prestigious; a few years before, that would normally follow with a New York gallery offer, but things were changing, and it didn't work that way. I did get enough work together, started making the rounds in New York and had a one-man show at the Amel Gallery on Madison Avenue. This was 1965, the heyday of the New York gallery scene, and galleries were blooming everywhere. The night my show opened, there were forty other openings in New York, November, the fall, all that year; people like Louise Nevelson, Andy Warhol, Frank Stella had shows. That's how big the scene was at that time. I sold three paintings, and got reviewed in *Art News, Art*, and *The New York Times*. The reviews were mixed; they said I couldn't decide whether I wanted to be realistic or abstract. In general, the critical responses was still better than the photo scene at that point. I was encouraged, and planned for a show next year. The gallery closed the year after that; they didn't have any backers, and were trying to make it off the wall, so to speak. I was unable to get another gallery lined up for that fall, so I began showing regionally; Boston, Providence, different art festivals, and did pretty well. I wouldn't say I was an overwhelming success, but I got respect, and response. I think my work, in looking back, was pretty interesting. It was really a fish out of water though. There wasn't any other work like that going around. Painting works very much, I was to find, in a tradition of developing this from that; I just shot in from photography. Most of the time, the people didn't know what to do with what I was showing. I think there were a lot of really exciting ideas. I see some of the earlier things I did, amazingly daring, a daring that's based on naivete, to a large degree.

TD: Had you somehow thought that photography wasn't respectable, is that why you went into painting?

SL: It was probably a little of that, yeah. I'll tell you, I really found myself in a box in photography also. I had done thirty or forty prints I really liked, plus some others that weren't as good, and I tried for awhile to continue working in the same way, but I was very bored with it. I didn't find anything new to go to, from that work. I painted myself into a corner. I couldn't see continuing doing that; there wasn't enough variety to it, and there're certain flaws, aesthetically, even in abstract photography as an idea. In a way, you're showing something that's real, and yet, in a way, it's not real, so you're playing this double-edged game all the time, and it doesn't really seem to be the strength of the medium; it seems you have to twist it, and stretch it out of shape quite a bit to make it function in that way. I think I'd explored all the ways you could twist and tug it to get it to behave in that way. I found it unsatisfactory. In addition, there's this factor, aesthetically. Philosophically, I decided I wanted images to be more what they were, to not be something else. A lot of abstract photography had a sort of poetic life, based on the idea that there was another picture in it. For example, that rock really looked like the head of a Greek god, or the torso of a woman, or you know, the picture wasn't the picture of a rock anymore, it was a picture of,—"Can't you see the face in there?" This seemed to be totally a wrong direction, one that I never liked, that I never did in my own work, but it seemed that you always had to try to bring that off, in a sense.

TD: It's almost like you're presenting a puzzle, and somebody's either going to find a picture in there, or they're going to define what the abstract thing really is. Is it a piece of a building or is it a rock, or is it a chipped wall, or whatever the hell it is.

SL: You have this schizophrenia going on. And it didn't seem to me like the right direction. I still feel that very much. A lot of the poetic abstraction of that period, I find really revolting, because there's this two-sided thing. I just don't want to play that. If you want a face, photograph a face, draw one, make a face.

TD: So actually abstraction led you back to realism.

SL: Yeah. I always felt my own color abstraction was not really abstract. It was dealing with what happened between the object and the film. There is something that changes in there, things undergo a transformation, and it was that transformation that I was really interested in. You could always tell pretty much what they were, they didn't have faces in them, if I could possibly edit those out. In painting I started getting it to more illusionistic forms and I became interested in what pictures really were. This goes back to the color photography, a picture isn't the real thing, and yet it isn't not the real thing, it's something else. I was involved in illusion in painting, because obviously a painting's flat, but yet you can believe literally that you see three dimensions, so I began working with a lot of illusions. I did a show at the Bridgeport Museum called, Vision and Reality, a large, extended show, which they put up a fair amount of money for. It involved both painting and photography, and a text that I wrote, throughout the show. It grew from quotations, poetry and philosophical thoughts on the nature of reality, and poetic reality. As a museum, they felt obligated to do some sort of educational show; as an artist, I had very little interest in that, but said, "OK, I can work with that idea." The show was really nice, a lot of people saw it, but mostly kids who came to see the helicopter, that was also on exhibit. The only thing wrong with it was that it was in Bridgeport. There wasn't any real audience there. It was another misfire in my career, but really enjoyable to do, a great deal of effort though. By this time, I was beginning to get back into photography. I used some new photographs in that show, and started getting back into photography, at least mentally, having a lot of interesting ideas of what pictures were, what illusion was, and what picture making was. I started doing graphics, based on photographic techniques, and on illusionary forms; I'd developed primary illusion forms, with the idea that you could build up a series of primary forms that would be building blocks. This is only on a theoretical level, not a factual one, but that all reality was nuclear illusionary forms and you could develop a vocabulary of these, and then shuffle them around, because they would all be turned into film, and develop a whole graphic art based on this. Well, in fact, I developed about eight or ten of these model forms, and then the idea didn't seem all that great. It's still a nice idea, not realistic, but I plan to do something with it, in book form, in some way. It's a little bit of a mad scientist idea, and in that sense, I think it still has potential.

TD: That you may create a monster?

SL: Yeah, right.

TD: So then you left painting, got back into photography?

SL: Well, not quite that directly. These prints were, again, neither fish nor fowl; no one knew what to make of them either. But I did get some play from galleries in New York and started selling prints. They actually had one commercial fling. I did a series of prints by offset, with a little bit of silk screening added, so they'd be art, for a place called Circle Gallery, uptown, which still has prints all around the place. And we ran a giant edition of 500, in five variations, and I got paid something like $10 a print. It was a really nice deal commercially; I felt like I beat the system for once. I was quite happy about that. These prints attracted Nathan's (Lyons) attention who, by now, was running the Visual Studies Workshop. They lost a teacher, Keith Smith moved to Chicago. Nathan called on short notice, and asked if I'd be interested in teaching print making. Well, I was a long way from being a photography print maker, but I said, "Sure." It was fairly good pay, and an assistant professorship, and I'd been so long out of the job market that I really doubted my own professionalism, in a sense. My kids would say, "Well, what do you do, Dad?" So, I took it with a fear that I would be inadequate. I went up with the idea that we would all start working on the offset press, because I'd developed quite a bit of knowledge about film techniques for offset. I was very much into Kodalith as a means of image making, although not primarily, yet in a photographic way. I expected, since this was a graduate program, to run into all these brilliant young kids, mostly a little stoned, a little high, but brilliant. Instead I just found that everybody was stoned and high, but not brilliant. And instead of being challenged by this brilliant group, the real job was to get anybody to do anything. I scratched around and realized what would get people to work, since they weren't up to doing anything on the scale of offset, was to start them in silk screen, and I'd be starting myself in silk screen, because I'd never done any. I quickly started trying to get my act together and began working in photographic images, since they were all there with photography in mind, on certain ideas that interested me, but related to the job also. I found a lot of stimulation and was very interested in what had happened in the photography field, since I had been, more or less, out of it. In the first place, there was this army of students, while not the hardest workers, at this period, the late 60s, but very visually aware, and a great deal of change, taste-wise, in picture making and images. There was a lot of input coming from them. The first year was getting the program going, the second I started launching more ambitious programs of my own, such as the Synthetic Landscape portfolio, which combined earlier tone form ideas with the idea of inventing landscapes with film. You can see that this idea goes back to making your own world with all these little units that I was going to make. But instead of these little units, you have the whole film world to draw from, which converted into Kodalith is quite usable as units. I found also that my time in painting was standing me in good stead, my ability to use color by selection, rather than by recognition. In color photography, you photograph what your eye likes to see; in painting, you have to decide what your eye will like, which is a different end of the process. So, it isn't particularly easy to work with color as an output element when you're used to being a receptor of it only. But the period I put in painting had bridged this gap for me, and I'd gone through that color struggle in painting, from the muddy black palette to being able to use colors brilliantly, in a free way. So, I began getting into photography as film, not as great pictures, but the fact that it was a medium that images traveled in, that you could pluck them out of, that you could work them into, that you could change them, change their size, or multiply them, make 100 little ones of something, if you wanted. All these things were similar to graphic ideas that I'd been working on. It was, though, a switch into a whole world of imagery, instead of just forms and formal considerations.

TD: How long did you stay in Rochester?

SL: I was there three and a half years. Particularly, I liked the middle period. I got a good group of students going, and we did some really nice work. Toward the end, the process of teaching started becoming a little repetitious. I found it less exciting, and wanted to work on my book, and do some other things. I continued to teach summer sessions, partly because I liked teaching; it sharpens you. You have to get your ideas together, and in usable shape, so other people can make use of them. I don't like the routine of it, frankly. As long as I'm being drained and it's exciting, I like it; if it gets easy, it gets boring.

TD: Do you like the routine of working the way you're working now, doing your own work each day?

SL: Oh yeah, sure, that's the idea. There are problems always for most people; I do have some income from my family's rapidly dwindling fortune, what's left of it. I have some income, although I'm not rich, but it gives me a little leeway in these matters. I can do something like this book project that would be a little risky, time-wise, for somebody else, a book as complex and time consuming as **Pleasure Beach.**

TD; You spoke briefly of influences, Weston being an influence. Was there anybody else who influenced you? Any painters, or writers, or whomever?

SL: I can just innumerate them almost. When I first moved to New York, the whole abstract expressionist scene influenced me, but not very much. I really didn't like it very much, but it was a great power in New York, and for the first time, American artists were becoming the immortals of the art world. That impressed me very deeply; Weston was not an immortal in Europe. I did not, though, like abstract expressionism. It seemed to have the same elements that abstract photography had, see the face, see the figure, and so on. I was very interested in the art of the 20's and 30's more, the modern movement in Europe, Paul Klee, Picasso, certainly.

TD: How about Matisse, his use of color?

SL: Not so much. I've always had a little bit of a blind spot there. I'm aware that people, whose taste and opinion I respected, loved Matisse. I think it's the fuzzy line I don't like; he doesn't really paint sharp edges; I like clarity very much. I went through, more or less, everybody. I would be passionately interested in Duchamp for a week, then somebody else. I went to museums, and looked at a lot of work. I don't consider myself a great intellectual, but on the other hand, I consider myself fairly well-educated. Almost all of that education occurred after college, however, I was totally bored at college, and didn't read anything. When I was at college, art didn't mean anything; it meant something that sissies were engaged in. But when I became aware of art, and the fact that all kinds of subtle inflections were expressible through it, these things started working on me. When you start getting into somebody's work, it really does move you. You're aware that all you're doing is looking at a piece of paper, and you're getting all this stuff. So, I got interested in writing and read quite a bit. I studied existentialism at great length, read a great deal of Sartre, fought my way through Heidegger, Jaspers, all kinds of stuff like that. I sought out people who would discuss it with me, and nobody had any interest at all. I got interested in French avant-garde writing, such as Robbe-Grillet and Marguerite Durreau, and the idea of a novel as an experimental form. There was a book in a box where all the pages were loose, and you could shuffle them. I remember I bought that, and everybody thought that was really ridiculous. I used to read it; you could shuffle it around, and it worked fine.

TD: It made sense, no doubt.

SL: Oh yeah, each page was a little vignette, and all the vignettes were a little related. It didn't matter what order you took them in, whether the girl was raped first, or kissed by her lover first. Of course, it was all very lurid. There were killings, and rapes, or automobile accidents, going on all over the place; it was very exciting writing.

TD: You read a lot of fictiion at that point?

SL: Yeah, a fair amount, I'm not a great reader, but I read a fair amount. I tend to skim a little bit.

TD: I have difficulty skimming, but it's a very good technique. I was reading somewhere that people who were educated in Catholic schools, where you had to read the book from page 1 through to the last page, couldn't just skim; they'd feel guilty. I do have that problem, although I'm getting over it, but it's difficult.

SL: Yeah, Barbara's that way. Not only that, but it gets people mad at you, to read from the back of the book, to the front.

TD: I do that. When I look at a magazine, I always start from the back.

SL: People get very mad when you skim. They say, "How do you read a book? That's not the way it was meant to be read." In the first place you want to know if you're interested in reading it, so you have to dive in and pick up key vibes from it.

TD: Yeah, I buy books like that, I skim them and read sections, and if I like the style or some part, I buy it.

SL: Yeah, you get a feel for the style. Another thing I got into heavily was classical music. While I was painting, I used to listen to classical music all day. These are all things I don't do now. I haven't read lately; I don't listen to classical music lately.

TD: Why do you think that is?

SL: I don't know. Classical music doesn't seem to relate much to anything right now. I think it will again, but right now it doesn't seem to.

TD: Do you listen to music now?

SL: Anything, yeah.

TD: Rock?

SL: No. Every now and then a song is really ridiculous, and it turns me on. The most ridiculous disco tune is now what I like; I can't think of the name, I never can.

TD: Do you watch TV now?

SL: Oh, a little bit. It's not very interesting though. I watch Midnight Blue, and stuff like that.

TD: Midnight Blue, what's that?

SL: That's porno movies on cable TV. I don't like TV much, I don't like movies that much either. I go almost into a high bitch about a film not being done right, like Barry Lyndon. It was OK for a couple of hours, the third hour, I just couldn't take it anymore.

TD: Have you seen any of the Wertmuller movies?

SL: No, I haven't, I haven't seen any of them. Do you like them?

TD: Yes, I saw *Swept Away* and was very impressed with it. I saw it right after I was sick. It was a very interesting film. I very much wanted to look at something that was well-done and serious, and that was a really good way to get back into life after being sick. I was still depressed, feeling weak and frustrated, and seeing that movie started to get my mind back into shape.

Is there anything in your childhood that led you to the visual arts?

SL: I don't know. I was not considered to have any artistic talent as a child. My brother was considered to be the one who drew better. There are some rich events in my childhood that might have had some effect. I'm just beginning to be able to use them artistically. I had a maiden aunt, Aunt Sally, who lived in New Orleans all her life, where I was born. She had this beautiful mansion that took up almost a whole city block, and I used to visit her once a week and spend the night. The house was huge, and she had a butler named Murray and a chauffeur named Myles. We used to have tea, listen to the radio, and play cards. I was about 10 or 11. She was very well-educated, a very cultured woman; she lived in Paris a lot. She knew Gertrude Stein, had correspondence with her, and autographed books from her, all of which burned up in my house fire. She had bought paintings, was on the edge of Gertrude Stein's circle in France in the 20's. She was a very kind woman.

TD: She bought Cubist paintings?

SL: I think so. She supported a thing called the Arts and Crafts Club in New Orleans, a bunch of semi-pros, semi-amateurs. New Orleans has always had a history as an art community. There was a sculptor there named Ricky Alfares, whom she used to support, and who people still know about. He's well known locally. I'm not especially interested in those things at all; I was more interested in all the millions of license plates that were in the garage on the wall.

TD: That's a kind of original thing.

SL: Yeah, but that's also what a kid looks at. I traveled around a lot as a kid, I lived in Maryland a part of the year, my grandfather had a farm in Maryland that my father and mother would go to every summer; I learned to ride, they had horses. I spent some of my childhood in California, some of it in Louisiana. New Orleans, where I grew up, is quite a colorful place.

TD: Do you think maybe that's why you're interested in color, more than black and white?

SL: No, I think it was circumstances, the original stuff I told you about, how I got into it. I think color is more interesting, don't you?

TD: I do, until I see something done well in black and white. For example, Ernest Haas' books don't really do anything for me, but then I look at something in black and white like The Gypsies **by Koudelka, and I'm very impressed. I told you about Danny Lyons' Columbian Prostitutes. I felt that series didn't make it in color; in black and white it would be very strong.**

SL: I think I like the technology.

TD: You're print-oriented, too, which is different.

SL: Yeah, I think it's very important. In color you have to think print.

TD: I like color, but I don't think it works.

SL: No, it mostly doesn't; mostly it's a horror show.

TD: When you were a child, were you a part of the crowd, or were you more of a loner?

SL: I think I was about normal, certainly not very much part of the crowd ever, but I think I was fairly normal until I was about fifteen, and then something snapped; I still don't know what. I really got totally pissed off. I was sent away to a boarding school, from eighth grade on, in New Jersey, called Lawrenceville, a very good boys boarding school. The first year or two I was a big shot, vice president of this, and that, and captain of this, and that. I always liked athletics a lot, and at that age, in the lower grades, not being so big wasn't a disadvantage. If you can run fast, you can be the star football player among eighth graders. The school was broken up into sections, so that the middle period, from sophomore to junior, you spend in another group of dormitories called circle houses, and I was once again elected as the first year representative in the circle houses. Then something happened. There was an incident, I reported some kids for doing something, busting up furniture, or something, and I was not supported by the other council members, and was really made to look like an ass. I got really pissed off, and resigned. I quit, and wouldn't go to football practice, I wouldn't do anything. There were a couple of other guys that I got in with, that I liked, and, of course, they were the real bad asses. They were great guys, though, intelligent and bright. Our main project from then on was how to sneak off to New York, and how to get enough money together to do it. We got into doing all that, and from then on, I felt somewhat outlawed from the normal stream. Toward my senior year I had gotten myself into a really bad state, I had three or four friends and didn't mix with the others at all. It was a bad situation, I still don't know exactly what happened. I went to college, and for about the first few weeks, I participated with everybody, and felt like I was on a new track. I met this girl and started spending all my time with her, and eventually married her, and, once again, became a total loner. When you're nineteen years old, and married, you're really not in step with anybody. I still find people very difficult. I admit now that I need them, but I continually am a little paranoid, or angry because somebody said something this way or that, I feel slighted. I find big events like parties or openings very threatening, in a sense. In a way, everybody else does, too. Teaching helped me get over some of this, I think. Also, truthfully, I find younger people much more enjoyable than a lot of the people I grew up with. I don't know why, but I think there's more of an artistic consciousness now than there was. You know, being in the arts, you had really no encouragement, at least I didn't, among the people I knew. You were considered either gay, lazy, weak, one of those three.

TD: Or all of those.

SL: Or all of the above.

TD: I have a friend who doesn't understand quite what I'm doing, and keeps saying, "But you don't show me any of your work." And I say, "Well, you're not around. I'm always working on something and if you're around, I'll show it to you, but if you're not around, I won't."

SL: What you brought up brings to mind a short story by Thomas Mann called "Tonio Kruger." It's over-melodramatic by today's standards, but it's the way I used to think of myself in reflecting back on that type of question. In that story, this young boy is desperately in love with a young girl, and they're all dancing in a room, and he's on the outside of the glass, outside of these French doors, looking in at all the younger kids dancing. And he wants this girl really badly, but he's been snubbed, and he knows he can never have her, and at that moment he knows that he forever is on the outside of that party, and that's the moment in the story when he realizes that he's an artist.

TD: I'll have to read that.

SL: It's very beautiful.

TD: I don't need any reinforcement though.

SL: No, in a way, I think today we're trying to get rid of some of that bullshit, and that kind of myth is not what you need right now.

TD: But everybody talks about that in the interviews. I always ask that question about being an artist, and the feeling that you see things differently. The average person grows up and goes into industry. Everybody talks about that, the feeling of being outside of that, and realizing it's necessary to be outside, but feeling uncomfortable that you are outside.

SL: It's a very complicated subject. I'm not sure it's that desirable. I'm not sure it's even necessary in the long run. In a different society, I think, the artist could be much more functional and not have this split scene.

TD: Well, the technological society, I suppose, is difficult because you're not providing anything useful. Do events in your personal life affect your work?

SL: Yeah, very much, for a long time it was way below the surface. Other people would point out how after my parents' death, I did a whole series of black and white tree pictures that were very somber, very sad, and a friend felt they were a litany for my parents' death. And I think that was true, although I'm not sure. But lately, in the last few years, I've come to feed upon my life very much in a conscious, active way, so that it isn't even a subconscious thing. I rely on me to provide myself with plots. I've gotten into that very actively. It's what I want to use at the present. The book (**Pleasure Beach**) is very autobiographical, and yet, of course, it's a pack of lies, at the same time.

TD: Yeah, which is what life is about anyway. Could you define yourself or describe yourself as a photographer, in terms of your photography?

SL: I don't see myself so much as a photographer anymore. It's funny, I feel I'm in photography, but I don't feel so much like a photographer. How can I put that?

TD: You feel you're just an artist who uses photography as his medium?

SL: Yeah, and I feel like photography is the soup I fell into, and some circumstances find me in photography, but I'm not that much interested in great pictures, but yet I am involved in photography. I can't see changing at this point. I've invested much too much in photography. In fact, the longer you stay in it, the more you're in that soup. I think we're all in photography, everybody, our time is in photography very much.

TD: Sure, even the painters are doing photo-realism.

SL: Yeah, and then everybody shoots pictures. That's life, life is photography, and I do that a little more than the average person. That really doesn't answer your question.

TD: I think that sometimes it's better to answer a question by not answering it.

SL: I don't consider myself a photo-stylist anymore.

TD: How do you define success, and how important is it?

SL: I don't consider myself successful really. I look forward to it. I find that, unfortunately, the more your ego feeds on success, the more it needs; therefore, you don't make any headway. It's like running in place. If I'm really into success, I need it, and I can get into it. If things go well a few weeks in a row, and I start feeling successful, then I feel I need it. Then if nothing happens for a few weeks, I get furious, so I realize what a trap I'm in.

TD: Are you talking about success in terms of selling stuff?

SL: Yeah, but right now it's in terms of the book, if I get good response on the book from a certain quarter. Sometimes I get several phone calls in a day, people comment, and my ego goes way up; the next time I have an experience like I had at Jaap Reitman's (bookstore) where I got the sort of bland refusal to handle the book, and I'm infuriated by that, and it's really just the other side of the compliment. I lapped up the compliment, so I'm forced to eat the shit.

TD: Well, you know the thing about that, I think, is that what's even more enraging is that it's indifference.

SL: I have a lot of ego and vanity, I think, and I'm very easily caught up in running in place, success. So, on one hand, I want it and on the other hand, I don't, because I know that with it comes an inflammation of my ego, and more suffering from the other side, because all you're doing is feeding a false appetite. It's kind of a hopeless situation.

TD: Is isolation necessary for your work?

SL: I used to think so. In fact, I used to work from that idea, but I don't think so anymore. It seems to me that I wish I had isolation sometimes, but it seems it just takes greater skill to get your work done if you don't have the advantage of isolation. Plus, with isolation, you don't have enough input from outside sources, so you start mulling over the same stuff much too long, you spend much too much time on the spot. I've been trying it in reverse the last few years, and my production seems up, and my idea flow seems to be up, although I feel I can't work under these conditions, I can't do anything this way, I feel that all the time.

TD: But now you prefer an active life?

SL: Yeah.

TD: See people and things like that?

SL: For the time being, I still feel I could go back into a monastic existence, if I had to, or wanted to. Maybe when I'm very old, I'd like to do that.

TD: Do you ever think of going back to New Orleans?

SL: No, I'd like to, though, for a visit. I would love to go back and see all the places that I grew up in, which I never have done. I haven't been in New Orleans since I was about 15 years old.

TD: Do you know Clarence John (Laughlin)?

SL: Yes, but I met him in Denver, when I was out in Colorado. I don't know him that well. I'd have to say, "You remember I met you that time when you were at so and so." And he would probably say, "Yeah, I think..." But he wouldn't remember my name at all.

TD: Could you discuss Pleasure Beach **from idea through completed book? You hadn't really dealt with books prior to that?**

SL: I did have the Synthetic Landscapes. The smooth screen portfolio I did of landscapes was, in a way, a beginning, because the idea of putting together these landscapes from film rather than from an actual landscape that you photograph, in other words, inventing landscapes. From inventing landscapes to inventing a situation based on a place or situations based on a place, isn't very far, and **Pleasure Beach** itself is a place, an abandoned resort outside of Bridgeport. Incidentally, Roger Mertin grew up around there, and he asked me the other day, "Is that Pleasure Beach anywhere around Bridgeport?" I said, "Yeah, that's the one." But there really isn't that much there, and there isn't that much really interesting about it. But I think most photographers have prowled around an abandoned amusement park once or twice, and I've prowled around quite a few of them, just because they're very rich places visually. I had a lot of pictures from different places, so I started with the idea of building an amusement park out of film. It appealed to me. Originally I was going to do a bunch of portfolios, prints of Pleasure Beach, which wouldn't really be Pleasure Beach, but it would be the film I had from there, and other places, in the way Synthetic Landscapes was done. Then, that gradually developed as an idea, into a plot for a story, using events from my childhood, fantasy or fictional events, shall I say. Then uncannily, things started falling into place. I left Connecticut and my wife about five years ago. **Pleasure Beach** is sort of the story of my internal life while I was there, and my looking back on it now. I don't know how much of this I should actually give away. In a real way, it's very autobiographical, the model in most of the book is my present woman, Barbara, and in a sense, a lot of the book was done in the passion of my new romance. I don't know if people really pick that up in the book, I'm sure they don't. See, the whole thing is very literal in many ways. I could work her into my fantasy woman. It's like using the props in your life to reorder your past. You can sort through it and use it as you see fit. I hate to give away too much because I like people to discover things on their own. I think it would be interesting if it dawns on people gradually. It'll probably only dawn on a few people who know me, but I feel that potentially I'm trying to fertilize a legend for the artistic fun of it. I've laid out some clues visually in the story that I don't want to be blatant about. I'll tell you another thing was, you were asking about photo style, what kind of a photographer I am. The trouble with style is it boxes you into doing that kind of picture and that's what I've not wanted to do. I wanted to make the style be some other place besides the photographs. For me the style is the shape of that book, its way as a book, not the pictures in the book. The book fell together for me, I don't consider it a perfect book in any sense, but I think it really does work well, it's 5/6 of the way there, or 3/4 of the way, it mostly works, and, for me, that's a big breakthrough over what I had done before. I'd never done anything that extended, in any sense. The Synthetic Landscapes portfolio or the illusionary forms are very timid compared to the complexity of a book. That central part of the book is the key element of the book. The first part, I've always wanted to do something about my early work. I think everybody has the idea of wanting to tidy up that drawer somehow. In addition, with color prints, dye-transfers, and so on, you have this nagging feeling of permanency, they're not really permanent, so you ultimately want to get them into ink in a book in some way. So, once the technical problems of doing these things by fine line technique were worked out, I originally was going to do a portfolio of them, but then with the writing beginning to flow from Pleasure Beach stuff, I thought, "Maybe I could reshape this to blend with that, in some way, that will relate, and deal with it in a different way." These were done a long time ago, before I started painting, before my parents died, before the house fire, way back there. It's pretty hard to get serious about publishing it as a brand new work, but as sort of a false history, the idea comes to life again, and I was able to get into it.

TD: Was it actually the writing that led you to think book?

SL: I would say so, yeah. The possibility that I could write, do these things verbally, opened up all kinds of doors for me.

TD: What got you into writing?

SL: I'd written articles, but I'd never attempted anything creative, so to speak, but I have written a lot, written a lot of letters. I've written articles for the *Encyclopedia of Photography*. I've decided a lot of things I wanted to say about photography, in a round about way, the writing is about photography, what it is and how it relates to me and the whole idea of making up a place with all these pictures, constructing a scenario of a place, like **Pleasure Beach** is a whole idea about photography, of what the stuff is, what film is, and what life is in relation to film. That's sort of philosophical and thrills me. I'd say once the writing got going, the photography stylistically started coming together, but stylistically, it's a print maker's way with pictures, with the writing making it a book. That's really what I want to continue doing. I enjoy writing very much, and I think that's what I have to develop better now. The actual quality of the pictures doesn't seem as important to me as the way in which they're presented, the context in which they're presented, and that context is formed by the writing, so take the **Wisconsin Death Trip.** Michael Lesy sets those pictures up in a certain way, so you see them in a certain way. The writing about what those pictures are, makes those pictures mean something; whether they are, or not, is another question. I think a good picture is a good picture, and it's always a great thing to have. It's not so important, to me, to have bells ringing, picture after picture, as it is to adjust their context to the writing. In fact, in the last part, "The Archeological Way," the pictures got pretty shitty at times. That's not really good camera work, but it still seems to work. That section was quite experimental. I had never done anything quite that casually. I've always had much more control, and the fact that I feel that I got away with it, and it works, that's very gratifying and liberating. I think the stronger the writing gets, the more that that liberation works visually, for me. Of course, I don't want to get into being a professional writer either, which is another thing, because then you have to do a whole other type of writing. My whole bit as a writer is that I'm really a photographer, and as a photographer, I'm really a writer.

TD: Yeah, when I first wanted to get into photography, somebody told me to be a photojournalist, because I was interested in photography, and I thought that meant that you're a photographer, and a writer. And that was always my idea as a photographer, I never thought that I wanted just to take pictures. And I never really changed that idea. I think the things that work for me best are the things where words go with the pictures, however loosely. Even sometimes when I don't appreciate things terribly, like I was looking at a book on Venice by Wright Morris, and I had been in Venice, and was reading the extended captions and it works pretty

well. But I think you did a lot more. The fact that yours is really related. I think the whole idea of its being autobiographical is important, it's in a really good direction.

SL: I think it has a lot of possibilities for a lot of people, because it seems to me that the variety of things that could come out of it is incredible.

TD: But, you know, what's interested me lately is music and I've been reading about and listening to music, reading a lot of interviews, and all of these musicians talking about doing an album as a concept, writing songs, and doing everything, putting the thing together, almost as if putting a book together, and it really became very exciting. I'm very impressed with Neil Young and the way he does albums; the fact that he's writing, and doing everything himself.

SL: They're farther out than book people are in the photography world.

TD: Your book reminds me of that.

SL: I'll say that it's a way of working I'm well aware of, in music. You know I really wanted to do a popular book, a book that'd be popular. I doubt if my book will be that popular, but I have to accept that whichever way it falls. I think it's not that far away. There's going to be enough of a good visual audience that books could be really big sellers at $5.98 the way a record album is, and I don't think that's impossible. It's got to be a more developed book.

TD: The big difference, I think, is that yours was really a huge project, whereas a record album is something that they work a month or two and put it out. That is exciting to me because I think you can approach a book like that. Do a book in a period of a month or two, taking an idea, that's not a major project; it doesn't always have to be a major thing.

SL: On the other hand, novelists; Kurt Vonnegut, has three, four or five years between each book.

TD: What about Joseph Heller, he had about—

SL: Twenty years.

TD: A long time, in terms of working as an artist. Vonnegut does a book and can live off the royalties; he can afford to spend five years. But I don't think, at the present time, that a photographer could.

SL: It doesn't look like it.

TD: But if you did a book a year, along with some other things, it's possible that you could make a living.

SL: I consider my book a financial experiment, too. If it sells out, my edition of 1,200, which is a really small edition, I will clear a profit of about $10,000 or $15,000, which I think is good.

TD: A good return on your money.

SL: A lot of books that are self-published can't make a nickel, in terms of what it sells for, in terms of what it costs. If the whole book sells out, they break even, or lose a little bit. It seems that to really work there has to be some kind of return or else there's no momentum. For other people who are working in the graphic arts, I think that if my book works out, I think they'll do books. If it doesn't they'll think twice. I think it's a model in that sense also.

TD: But would you be encouraged if you hit a break-even point?

SL: No, I'd be encouraged if I sell out the edition and make that amount of money, $10,000 or $15,000. That's what I figure I need out of the enterprise to make it worthwhile, and that isn't that much, that's not really a great wage.

TD: Are you going to try to work cheaper next time, or are you going to wait and see what happens here?

SL: I can't really work cheaper. The book cost around $12,000 to make. The only thing that could make it cheaper is more copies. I don't have any way to get rid of more copies.

TD: How about if you worked in a smaller format, or used less color, or whatever, to cut costs down?

SL: It's not going to cut it that much. You'd get down to around $8,000. The average black and white book, like the Koudelka book, (**Gypsies**) cost $12,000. My book isn't that expensive, but they printed 40,000 of that book, something like that, 30,000 or 40,000.

TD: That's because it's Aperture.

SL: Yeah, and they'll move them. That's where the real stinger is. I'm going to try to get a larger edition published of this, which isn't ideal. You should get it all run at that first run, but if you just break even for 5,000, you could cut the price down to $20.

TD: I guess it depends a lot on how well it's distributed.

SL: Yeah, and my distribution is just through the (Visual Studies) Workshop and a few smaller places, like Witkin Gallery, Wittenborn bookstore, Museum of Modern Art, places like that, and that's really hard.

TD: It's limited.

SL: That would be OK for this size, 1,200 copies. It should work, but I wouldn't care to have any more printed. The economics of the whole thing is very important, because in the end activities survive or don't survive to some degree on that basis. I think quite a bit about distribution situations. The audience is getting quite developed with all these students, and it seems to me what's really needed is a way to pinpoint your sales to them, like if I put my book in Brentano's, it's reaching mostly waste audience, you might say, who are not going to buy it. But, on the other hand, if you reach the student audience or post-student audience, or the museum and academic worlds, or the photo world, if you reach that with a really high degree of accuracy, you should be able to market things well. But just a mail flyer won't do it. There should be some great book store where everybody would go for those books, whereas they'd go to another book store for another type.

TD: I wonder how Time-Life would handle that book?

SL: They'd put it in photo stores, and I don't think it would sell that well there.

TD: They would send an elaborate brochure out to some mailing list.

SL: I don't think that's the audience I want though. There's something about things getting spoiled when they get into those kinds of hands. Maybe it's just my artistic snobbery. I think that what you want is a really good audience, but you want them to buy also, you want them to pay for it.

TD: So, if this book sells out, then you'll be encouraged, and feel you'll be able to continue to work, you'll know there is an audience out there.

SL: Yeah, if it doesn't work out, I won't be that eager to do another one frankly. If I just get my money back or don't quite, I don't feel inclined to do it again. I'll probably try something else.

TD: Will you also do a portfolio of Pleasure Beach?

SL: No, not really. I thought of it, and may still; I didn't, no. I have another print portfolio idea that I've been kicking around for this show from Boston that I'm doing. A print is being done by offset which they're going to do in a large edition, 750 prints, and sell for $10. Its title, in small writing on the bottom part of the print, Part of the Labyrinth, from Film Labyrinths Number 3 and, of course, there aren't any Film Labyrinths Number 3, but the idea started appealing to me that I might really enjoy doing film labyrinths. In other words, doing these prints that are endless images organized around the idea of a labyrinth and try to develop these film labyrinths and have the prints, so they could be joined ultimately, but really they're separate. Do ten or twelve piece prints and have a really giant exhibition piece or do a portfolio, according to how you choose to want it up on the wall. But the idea that appeals to me is that we all live in a labyrinth of imagery and it takes its material form in film, in our time, in our society, and so we live in this film labyrinth, and we're lost among our images, and continually trying to find our way out, by making new images, or by looking back to the ones we have made, and trying to understand them in some new ways. In any film labyrinth, there would be all kinds of pictures, all those that you wouldn't use for "serious photography" you can use in your labyrinth. And that idea of being able to reuse a lot of material appeals to me greatly. So that's my idea of about the last two days.

TD: Do you find anybody who really appreciates your work? Whom do you show your work to?

SL: Mostly I show work continually to friends that drop in. I generally don't show it to people in authority before it's done, but many of my friends know circumstances of my life and have an inside aspect of looking at the work in the book, and they're very delighted to see how certain events are transformed into events in the book. For example, a few of my friends know that the Manhattan Transfer that appeared in "The Archeological Way," double-exposed into Egypt are a group of people I know from when they were just beginning as a singing group in New York. Barbara and I went on a boat ride called, Three Decks of Midsummer Night, down the Hudson, with different bands, and mostly it was a real disaster; it was one giant cloud of dope floating down the river, about 50% a gay scene, very outrageous, the boat was a really creaky old thing, and the decorations were extremely limited, the drinks were really expensive and very weak, and the entertainment was pretty bad, Jackie Curtis and his band. Do you know Jackie Curtis? Andy Warhol's friend, a transvestite. Then the Manhattan Transfer came on and they were fantastic; they were doing old stuff from the 30's and 40's, really a sensational group and a very original concept. We were just overwhelmed. I made a point of getting in touch with them the next time they were playing in town, at a little dumpy bar, with about eight people there, so between sets, I got to meet Tim and said I would like to do some pictures, because they were very extraordinary, theatrical-looking people. He said, "Sure, we'll pose and you give us some free prints for our publicity." I said, "Fine, deal." He came down with their manager, a lawyer who had studied photography with Minor White; I did a lot of pictures of them. We used to go watch them play until they started getting successful, then I lost interest totally in them.

TD: I know the feeling.

SL: Anyway, people that I know would notice that in the book, and would get a big chuckle out of it. The only time that I sent something to a person in authority was when I had a brief conversation with Robert Sobiezek from Eastman House, and I really felt that we had certain things in common. When the first two sections of the book were done, I sent him those pages and asked for his comment. About a month later I got back three typewritten pages of discussion about what I was doing. It was really exactly on the nose of what I'd love to hear a critic say. It was a type of letter that you could only write to yourself; it just doesn't happen in normal life. I do think there are people who will understand what I'm up to without being unduly primed to my way, like knowing me too long.

TD: How does Nathan Lyons respond to your work?

SL: Nathan never gives direct answers. I don't know, he would never discuss it. He's very supportive, and very helpful, of my work in general; he's marvelous. I think for many people in photography, he's been a great catalyst and a great encourager, but, at least with me, he doesn't get into discussing details of my work with me. I feel great overall support and great overall help from him, but not in any specific sense. I always have the feeling that once he believes in you as a person, he overall believes in your work; as for specific details, they're not really that important to him, I don't think.

TD: You think he just wants people to work.

SL: He believes in their creative processes, and he wants to see that happen, yeah.

TD: Did that ever fluster you? Did it ever bother you? Did you want him to say more than he says?

SL: A little bit, but in the long run, I find it pretty much right. In the long run, nobody can tell you anything anyway. I'm so paranoid that even a compliment, if it's not done exactly right, I consider not worth anything, because the person is obviously an idiot if they put it that way. It's sort of pointless. Really good criticism is very hard to come by also, for somebody to give you a negative comment that's really accurate, I think is very valuable, painful—but valuable, but that's very rare that you find somebody who'll do that.

TD: They're liable to say something positive or they won't say anything?

SL: Yeah. To pass a pleasant day, I'd prefer that.

TD: Do you still work with a view camera?

SL: Sometimes, a little bit, very little though.

TD: Mostly 35mm?

SL: Mostly 2¼, 2¼ x 3¼, 2¼ x 2¼ or 35.

TD: What kind of 2¼?

SL: Well, I had a Mamiya Press for a long time, with the roll film back, and I have an old Plaubel I used throughout "The Archeological Way," the last part. That's a really nice camera, it's a 2¼ x 3¼ format, and very compact. Recently I got a Hasselblad which I have mixed feelings about. It's a beautiful camera to look at, and to fool with, but 2¼ square format is not my favorite format. It's also so expensive. I border on selling it every few weeks. The Plaubel I really liked because it's fairly cheap; you can pick up an old one, they're not being made anymore, but you can find a used one. It's a very versatile, good camera.

TD: Do they have Schneider lenses?

SL: Yes, good lenses, it's a well-built, nice camera. In 35, I have a Leica that was my dad's when he went to Europe about five years before he died. It's a first F. Is there an F Leica?

TD: Oh, yeah, does it have a split view finder and range finder?

SL: Yeah. It has very little mileage on it; he never used it.

TD: Don't you find it difficult?

SL: Yeah. I don't like the camera especially, but it's compact and it's accessible. I got offered $50 for it used, and it's worth more than that as a functioning machine.

TD: Do you still work with black and white?

SL: Yeah, I shoot a lot of black and white. In fact, I've always done quite a bit of black and white, but my reputation has been in color. Color isn't a crowded field and black and white is, so I have not had too much work shown in black and white, nor have I really pushed for it that hard. In fact, I really haven't worked that hard at it or in it, but I've had black and white shows occasionally, and I always get secret pleasure out of having a black and white piece included.

TD: Do you work fairly simply, like limit yourself to one film?

SL: Yeah, pretty much. Lately, I've been working almost entirely for graphic arts use in the long run, which means the film is developed to come out very flat, so I can make fine line images from it. This means shooting Tri-X at E.I. 200, so you can develop it in very low energy developer.

TD: You don't develop it normally?

SL: No, I develop it way under. I develop 1 to 5 in Acufine for about 5 minutes.

TD: What kind of negative do you get?

SL: A really flat negative, and then I can make a Kodalith directly that has about the right tonal scale, and that's ready for the press right away. In other words, I can make contact sheets which in fact can be used on a press at some point in some intricate part of a labyrinth. It gets me there right away. Then if I want to make a black and white print, I whip out a #6 paper and the strongest Beers developer I can mix, and make a decent black and white print.

TD: Do you still use Ektachrome?

SL: Yeah. I don't really like the color films that are available. The old E-1 I think was a really good film, even if it was incredibly slow, ASA 10 or 12. I could develop it in 55 minutes, six chemicals. It tended to get too blue, but otherwise it was very good, and I could guard against the blue by being aware of heavy north light qualities, and so on; I could filter it off or something. I use E-3 or I like Agfachrome, but it's a little slow for a hand camera, 64. I think Agfachrome is a really pretty color film; it's more subtle and subdued, yet has fairly high contrast. The colors aren't punched up in it and yet the tonal range is really vigorous. I tend to use Ektachrome now. Many of the pictures I make have to do more with the graphic manipulations they've gone through than with the film that was used to begin with. It doesn't matter all that much, although the ideal for me is Agfachrome right now.

TD: Do you still make color prints?

SL: No, I haven't for about five or six years, not any dye transfer processing either.

TD: Tri Carbro either?

SL: No. Tri Carbro materials aren't available anymore. They used to be put out by McGraw Color Graph, a subsidiary of Pet Milk. That's absolutely true. And then I think Pet Milk decided it wasn't such a good product.

TD: Do you work every day?

SL: No, I used to. When I was a painter, I worked every day, but now I don't at all.

TD: When do you work now?

SL: When I'm forced to.

TD: What forces you to?

SL: Lately I have a lot of deadlines and schedules. For a long time, completing the book was a force factor. I had a certain time allotment that I wanted to complete it in, partly for sales reasons, marketing, which ultimately turned out to be not that important, but I thought it would be at the time. For example, I hoped to make Christmas, but I didn't, but it still made me do a lot of work, so that I was ready by the first of January; Christmas next year.

TD: And you edit as you go along?

SL: Yeah, I worked on the three sections separately.

TD: As separate entities?

SL: Yeah, they were printed as separate entities. The last section I worked on after the first two were done. I have exhibitions coming up that I have to make a few more prints for. Currently, I've been doing some lecturing at universities, and I've gotten a slide show together from **Pleasure Beach,** and that's the force factor again. I'm very much in there trying to make money off this thing now.

TD: Did you have a show at Nathan's (Lyons - Visual Studies Workshop) on this, or

are you going to?

SL: I'm supposed to, yeah, that's been put back a couple of times because of scheduling, but it's supposed to be, I think, in May. It may be put back again, I don't know; it doesn't seem to be that crucial when it's done.

TD: You did everything on the book.

SL: Everything.

TD: What didn't you do?

SL: Well, I didn't run the press.

TD: But you did everything else.

SL: Yeah, but I didn't bind it, of course. But the whole look of it, in every sense. I picked out the binding certainly, and so on. Any book is made from stripped-up film flats, so it was done as though I were making a print. In most cases, there's no original picture, there's maybe a slide to begin with, or a black and white negative, or something like that, but ultimately Kodaliths were made mostly by the fine line method, and then are worked with until the page is decided upon, and then the page is stripped up on a flat and ultimately the four pages in a group are put together, and from that flat the plate is burned. I don't do that either, that takes five minutes, then it's run on the press. No decisions were made on the press. The press was run with all the colors running in, more or less, full strength. But the nature of the economics is such that no changes can be made on the press without costing you a bundle, so everything was run just as it came out of the can, so to speak. So any decisions, any changes, I made on the flats ahead of time. In other words, the making of the flats is the making of the book. The press runs essentially automatically. That's not that the people who printed it, Meriden Gravure, didn't do a really Grade A job, they're very good printers, they run the presses very well, but there were no printing decisions made, because, unless you owned your own press, you couldn't get into doing that in any sort of economical way. I didn't even go there. I went when the first four-page section was run, and it became clear to me that there was nothing I could do except watch, so I didn't even watch them do most of it. And by the third section, we were pretty well-coordinated. I knew they wouldn't screw up, and they knew I wouldn't screw up my flats, that it would all work out all right, so it went pretty easily.

TD: What happened to the stuff while it was waiting to be bound, while you were working on it? How long did it take to be printed?

SL: Well, it was printed in three sections over a year's period.

TD: And you stored the stuff?

SL: No, they stored it

TD: They stored it for you.

SL: Yeah, they'll do that normally.

TD: Was there a special deal because you did everything else on it?

SL: Oh, yeah. The price was much, much lower. The price of the book was the price of doing a black and white book.

TD: Did you pick out the paper and all that?

SL: Yeah. Two-thirds of the cost of printing is in all the make-ready, not in the press stage of the process, so I took on those costs, much of which is labor, myself. Otherwise this kind of a book could never have been done. In the first place, you couldn't have made it anyway, because you'd have had to make a silk screen print or something first, there's no original.

TD: What was the most difficult aspect of the book?

SL: The techniques get tedious and tiring and boring, stripping things up, registering, all the film, organizing it so it doesn't get all lost and strewn around, keeping the routine. The routine's difficult.

TD: How do you feel about Pleasure Beach **now that it's finished? Are you satisfied?**

SL: Yes, I'm quite satisfied. There are no disasters. Doing a book in this way and having it run on the press with no proofing, in the way I described to you, because the cost of proofing would be the cost of doing this book, practically, the only saving would be in the paper. You're leaving yourself open to some great disaster, like printing a whole bunch of pages upside down. That's the big danger, the sort of thing I worried about. But, artistically, I'm pretty happy with it. There are things I would have done a little differently, but there's nothing major that I don't like. There're some typo errors. That's OK, it's inevitable the way the book was done.

TD: What do you expect or hope it will mean in terms of the future?

SL: I hope it will mean that I can continue to work in that medium, that it's a viable medium for me. The key is that it sell enough to warrant continuing to work that way. I hate to put things down to money so much, but when you get into a project like that, it is money, and there's no way to get out of it. I'm not going to put up money again, in that way, if I don't get it back. I would much rather take the money and put it into a horse, or something like that.

TD: How important are books to reputation, do you feel?

SL: I don't know. I think a lot of people do want to get a book out for their reputation. I think that's the wrong way to approach things. All you're going to do is have a book of your greatest masterpieces, bound together, which is like an exhibition. I don't think that's really interesting as a book concept. A lot of people do it, and sometimes pictures are nice and so on. I'd rather see them in an exhibition. It doesn't interest me that much. When things are done that way, I don't think it really helps a reputation very much. If a book is exciting, then people are excited about who made it, but generally, it has to have some other quality than just a collection of their pictures. Even straight picture books, like Bill Owens' book, they have a theme, and a viewpoint. That's a perfectly good book in its way. It doesn't appeal to me particularly, because I feel he's laughing up his sleeve at those people. But that's not the point, the point is, it is a book, not just a bunch of his photos made into an album collection.

TD: Will you do more portfolios?

SL: Again, if that seems to be a viable direction. The portfolios I've done have not sold that well. For the amount of work and the amount of exhibition use they've had, I don't feel too happy about it, really.

TD: How many do you usually do?

SL: Oh, 20 or so. Like the Synthetic Landscapes sells for about $1,000, and it's about half sold and half unsold, which over a 3, 4 or 5 year period is not really good. Of course, it depends. If I find an idea I really want to do, I'd do it anyway probably. If you want it badly enough, you do it.

TD: Do you have dealings with other photographers, do you count photographers as your intimates or friends?

SL: Yeah, quite a lot.

TD: Who do you see or deal with?

SL: It's hard for me to single out names, because there're many people, but Scott Hyde is a long-time friend of mine; he lives in New York. There're many others, but in general, I consider myself as part of the photography community, and it's a world in itself, in a sense. Most of the people I know, well over half, are related to photography in one sense or another.

TD: Are there any photographers you particularly admire? Or books, current or otherwise?

SL: No, not really. There are things I admire about certain books, or certain things often. It's really hard for me to give one thing that I particularly like, but I can recall a few years ago being turned on by Eikoh Hosoe's book, **Killed by Roses,** as being a really creative book. I liked (William) Klein's books from years ago, very grainy pictures. I haven't seen any of that work in a long time.

TD: Last week you said you started doing some writing for your next book. Could you say anything about the new project?

SL: Yeah. The tentative title for the new book is "The Sporting Life." Did I talk to you about this?

TD: Um hmm.

SL: It'll sort of be a fantasy of extravagant living.

TD: You're getting more autobiographical?

SL: Right. But again I think everybody has this sort of dream of glorious living. On one hand, everybody wants to be a real person, so they wear jeans and all that; on the other side, they have this inner dream of what auto racing and those things are, horse racing, things connected in that way. I want to build a story around that dream I think I share with other people. Of course, all these things never quite work out, but in book form, they should work out, at least in some way. I'm not quite clear whether it'll be more fictional than the rest of the work has been. I think, increasingly, my tendency will be to become more fictional, and less autobiographical, or factual, and extend into a cinematic form more and more.

TD: Will you basically be dealing from a framework of experience?

SL: Oh, yeah.

TD: What kind of a background are you from?

SL: Myself?

TD: Yeah, how are you economically?

SL: Oh, well off.

TD: Upper, upper middle class?

SL: Something like that.

TD: Above that?

SL: No, not supreme.

TD: Were your parents wealthy?

SL: My grandfather was wealthy, I'd say. I'd say my father was, too, but my grandfather made a fortune in this country, so to speak.

TD: Where was he from?

SL: He was from France, but he wasn't an immigrant. He didn't come over on the boat, as they say. I mean, everybody came over on a boat, but the thing is they were moderately well off in France, and he was educated in France, and there was some family over here from previous immigration. He had an engineering degree when he came over and spoke English, and he would go back to France periodically. It wasn't like rags to riches. They were a comfortably well-off family in France, southern France, the area is Ardeshe. Do you know where that is?

TD: No.

SL: I don't either, for that matter. I haven't been back, but my brother went back to France and there's a Cafe Labrot in the town there, and he was embraced and kissed on both cheeks and all that, distant cousins. Let me trace something for you that might be interesting. My parents were pretty well off, but as a boy of around 18-20, I was an ardent radical, subscribed to the New Republic, **campaigned for Wallace in** the '48 election, I guess it was, the '48-'52, and was interested in Socialist politics. My interest in Political Science in college was so that the working class and the new world would come to be. I became disillusioned with that. That type of politics was dying in the country following that period in the 50's. Politics got very conservative. You could work for Stevenson and be a loser, which I didn't want also. I still have that interest in politics, the real politics are on the left, always the interesting thinking, the vitality in politics is on the left. The politics on the right are primarily trying to keep things patched together, so we could play it out a little longer. Increasingly I found myself more conservative, doing a double take on myself all the time as I've become more conservative. It isn't so much a conservatism of belief as of circumstance. I find artistically there's a little more fun, there's a little more play on the right now suddenly than there used to be. For example, an idea such as "The Sporting Life," to fantasize a life of gaudiness and decadent living, is really something that hasn't been done at all since the British in the 1890's or something, so there's a great deal of play in that area suddenly. It's also an area that I'm not really unqualified to relate to, in some vague sense, although I wouldn't have admitted this during the revolution of the 60's. In the period of the 70's, it seems like something worth tinkering with creatively. I do this with the idea that it's going to be the sort of thing that everybody will identify with secretly, but never publicly.

New York City
March 29, 1976

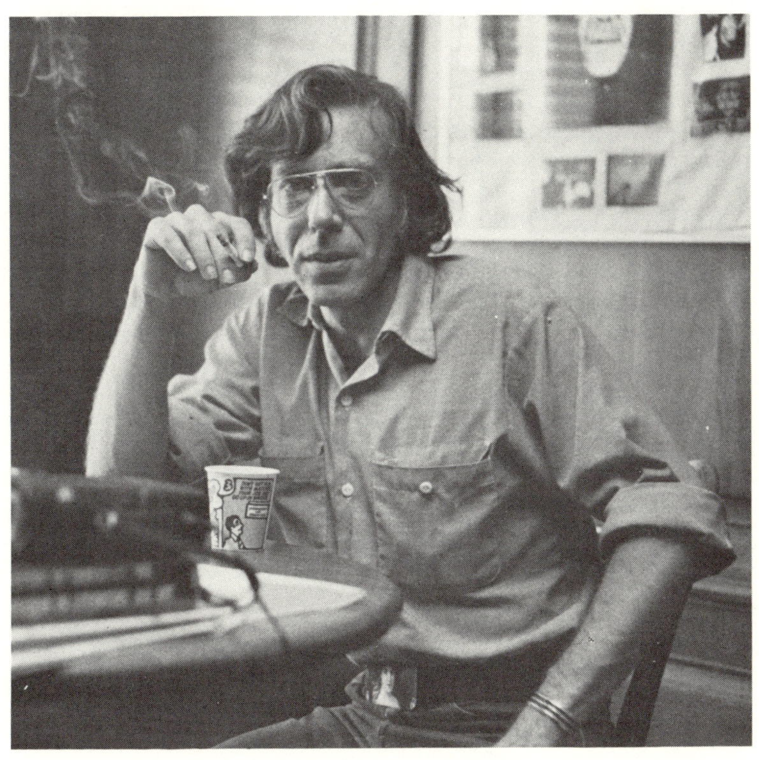

Nathan Lyons

Interviewer: What was the most difficult aspect of Notations in Passing?
Nathan Lyons: Being patient enough to let it develop.

The conversation with Nathan Lyons took place in his cluttered office at the Visual Studies Workshop, Rochester, N.Y. in July 1974. On several prior occasions we discussed the concept of the interviews I intended to do. It seems appropriate that I begin the series by interviewing him. This interview, which I tape recorded, lasted one hour, the shortest in the series, and appears basically as it was recorded. The few changes concerned the clarification of an idea here and there. At the time of our meeting Nathan had completed **Notations in Passing** and publication was a couple of months away. This is the single interview conducted before the publication of the work discussed, but I had seen the series on a number of visits with Nathan.

Nathan Lyons is a supremely complex man, unassuming by nature, yet possessing a regal, quiet dignity. Reserved at times to the point of aloofness, he is sensitive and supportive of those he considers serious, and, at times, surprisingly talkative. He always appears busier than it seems possible for one person to be. He is slim, of medium height, cigarette and coffee cup always in hand, boyishly handsome in his jeans and long hair, a hand softly, incessantly pushing back a cowlick that prefers a place over his eyebrow.

Born: Jamaica, N. Y. January 10, 1930.
B.A. Degree: Alfred University, Alfred, N.Y., 1957.
Books:
  Under the Sun: The Abstract Art of Camera Vision. With Syl Labrot and Walter Chappell. Braziller. New York, 1960.
  Photography 63. George Eastman House. Rochester, New York, 1963.
  Photography 64. George Eastman House. Rochester, New York 1964.
  Aaron Siskind, Photographer. George Eastman House. Rochester, New York 1965.
  Photographers on Photography. Prentice Hall, Englewood Cliffs, New Jersey, 1966.
  Toward a Social Landscape. Horizon Press in collaboration with George Eastman House. New York, 1966.
  The Persistence of Vision. Horizon Press in collaboration with George Eastman House. New York, 1967.
  Photography in the Twentieth Century. Horizon Press in collaboration with George Eastman House. New York, 1967.
  Vision and Expression. Horizon Press in collaboration with George Eastman House. New York, 1969.
  Notations in Passing. M.I.T. Press. Boston, 1974.
Currently: Director, Visual Studies Workshop, Rochester, N.Y.

Tom Dugan: For starters, how about discussing your background as a photographer?

Nathan Lyons:The interest began when I was about 15 or 16. I can remember processing film in closets and working very independently, no formal training whatsoever, and gradually becoming more and more involved. There was even a period of time when I was doing custom processing for a few people who were too lazy to do their own. I guess the big transition started to form when I left New York City and went off to a small college (Alfred University) in upstate New York. I set up a darkroom there, tried to retain my interest in my formal studies while I was photographing, which wasn't the easiest thing to do sometimes. The real turning point, strangely enough, was going into service as a photographer for about four years and involving myself in a lot of different work, some issues involving aerial reconnaissance, being a base photographer, doing a lot of specialized photographic work, having access to a wide range of equipment, but strongly not feeling that what I was going to do at all was to become a photographer. I had originally projected returning to college and working in the communications area, editorial areas.

Returning to college I worked almost full time for the university as a photographer, doing a lot of their publicity and public relations work and again specialized work, involving myself in theater, poetry workshops, running the college newspaper and, upon leaving, having some feeling that I might go to graduate school somewhere, but the entire school situation was getting to me. I had been out of school for almost five years, came back, completed my degree in an accelerated program and the only place you probably could form any continuation was in a graduate program. I probably should say one of the more stimulating experiences for me at that time, in relation to certain ideas and concepts, came from one or two people in the English department, and one person in the design department. I took a number of courses in the design department; the person who was there was a fellow by the name of John Wood. I think probably through the kinds of questions he was able to pose, the timing was very right in my head to form some shifts and some considerations about direction, what I was doing, the relevance of the kind of picture I was making. He recommended that I visit a few people, and one was Steichen in New York. I never could make contact with him, but I spoke to somebody working for him. I brought in a raft of photographs, models of exhibitions I already designed and executed. I'd been combining elements of theater in varying performance ways. I guess I was fairly involved in a kind of communications position that cut across everything from journalism to poetry to theater to exhibition design, at that stage. He'd also indicated I should talk with Minor White, whose work I hadn't known, but for some reason he felt that, in the way that I was moving, Minor (White) would be a good person to speak with. Also he suggested a visit with (Aaron) Siskind and (Harry) Callahan. So I had a direction that was going to get me ultimately to Chicago.

My car had died. I can remember very distinctly getting it in enough shape to drive it to a car sale where they would take mine in trade, give me a brand new car and I didn't have to make the first payment for three months. So I left Alfred with this oversized station wagon with everything I owned in it, a full tank of gas, fifty cents, and three months to get a job and make the first payment on the car. I wound up in Rochester living in the basement of a friend, met Minor — spoke with him. He asked me if I wanted to study with him. I thought the idea was kind of intriguing because he was one of the few people who was considering the medium on terms that I thought challenging. But ultimately that only lasted for about two weeks. Somewhere along the line he asked me what I thought of his workshop. I told him I thought it was terrible. He said, "All right, next year you teach the workshop," and Minor and a number of his students were my first students. Minor was probably more active than most of the students, which was kind of interesting as well. He worked along, participated in a number of problems that I laid out for the students and we established a good working relationship. At the same time, Walt Chappell was here, Paul Caponigro had just come by, Carl Chiarenza was here as a student, and we all sort of intersected. I can remember a few long evenings with Ralph Hattersley, going at some issue that he took exception to in what Minor was presenting. It was a very, very good climate of activity, having all of those people at one place at one time. I had to get a job and I was looking for anything. My thought was to become a clerk in a grocery store, at the check-out counter, just to get enough money to keep things going and get some work done. I also went around to a number of places in town for interviews, one of them was the Eastman Kodak Co.

I was looking for someplace in this city where people were interested in what effect photographs had on people, and it was very hard to find. I brought this up during my interview with Kodak and they seemed to be a little puzzled, and suggested that I check in at the George Eastman House which I hadn't visited yet. I had gotten lost periodically and noticed this sign which said, Museum of

Photography, and I thought that was kind of strange that there would be a museum of photography. I made an appointment with the director, General Solbert and met Beaumont Newhall. I went through three interviews at the Eastman House. They had already made up their mind to hire someone the day before. I had come in the next day and they started to get interested in the range of my working interests. I ultimately was hired as something between a publicity coordinator and an associate editor of the publication they had at the time, *Image* magazine. My responsibility, with regard to the magazine, was to straighten out the production flow and the economics of it. It had been a financial disaster. Gradually I worked the magazine back on a more solid footing, straightened out the distribution of information, moved to redesign the magazine, making it a quarterly. It was becoming economically sound when one issue offended a few of the trustees for a very personal reason which had to do with someone who was featured in the publication, I think. They used the fact that *Image* was economically unstable, but hadn't looked at any recent figures, as an argument in a very pressured way to destroy the publication. The only foothold was the fact that it was by subscription. There was a nucleus of funds, and they agreed to permit the publication of the photo secession book, and I parlayed that into a publishing program which resulted in, subsequently, the publishing of about 18 titles over a period of eight or nine years.

Simultaneously my own work was developing, but there was almost a strange kind of counter-pull that I sensed. Because of the direction of my own work, a number of other photographers were not responding to the potential of the Eastman House thinking that that would be a bias which would be imposed on my response to their work — which really wasn't the case. I've always enjoyed interesting work no matter what direction it's pursuing. Of my own choosing, I limited access to my own work. I put most of my emphasis in developing a series of programs at the Eastman House. Now that I don't find myself in that kind of position, the work is coming forward again. This context (Director — Visual Studies Workshop) doesn't carry all of the associations that people might bring across the street (to George Eastman House), so I feel a lot better about that in a more total sense. I don't make any separation with what I'm doing, it's all part of the same thing, whether I'm teaching, doing research, writing, photographing — it's just an approach I've come to that's very important to me. If I'm working intensely on one project I don't get upset because I'm not out photographing. If I'm out photographing I don't get upset because I'm not working on something else. There just seems to be a kind of rhythmic pace that usually finds me and I don't consciously schedule this in. It has to do with the issues, what's important at the time for me.

TD: Who are the people who inspired you?

NL: I really didn't have any; I got to be too old to be inspired, I guess. There was no formal training; there was no access, or resources on the terms that they exist today. It's very characteristic of most people who involved themselves in photography that they were loners. I could say the one who influenced me the most in the early period was some anonymous clerk at Willoughby's. I'd go down and try to listen to what he was saying, while looking through a magazine or something, to pick up any tips from the pros. But it wasn't until much later that I began to recognize and identify the work of individual photographers. That was probably an interesting factor developmentally because I had already had a very extensive background in another field when I came to a point of recognizing certain things about the photographic medium, part my own needs, recognizing and coming in contact with other people who were working. I have a high regard for anyone who has sustained a working position in the field and has contributed something to the history of the medium, and the people who have affected my thinking and my responses, or challenged my thinking, aren't exclusively photographers. Poets, philosophers — again, I don't make that separation.

I think the first exhibition that I saw was *The Family of Man* in the early 50s, when I was just going overseas or coming back from overseas, I can't remember. I was very excited about the implications of the kind of picture environment which was created. I saw a very small show of Weston photographs in a tiny gallery somewhere and I remember being very taken by the vision — the way he was seeing things. Those were probably the only two exhibitions I saw well into the late 50s.

TD: Perhaps we can clarify some of the terms which will come up as we go into your photography. For example, reality in photography; abstraction; the snapshot aesthetic; and spontaneity?

NL: Well, probably if we had talked ten years ago the emphasis would be different when utilizing the same terms. One thing I'm finding is I'm less and less interested in terminology. The other evening I was trying to tell a group of people that one thing I've noticed is that progressively, in terms of anything I've written, it gets briefer, maybe more complicated—but briefer. The subsequent book which is coming out, (**Notations in Passing**), has absolutely no writing in it at all. We get confused about the relationship between clarifying our concerns, one of the earliest instincts seems to be to establish a verbal display that assures everybody what the work means. I'm probably now more interested in establishing more of a visual verification of those issues. I've spent a lot of time speaking with people, teaching and lecturing. The thing you begin to sense is that it may be an inappropriate form for the exchange of certain ideas.

It's quite possible in a few years I'll cycle back and feel the need to clarify something, but I think the issue will be out of a range of work, and a totally different approach to the discussion. I'd like to find another way of dealing with some of the issues and ideas. Just in terms of what you've asked, we continually deal with all functional issues in relation to terminology. If I can convince you about what I mean by using certain terms, that's one thing. But usually in terms of larger groups of people there's a breakdown even in the implications, the utilization of certain kinds of terminology. And you're not always in a position to clarify everything you're saying, simultaneously with you're saying it. Historically, we've developed a wide range of considerations about the terms to which you allude. And there are still people who are very involved in trying to penetrate issues regarding the nature of reality in our lives. I don't think I can just trace the extent of thinking that I've been exploring regarding all of these issues. It would be almost an endless conversation. Briefly it has something to do with trying to understand issues regarding relative meanings of things, the pictures we make, the effect those pictures have on other people, even the effect their response has on us. I think we've been willing to make a wide range of assumptions about meaning and effect in areas of visual communications and I'm still actively pursuing, trying to understand some of these issues.

TD: The reason I brought them up was because in looking at your work I would come across certain terms, for example, in Under the Sun, **the focus is on abstraction.**

NL: The issue of abstraction, yeah, but if you go back into that you'll recognize that I'm suggesting the concept of a process as opposed to product and in another article

I wrote, in response to the exhibition, "The Sense of Abstraction," that we're all involved in the process of abstraction, and I think it changes certain implications, which I tried to clarify, to some degree, in that article.

If you're photographing and using the medium directly, the order of what's being observed shifts and the relevance you bring to it through your responses is what's informative. The earlier work progressively was dealing with removing a lot of familiar associations and providing a very personal kind of experience for someone. Often the pictures look very complex, often, for me, the issue of the picture was very simple. Well, through that whole cycle I gradually became concerned about reinvestigating the effect that objects might have, and became very interested in dealing with simple pictures which were subsequently very complex. So it was kind of an inversion of a working premise, going from complicated images to simple images. That's been a working position for a long period of time. There is evidence of the concern as early as 1955.

I was concerned about both issues simultaneously, then I moved and explored one main consideration, and then came back, it seems, and started to pursue the other. I haven't thought about it that much, but the exhibition which clarified a lot of it was one I did in '58, entitled "Seven Days a Week" and, going back in my own head, a lot of what I worked on since then was declared at that time. I've just been investigating it more fully, more totally. There's always been an interplay between the recognizable and familiar to the unrecognizable and not so familiar, having to do with what associations we can form out of both realms of experience and what relationships might exist between them. It's also the involvement with series somewhere in 1955 and has a strong relationship with understanding certain issues regarding poetry and a number of conversations that I had with John Wood at that time, and they're both coming together and recognizing that I was concerned with the interrelationship between words and images; the interrelationship with images. My main interest was not just making a picture.

TD: How did the concept of this book Notations in Passing **evolve?**

NL: You got the sense of its connection back, but besides the work that people might recognize or remember from **Under the Sun,** there was another concern that was developing. A lot has to do with the way we articulate space, the human landscape, and it was at a time when cities were just going through the first stages of transition. I did a series of photographs that had to do with that kind of transition; things being torn down, things being revealed, the juxtaposition of elements within a city. As man builds a city certain things come together for very strange reasons, or there's no consideration as to why one thing relates — exists with another thing. And I did a fairly large group of photographs which have appeared in two exhibitions, dealing with the city, one with Charles Eames' "Photography in the City" (1969) and one that came out of M.I.T. called "The Innermost House." I was still working with 4 x 5. It was a time when I was starting to move around the country a lot more, and the prospects of taking a 4 x 5 camera with me were next to impossible, so I came back again to the 35. I would time it to do a day's work or two days' work shooting, and **Notations in Passing** covers a lot of physical territory. What I was concerned about was probably an extension of that city landscape concept, and then not wanting it to be regulated by that thematic position, and started feeling the need to deal with the kind of social horror that we were existing in, and wanting to photograph fragments of that in some way. But then, very quickly, as the thing developed, there's no preconscious involvement, just a feeling that what I had to do was carry out this visual journal — just openly responding to things I was seeing, and then beginning to understand something about my own responses and bringing that together. It was really dictating more about what was happening than I was.

There's a whole range of sequential considerations that I'm bringing to bear with this work. It, at one level, I hope, looks very simple; at another level I think it's an incredibly complicated work and I've always tended to respond to that issue because then you don't drive anyone away. Somebody looks at it and thinks it's charming or funny, fine. Those who begin to pick up on it or come back to it will probably begin to discover there's more there. I am interested in the potentials of an imagistic form that you can return to and discover more. It's not just a question of simple recognition factor. I'm kind of concerned about implications, relationships, developing issues, and hopefully somebody may come back to that book ten times and still discover something they hadn't seen before.

TD: You were working on a book all along.

NL: Yes, I knew that was the form, that's an important point, too, because most of the other work was transmitted in terms of framed prints on a wall and that started to bother me. I've been, for a very long time trying to encourage people to consider the potentials of the book. I can remember arguments that go back 10-12 years, 14 years, saying much more serious attention has to be paid to the development of this potential within the medium and, even here, (Visual Studies Workshop, Rochester, N.Y.) we make a very strong commitment to encouraging people to begin to pursue and investigate a number of these issues and ideas, because I do ultimately feel that it can form a shift from the preconception of the photographic medium only exisiting in the traditional fine art context. Matted prints, framed, under glass, on a wall, are only one aspect and, for a long period of time, I think it was the singular direction that everybody felt their work had to move towards. I like the book because of the way in which a work can develop. It's an exhausting proposition, developing something that totally, rather than having six photographs on the wall, but I think ultimately there are a number of very distinct differences between the two activities.

TD: Did this actually take from 1962 to approximately 1972?

NL: I think '74. There's a photograph in the book, I'm quite sure, from 1962 and the last photograph I did in early '74. So it's about 12 years.

TD: What were you looking and aiming for as your vision evolved? It's a long time to hold an idea in your mind.

NL: Well, the developmental issues, the form itself, is a very demanding issue. The concept was one of an extended series, but also incorporated certain considerations regarding, not only the serial development of images, but a notational system, that's why it's called **Notations in Passing.** You see the thing that keeps you going are the issues of your life, what's happening around you, what's affecting your responses. I don't think it's completed, I think I'll probably continue working on the terms that **Notations in Passing** represents, and that will surface again at a later period. I'm already starting to go back over a lot of other shooting I've been doing over this period of time that deals with some other issues and I'll bring that forward. But a lot has to do with the total concept in terms of what I was working on, and because it was demanding, it was very interesting, and I could sustain an interest in it. I didn't say, "It's finished." It just felt right, now is when it should come together. There have been intermediate versions of it. In print form, which isn't my primary concern, the book being new in relation to those exhibitions, I think, can even establish another interesting dimension, because the two exhibition forms of it appeared at different times, even are utilized in very different ways from one to the other, to the book, where a number of the photographs in the exhibitions are not in the book, the relationship to other images changes and it's hard to describe something to you really that is involving itself with about a 98 or 96 print series.

TD: You're working for a period of twelve years and all of a sudden you bring all this material together. Did you have the feeling that "I have a book here," or "The time is right for this book?"

NL: It's not that the time is right for the book, it's just that I think it clarified itself to a point that it could kind of move out at this stage.

TD: It's a very fascinating thing to talk about the process, and then say this is a notation in the process of the book. The title, Notations in Passing, **is such a complex title, and throughout the process you put out the work in different forms. It's an incredible phrase that can be applied in so many ways as it related to your work, to photography in general, to just about anywhere you want to look. The assembling of the book took how long? A year?**

NL: In the final form, no. It evolved probably very strongly over a five-year period, and it wasn't necessarily in directing it toward completion, it was in trying to get a better understanding of what was happening, what was clarifying itself, and then I put it aside, and just pulled out work, not to fill in gaps, not to find the missing links, but in a strange way, in response to what I put together, but not as a conscious intellectual position. I received an N.E.A. grant last year which enabled me to continue a stage of shooting. I felt I hadn't looked at some things that I should take a look at and I did, and it added another dimension to the overall thing and I was able, about this time last summer, to do a lot of printing, and the gradual progression of it has been very pronounced over this past year and a half. I actually finished it six months before it went to the publisher. What I'd do is not look at it for periods of time and try to come at it as if I was looking at it for the first time, also asking a few people, very different people really, in terms ot their interests in the medium, to take a look at it.

TD: Who, for example?

NL: Larry Clark went through it, and seemed very enthused. Ralph Gibson went through it and actually wanted to publish it, but couldn't handle the size of the project. Hollis Frampton looked at it. Carl Chiarenza, and John Wood.

TD: When did you approach a publisher?

NL: I didn't approach a publisher. Gibson saw the work at an earlier stage, was enthused, and wanted to publish it. I had prior commitments to another publisher in terms of other books I had done, so I felt responsible to show it to him. He wanted to publish it. Gibson convinced him that it would be very important for Lustrum Press (Ralph Gibson's Press) to do it. I don't know how he convinced them, but he did, it seems, and it might have been the size of the project, which still isn't that large, but in terms of certain publishing issues it might be considered that. Then Ralph couldn't hold to it and he relinquished it, and Bill (Edwards) and Lionel (Suntop) at Light Impressions, who were handling Lustrum, were very interested in it, and took on the responsibility of finding a publisher. They made the arrangements with M.I.T. (Massachusetts Institute of Technology) Press. I spoke to Muriel Cooper who was in charge of production when I delivered it. I don't think I've had any kind of formal meeting with M.I.T. Press.

TD: How about your control over the layout, design et al?

NL: Everything was sequenced, I've laid on certain specifications about the printing of it. I did ask them to respond to the issue of it in the design of the cover, and the title page — half of the title page really — because part of it I designed and wanted to see how they'd respond graphically to it. 95% of the book was handed to them complete, sequenced, paged, designed, format; all of these things were worked out by me.

TD: Does the editor, Nathan Lyons, get in trouble with Nathan Lyons the photographer?

NL: Probably, but we get along pretty well. We seem to understand one another.

TD: You have primarily done editing of books and your editing is so strong that it sort of takes control, I think.

NL: Oh, I came down on the photographer pretty hard. Sounds like a song. 'The photographer in me,' and the photographer took a lot of stands with the editor. Probably there was no distinction between the two because I think what I've even alluded to in the preceding books, that I'm working on certain issues within them, and trying to understand something about overall work that an individual does, the relationship of that work to other work that they do. Yeah, I probably could have rushed off in the first three years and produced an acceptable book, but that isn't what work is about for me. There are important issues that take time — you work at them. I'm not selling anything and I'm not trying to. Often people working feel that they have to be continually calling attention to themselves in their work. It may sound funny in a sense, because probably more people know me than I know them, but I generally tended to try to be more anonymous publicly than people realize.

TD: Well, you are certainly anonymous as a photographer.

NL: In certain areas, yes; not in Europe, not in Japan. I'm probably known better as a photographer in Europe and Japan than in this country. And that may have something to do with the books or the appearance, in publications, of work. And it seems strange, I've been at it a while, so there's a whole mid-generation that probably hasn't seen any work that I've done.

TD: Is your visual material a record of your life and is it necessary for your sense of being?

NL: You said that, I didn't.

TD: For example, you talk about traveling around and I got the impression that photographing gave you a sense of being.

NL: No. Photographing doesn't. Living gives me a sense of being. I'd put that first. Photographing is related to that whole process. I feel the more I can relate that and integrate that, the more totally you can make that, maybe the more you can really understand.

TD: Do you feel it necessary to document your existence as you plunge through life?

NL: Everybody feels the need and they do it in different ways. The way somebody creates a physical space for themselves is another kind of record but, I'm not only concerned about myself, it's not a totally egocentric involvement. I'm concerned about a wide range of corresponding issues in everyone's life.

TD: I felt that in your earlier work Under the Sun **(Braziller (1960), for example, you were more contemplative and deliberate, and now with** Notations in Passing, **you say there's a more casual and spontaneous reaction to the process.**

NL: Yes, I probably could go along with you on that. It's funny, past the more obvious aspects of each, I think the same things are functional. I think there are people who know my earlier work fairly well and, although issues of subject matter have changed, they see the relationship between the work because there is, for me, a very definite relationship back, even to **Under the Sun,** and earlier than that and later than that. I don't see it as separate. That work was and is very important to me, even now because it did help to clarify and raise a series of questions. I'm intrigued with the possibility of even reinvestigating some of those issues in another way, whatever that means. I can't see the pictures yet, but I know or I guess some issue is going to be made over the fact that they'll look different. I'm not sure I'm totally the same person I was then. I'm that person plus another span of years of experience. The first time that ever came up in my life was when I returned from overseas and a few people said, "You've changed." I said I'm kind of glad I did.

TD: Do you feel Notations in Passing **is a major statement by you?**

NL: I'll be willing to wait to see what the response is. I can accept the fact that it may be very important for me and it may not be for others. The people that I've shown it to seem very enthused about the implications of it.

TD: Were you influenced by Robert Frank or Walker Evans? I see this body of work as in the tradition of Frank's The Americans, **though more contemplative, and in the tradition of Evans'** American Photographs, **although more spontaneous and stark. Frank I see as gray, grainy prints; Evans as full tonal range, everything sharp; your work, deep blacks, sharp, dark, stark, contrasty, and reflections. Is this** The Americans **or** American Photographs **of the sixties?**

NL: It probably, in some sense, characterizes aspects of a time span, but there is more of a time span than just that in it. There are a whole series of artifacts that allude to culture, from pictographs through, even a dinosaur surfaces in the thing. So I'm setting up a very long time span, but I'm setting up that time span through a reference of the late fifties, sixties and seventies because that's an important issue in my mind. As far as I've had a lot of respect for both Evans and Frank in terms of the work that they've done, I don't think the issue was influential as much as it was supportive. And there's a distinction there. I have a high regard for the work that both Frank and Evans have done, but I really don't think I did this because their work existed. Sometimes you feel you're preoccupied about something, and you see something and it's supportive. You say, well, somebody else is seeing that in a kind of way. I think I've acknowleged it publicly in another way. **Toward a Social Landscape** grew out of a range of concerns trying to help clarify work going on in the field, and from there the next book that I did was another aspect of the work going on in the field. Maybe something about finding yourself in that kind of a situation where you're trying to be responsive to a wide range of work that's going on and how you're trying to deal with your own work establishes something, the influences are influential, but they just seem to be supportive in my mind.

TD: Do you define Notations in Passing **as a personal thing?** Notations in Passing— **and this I'm reading from** Aperture — **(1971 - Vol. 16, #2) "Snapshots done as part of a process, unpretentious and yet important, aspiring to nothing, a notation in passing. Do we see things as they are or do we see what we make of them, a continuity of impressions, it could be about me, but I think it is probably a series of questions about us and our stuff, fixtures, objects and things. They may question us for an answer that we cannot tell." I feel here that you are asking a deliberate question. These notations are your concerns, perhaps your symbol of what we are about. I feel a definite statement about us in your questions, they may be your questions, but you also know the answer. Over and over I'm reminded of Robert Frank, the same concerns, but a different personal vision, beautiful, biting, powerful; your photographs are cold, they must be read carefully, consciously, no casual glance will deliver the message, reflections play a large part in the statement. I feel the statement is a reflection of your concerns and a reflection of us.**

NL: Sure. It's out of an issue of concern — concern about a lot of things, not just myself. I think a lot of work that I've done does relate to a concern for other people, something more total than one's self and as I tried to allude to previously, all of that connects up for me. It's not separate or distinct or this is more important than that, and the whole range of things. It's not a question of a personal aesthetic, it's a question of a personal philosophy. The issue is philosophy, not aesthetics.

TD: And aesthetics being a part of the philosophy?

NL: Yes.

TD: Could you talk about the actual printing of the book? Did you insist on a particular standard of reproduction?

NL: I've put on certain specifications about it, but I've done enough books to know what the variables are. You keep your fingers crossed at this stage. I'll check back in certain stages of production and, I'm hoping we can work it out so that I can be at the printer's when they print it.

TD: Who's printing it?

NL: I think Rapaport. I think that was where the last discussions were, with the promise that there would be certain kinds of control factors, but there's a reality in that and there's a fantasy. The only way you can assure any response to production is that you stand at the press during the entire run and check sections of the run as they come off. This is what I've done on sixteen books already. I've spent so much time worrying about everybody else's work on these terms, it would be nice to have someone worry about my work, and I feel fairly confident about the production people at M.I.T. We've talked. They do have a level of standards that is high in publishing, and I'm willing to not impose, just keep an eye on it as it proceeds. There are stages that I have to review. The other thing is the nature of the book. I want the reproduction to be certainly more than acceptable, but it doesn't have to be a kind of overstated printing situation. I don't want to get caught in that trap in relation to what this book is and the nature of the photographs. It has to be well-printed, but I don't want to make an issue out of the printing, because that puts an emphasis on it that I don't want to call attention to.

TD: Were there any restrictions on you in putting the book together, or did you just deliver the dummy and that was that?

NL: Yes.

TD: As you delivered it, that's the way it will be published?

NL: Sure, yeah, that's it. I'd written a novel and...

TD: Well, even a novel is edited.

NL: Certainly, but there may be some different issues about the photographs, and it may be also that there aren't enough editors around yet who can deal with the problem of picture-editing intelligently enough.

TD: How much do you photograph?

NL: It's usually in blocks of time when I'll shoot and there are blocks of time when I'll print, but there are a number of other things that I also was working on at the same time. This is one thing that has come out of that period of shooting. There'll probably be two or three other series to come out of the same period of shooting.

TD: How did you decide on the structure of the book? Do you consider the form a traditional one?

NL: It is and it isn't. I've indicated that it has something to do with structures that have existed for a very long time, and that's like a two-day conversation in itself, back over the ways in which images can go together, trying to have something function in one way, and restating aspects of it so it functions in another way. You can analyze these issues probably, you can isolate aspects of it, but I don't think you can tell someone why it happens that way. That's part of a very complicated activity that has to do with whatever it is that I understand about the potentials of structure, and bringing things together, of challenging some of those things internally within a work. Setting up things for people to anticipate and then changing that very dramatically, or very subtly. These are all working issues, while the photographing is problematic enough. The structural position is equally problematic, and people would understand that after they went through the book a number of times. The structural premise is a series. It has to do with the order of presentation of images and how that can affect the viewer. I'm quite sure, beyond what the working premise is, that that may be totally unimportant to how that attention to the total work is going to affect a viewer, who doesn't consciously pay attention to how I put it together. It's a combination of the mechanics of something, plus the responsibility of one's craft, like a writer has to deal with many issues beyond what he's writing about. Well, the photographer on these terms faces the same problems, but they're different, yet they're related.

TD: How do you think this book will affect your reputation?

NL: Oh, should I really worry about that? Do what you have to do. If people respond through an interest, that's supportive, but I'm trying to say sometimes the most dangerous aspect of trying to continue working is being deluded in what responses represent. Some people who respond to what I do make me very nervous because I don't really have a positive sense that they're really that involved. Other people can look at something that's taken me a very long time to do, and just smile and nod. It's really nice. I'm quite sure other people will have to go through a very detailed analysis of what it is they think I've done. I want to be responsible to that, but I don't want to be misled by any of it. I just want to keep working.

TD: Do you ever have a desire to simply be a photographer, instead of an educator/photographer, et al?

NL: No, I tried to convey an aspect of that previously in the conversation; it's all important to me.

TD: And you don't have any conflicts?

NL: No. I've tried not to impose my problems on anyone else. It's something that I'm trying to deal with, and continually try to work out, and it seems to be continuing.

TD: Where do you see picture books going?

NL: I think we've already started to get an indication that they can be much more interesting than they have been, and I think it's going to necessitate people getting past just photographing and start dealing with some of those issues, but the main attention that people bring now has to do with making the picture. I try to encourage people to explore ways in which that picture can be transmitted. In general, there have been specific photographers, but very few, who have brought attention to the context in which their work appears, and the photographer has to become more and more responsibile for those issues. Too often somebody's work has been distorted, misinterpreted, not given a chance to develop itself fully, in terms of all these implications and hopefully, what I have been trying to suggest for a very long time is the question of authorship, where the issue of the philosophy of one picture maker can be dealt with as a very full and total kind of an experience, and he's not an anonymous ingredient in the society, but his observations are important observations to present to other people, not just to satisfy something in terms of that audience, but to challenge something in terms of that audience, to get them to see more than they've seen before.

TD: What are some of the important picture books?

NL: In going back, I'm very interested in some of the earlier picture book forms, from illuminated manuscripts to emblematic books to earlier pre-photographic attempts where words and images or sequences of images were presented. Photographically, books that I think have been very important, possibly for very different reasons, have been Brugiere's **Beyond This Point,** which not too many people know, but it deals with some interesting observations. Certainly both the (Robert) Frank **(The Americans)** and the (Walker) Evans **(American Photographs)** books. Some of the issues serially that some of the historians have been working with. There have been a few, like **The Columbia Portrait of New York** (John A. Kouwenhoven), the kind of collection of images that that represents. On other terms Grace Mayer's book which I think is a superb book, **(Once Upon a City: New York from 1890 to 1910 as Photographed by Byron.** Macmillan & Co. New York, 1958.) There's a whole bibliography you could bring forward. Some of the more spontaneous things that are occurring now among a number of photographers, doing little private books and some of the activity that we're generating here (Visual Studies Workshop). These are all very encouraging indications.

TD: What was the most difficult aspect of your book?

NL: Being patient enough to let it develop.

TD: What are your plans for your next book?

NL: The next book will probably deal with visual history, which I don't want to get into here because I'll go on for four days about it.

Rochester, New York
July, 1974

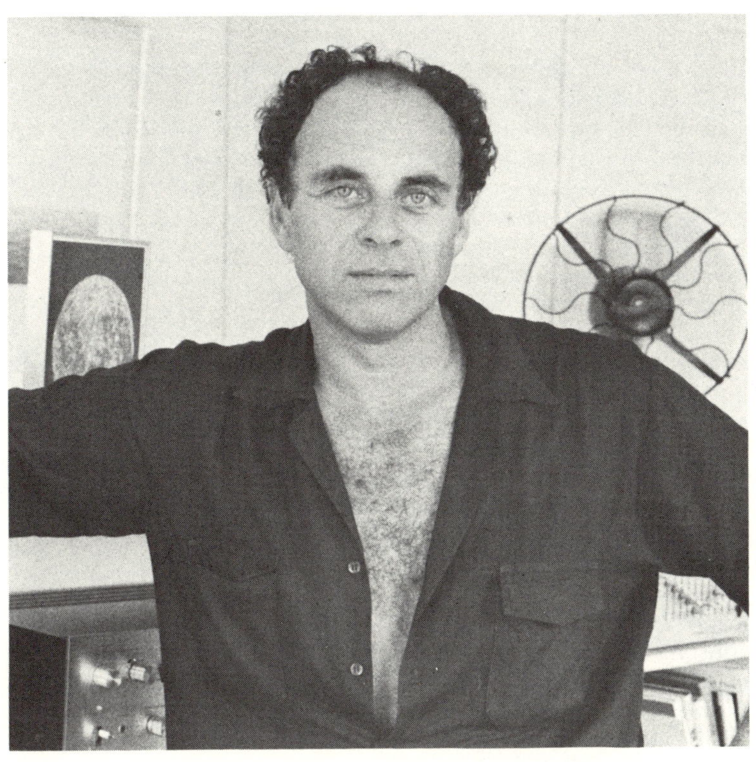

Ralph Gibson

Interviewer: Did people appreciate your imagery at that point?
Ralph Gibson: I worked on the dummy for three years, the sequence of **The Somnambulist,** continually adding, changing, and, during that period, I was also a freelance photographer... I had a peer group of photographers you would know who were highly critical of my contrast and grain and the surrealistic quality of my images. There was a point where I stopped being a documentary photographer and abruptly became what, for want of a better word, we'll call a surrealist, and, at that abrupt change, my peer group put enormous pressure of a negative sort on me. I don't see those fellows anymore. I have a much more interesting circle of friends now, as a matter of fact.

The interview with Ralph Gibson took place in his Soho loft in March, 1975. It was a cold, blustery New York winter day. Initially the most striking aspect of Ralph's personality was his intensity and seriousness of purpose. He displayed a facility for total involvement, even when a question might bore him, and I felt we achieved a degree of intimacy unusual for a tape recorded conversation. He had recently completed his trilogy with the publication of **Days at Sea.** This interview lasted two hours and appears almost verbatim. Any changes served to clarify a point here or there.

Ralph Gibson is a tall, athletically-built man bursting with energy, confident, and with an air of remarkable self-assurance. He is exquisitely articulate, honest, open, entertaining and charming. A sensitive man and artist making his mark in a modern, technological culture and society, a recluse of sorts, dedicated to his purpose in life. Everything appears to be sublimated to his Art. Throughout the talk we sipped wine and nibbled crackers and cheese.

Born: Los Angeles, California. January 16, 1939.
Attended: San Francisco Art Institute.
Books:
   The Strip. 55 photographs of the Sunset Strip. Roger Kennedy Inc. Los Angeles, 1966.
   The Hawk. 50 photographs from the play by Tony Barsha and Murray Mednick. Bobs-Merrill. New York, 1968.
   The Somnambulist. Lustrum Press. New York, 1970.
   Deja-Vu. Lustrum Press. New York, 1972.
   Days at Sea. Lustrum Press. New York, 1974.
Currently: Photographer, New York City.

Tom Dugan: How did you become a photographer?

Ralph Gibson: Quite by accident. I went into the Navy when I was very young and they sent me to photography school, as a result of an aptitude test. I got thrown out of that school, but tried very hard and got back in—I was 18 then—and I decided I would try, for once, to make a go at something in my life and I've been at it ever since, still trying.

TD: In one of the magazine pieces on you, you're quoted as saying you became a photographer because you wanted to succeed at something. Had you had problems in your teen years?

RG: I had been a very good magician and a very talented musician, and could have really gone far in music, if I had tried; I had some skill as an athlete, things like that. I had a tremendous sense of never having accomplished anything and a feeling that I never would, unless I drastically changed my attitude. I went into the service when I was young, I got thrown out of the house, and it's a very sink or swim kind of thing, early in your life, it's heavy and painful and you have to survive.

TD: What was the problem? A problem with authority?

RG: Stuff like that. I didn't study, I was smart, I'd be good for the first few weeks and then I'd dope off, get arrogant and start failing tests. It was a very intensive, very rigorous course in photography that just covered everything. It's still the very basis of my technique. It gave me a very sound footing, plus I did get interested in photography and continued to read, while in the service, anything I could get my hands on.

I was in Turkey, got hepatitis, and had to go into the hospital for six months. They happened to have had an extensive photography library at the Air Force Hospital, so I came out of the service pretty well-tutored technically.

TD: Then you went to the San Francisco Art Institute?

RG: Two semesters, then decided I had to do it for myself. I saw people around me had a tremendous amount of talent in a way I didn't. I've said this many times: I had a very clear vision that there were a certain number of clicks, decisions of the camera, exposures made with the camera at my eye, between where I was and where I hoped to be. The best thing to do would be to start making those clicks, so I quit school and shot a lot.

TD: What kind of direction did you have at that point?

RG: I was very into the idea of becoming a great documentary, photojournalist-type, Magnum photographer.

TD: Who influenced you at that point?

RG: I was crazy about Robert Frank. His book **The Americans** really hit, made a big impression on me, and my contemporaries, at the time. I was working for Dorothea Lange around then, too; I was her assistant. It was generally thought that the ideal one could aspire towards in photography was to present a social truth.

TD: Were there any experiences in your childhood that led to photography as a career?

RG: I grew up in Hollywood. My father was an assistant director and production manager for 35 years at Warner Brothers and I was a child actor. I'd been around a set, I'd been around the image-making community.

TD: Besides Frank, did anyone else influence you? Did Cartier-Bresson influence you?

RG: Yeah, Cartier-Bresson. There was a period in French photography, right after the war, in the fifties, when photographers like Edward Boubat, Jean-Philippe Charbonnier and Robert Doisneau caught my fancy; Ed Van der Elsken with his book, **Love on the Left Bank.** There was a time when I was interested in what was going on in Europe very much; Gene Smith, but then came Robert Frank and he just absolutely eclipsed everybody.

TD: You subsequently met Frank?

RG: Yeah, we've become very good friends.

TD: Did you seek him out?

RG: Once he came to San Francisco and I did briefly meet him. He said, "If you ever come to New York, call me." Then I came to New York and ran into him at a party and referred to that time several years earlier. He said, "Oh, yeah, I remember. Well, come on over, show me your things."

I had done a book **The Sunset Strip,** a documentary-type reportage and I showed it to him. He kind of liked it, and offered me work on his films. I didn't go seeking this work, I just wanted to know the guy. I started working with him and eventually traveled to Mexico with him, and I've flown around the country with him and his family. I wound up living at his place for a few months one time. We're very good friends. I saw Robert maybe a month ago. He stopped in here. When he's in town he comes by.

TD: Is he just into film-making now?

RG: Yeah.

TD: When you were growing up, did you feel outside the crowd?

RG: Very much, extremely. In fact, it is only in the last five years that I've lost that sense of being a pariah. I think, for want of a better word, recognition of the thing that you try hardest and take most seriously about yourself, to have affirmation in that specific area of one's life is a remarkable thing.

TD: Is your success something that with this new book you have proven yourself again?

RG: I really worked in the closet for twelve years. I didn't have any recognition until **The Somnambulist** and it just hit overnight and my life changed from black to white. I couldn't begin to tell how drastically the change in my reality became. Endless. Things like I had money, I could travel, I was invited, people knew me. Best of all, it gave me confidence to go ahead and do other, more difficult projects. For me, each successive book that I've done is more difficult than the former, the previous. So that's absolutely the best thing about it.

TD: Did you think The Somnambulist **would be successful?**

RG: No, absolutely, couldn't have cared less. I just wanted it published. It was the first time, though, that I had ever made anything resembling a major effort in my life. Some people have made great efforts in their lives, climbed mountains, overcame handicaps, shit like that. I had never made a great effort in my life before and I was amply rewarded.

TD: Did anybody appreciate your imagery at that point?

RG: I worked on the dummy for three years, the sequence of **The Somnambulist,** continually adding, changing, and during that period, I was also a freelance photographer. I had worked as a freelance photographer for seven or eight years. I'd even been in Magnum at one time. I had a peer group of photographers you would know, who were highly critical of my contrast and grain and the surrealistic quality of my images. There was a point where I stopped being a documentary photographer and abruptly became what, for want of a better word, we'll call a surrealist, and at that abrupt change, my peer group put enormous pressure of a negative sort on me. I don't see those fellows anymore. I have a much more interesting circle of friends now, as a matter of fact. I got rejected from a lot of shows and had a very hard time getting work. It was really a grind until it got better.

TD: And it got better upon publication of The Somnambulist**?**

RG: Sure.

TD: How did you get into self-publishing?

RG: Because other people, who were willing to publish it, wanted to change the book. I had done a lot of essays for the magazines in town; I'd been working and knew my way around the business, and I knew that this was one time that I didn't want to have any apologies, no excuses; I didn't want to blame anybody for fucking up, cropping, lousy printing, whatever. Most professional photographers are always saying, "Hey, I saw some of your spread in *Life* magazine." "Oh, yeah, but they didn't run the good ones." I mean you've heard it a thousand times. And they're all pissing and moaning and bitching all the time. Well, I was such a person and this was the one time in my life I wanted to have autonomy. I was going to take all the bows or all the knocks, but I wasn't going to pass the buck or let anybody else take the credit. I was very fortunate in that I was able to get a deal together and it came out rather well.

TD: How much money did it take to publish the book?

RG: Very little, surprisingly little, could never be done that cheaply now, but I produced that book for about one-third of what it costs me to produce a book now, in a similar edition.

TD: Which is how much?

RG: I don't know if figures are relevant to this. I mean you can go to any number of printers, I don't want to compromise the printer who did it for me or the one I'm working with now. Everybody makes different price deals. As a rule of thumb, you could probably take any fifty page photo book and do a first class job for around ten thousand dollars for five thousand copies. That's a sort of ball park. It could be more, it could be less, depending on many, many, many variables.

TD: How did you first distribute it?

RG: Light Impressions were my distributors at the time and they had just started. As it turns out, Robert Frank took a copy of the book and showed it to Nathan Lyons, who showed it to Bill Edwards and Lionel Suntop, and they took it over. In fact, it was quite easy getting distribution. A lot of distributors wanted it after it was made. The book came out very beautifully produced and I had absolutely no trouble. I took it around, distributed it myself in town for about a month or so. I would say nine out of ten stores that I went to with the book immediately ordered it. I placed it all over.

TD: Do they take it on consignment?

RG: Yeah, they take it on consignment or would buy a very small number of copies. I placed it in the Museum of Modern Art bookstore. They were my first big order. They started with fifty and then bought another hundred after that very quickly. Usually a bookstore will take one or two copies unless it's an old trusted salesman come to see them, a guy they've been doing business with for years. He says, "This is going to be a mover" and they might order six. It's hard to sell books.

TD: How many copies were finally sold?

RG: Three thousand.

TD: That was the whole first edition?

RG: Yeah, I've subsequently reprinted it in a much bigger edition. The second edition is now on the stands.

TD: You'll continue to reprint it?

RG: That's my intention, to keep my three books on the stands. They're all very steady sellers. When you bring out a new book, it takes a big jump in the first month or two, then sets its pace which is a much more realistic indication of what the book's going to really do, how many are going to sell a year.

TD: Distribution seems to be the big problem. Photographers feel if they get the book out on the stands it will sell.

RG: Yeah, that seems to be true, certainly up to a certain quantity. Even though we're in a relative boom period, it's never been quite this good, it's still new. The book thing is still new, especially in the quality of books, content-wise, that we're discussing, the so-called fine art photography book.

TD: It seems to me that your book would be more difficult than most. I was surprised that you were successful in distributing it, because you would seem to need a more sophisticated "looker" to buy your book than to buy a more traditional book like George Tice's Paterson. **The person buying the book would have to bring much more to your books than to some of the others.**

RG: I think people like to do that, as a matter of fact. One of the things I discovered when I was trying to get the book published, and I had the dummy with me at all times, I'd be on trains or planes or elevators, I'd just show it to all kinds of different people, straight, normal, ordinary folks and I was amazed at the level of response.

TD: I've shown your work to friends and they all have difficulty. And I can understand them not understanding. I deal with it in a very personal way, probably unlike what you had intended. I was thinking of how I respond to your work? When I'm driving I find myself looking at something along the way, as though through a 50mm lens, and I do this all the time. The pictures I see don't make any coherent, logical sense, and I always wish I could record those images on film, but, while driving, I can't. Someday I'd like to be a passenger and shoot those things.

RG: It never works that way.

TD: That type of seeing reminds me of your books, a cinematic, surreal series of images, a daydream as I go through my life. I like to show your work because of the

responses they elicit. People seem somewhat shaken in their preconceptions afterwards. Non-understanding seems very difficult for people to deal with.

RG: I was completely prepared to be a misunderstood artist, but I can't seem to come up with that conclusion anymore. The response is very favorable to my efforts, in all truth.

TD: People understand your work?

RG: Even if they don't understand it, they seem to like it. Some people loath it, I know, some people actually hate what I do, but they seem to be in the minority. I sell prints, I have exhibits.

TD: Whom do you sell through?

RG: I sell to private collectors and I sell through galleries. I sell a lot in Europe, I mean, really a lot.

TD: What personal characteristics do you feel made the choice of photographer a logical one for you?

RG: I think it more has to do with the fact that I'm visually more developed, my sight is more developed than any of my other senses.

TD: Why do you think that is?

RG: Probably has to do with previous lifetimes, things like that. Mine is the first generation to have TV; we got the first TV the minute they hit, I was about five or six and I'm glued to it ever since. I might be one of the first of the media babies, now they're in the womb. You've got two generations old of visual input, TV input.

TD: How would you describe yourself as a photographer?

RG: I work out my most serious and pressing concerns through my art, and my photographs are descriptions of the most serious concerns in my life, at that given time, things I'm most involved in trying to define. I don't get solutions to my riddles, but I get definitions that I can accept.

TD: Do you think you'll continue to work this way?

RG: The work tells me where to go next. I'm very involved and over my head in a new project now, and for me, the thing is to continue to stay inspired. As long as I'm inspired, I'll continue to think intensely about the things I'm most concerned about, and I'll be alive on a more intense frequency than if I weren't.

TD: Is inspiration a problem?

RG: No, but it's been the key to every artist. Certainly as I read the lives of the great artists, there's no doubt about it. They call inspiration the greatest piece of technique, their ability to inspire themselves.

TD: Is there a chance you'll go dry? Is that a fear?

RG: No. I don't worry about ever going dry, but just since I've finished my book, I started to think if I did it right, I could accomplish a great deal. I've seen this glimpse down at the end of a tunnel, just a little point of light, and on the other end, there might be true, true magnitude, true greatness. I'd like to know what the air is like up there. I'd like to know what it feels like to have produced a tremendous amount of work of a very high quality. You take somebody like a Picasso, well, he knows something we don't know, he knows something that you can only know, having produced a tremendous amount of work for many years. Now I would like to ally myself in such a pursuit, that's my intention as an artist.

TD: It doesn't seem any photographer has done that to date.

RG: That's true. There seems to be a pattern where they're hot for a while. I know I have certain of the key ingredients like ambition and shit like that.

TD: Something goes wrong, along the way, with photographers; for example, Walker Evans produced very few books and didn't produce a large body of work. It

seems that most photographers can't sustain the effort. They may be successful commercially, but they don't seem to continue to do personal work, except on a limited scale.

RG: I will avoid that pitfall, I haven't done any commercial work for five years, never will do it again. You just can't get me to do it, I'll teach before I'll be a hack.

TD: How much teaching do you do?

RG: I just do lectures and workshops. I don't even want to teach. I don't consider workshops teaching. Somehow or other, they're so intense that they're beyond simple teaching. But I have started a few jobs as instructor of visual arts and craft, I find it very stultifying and low level stuff. I don't like it.

TD: So you make a living from your books and sales of prints?

RG: And lectures.

TD: How many lectures do you do a year?

RG: About fifteen or twenty. I appear in a lot of photo magazines too, quite a few, and that does account for a part of my income.

TD: Do you see the photo magazines as a way to introduce new work?

RG: Absolutely. I don't care about the lousy reproduction. They put your pictures in front of a large number of people that you wouldn't reach any other way. I'd rather have a third of the content come through and hit a wider audience. It's more educational. The ones who are interested can always find the books. They can go further, if they're inclined.

TD: Who selects those portfolios?

RG: I do, absolutely. Sometimes we collaborate a little bit, but I have total autonomy. I say what size the picture should be, what sequence they run in, how big on the page, sometimes I mix the inks. It depends on which magazine and what my relationship is to them. There was an excellent magazine, *Photo World,* and I was extremely pleased with that spread (Jan. 1974). That was one where I got to select the inks. *French Photo* is very good to me that way. I had one spread in the Pop Photo annual (1972), the reproduction isn't very good, but at one time, they had several of the photographs blown up and bled and I asked them to change it and they did. There's a big difference in quality gained at such a moment. I discovered if you insist on certain things, you get them; if you don't insist on them, you don't get them, period, regardless, I don't care who you are.

TD: Is isolation necessary for your work?

RG: Most of the time I live alone, you see how I live. I'm always thinking about my work. I have it to the point where I never stop thinking about it, hardly ever stop thinking about it. Everything I do, I live in my studio, I live my work.

TD: Is the major portion of your work the thinking out of things?

RG: I fooled with my board today, put up some prints, took some down. I'm continuously rearranging, studying, trying to understand, make a next step, grow. It's very hard to grow.

TD: Once you get a book out, is there an emotional letdown, are you drained?

RG: I try to avoid it. I immediately, immediately fling myself into a new project to avoid that and usually can. I do happen to have a lot of energy. I was going to go away this winter to South America, but I said to hell with it. I think I'll stay here and work because I'm involved and I'm feeling it. This was the one time I felt that a trip would have been an interference.

TD: Do you go on extended trips?

RG: A couple of months at a time.

TD: And do you work while you're away?

RG: I shoot, sure, I always shoot when I'm traveling, sometimes more than here. However, if I'm shooting very well here and I'm very involved, it's foolish to go away.

TD: You said you're ambitious, so I assume success is very important to you.

RG: Let's say it makes it possible to do things. I had a tremendous sense of frustration before that I could never do anything. Now if I want to go somewhere, if I want to do something, I can do it.

TD: Do you remember what that frustration was like?

RG: Vividly. If you felt as bad as long as I did; I refuse to feel that way now. I never get depressed, I refuse it, I blast it out. I won't be, I shan't be depressed. I'll take a cold shower. You can't take a cold shower and come out depressed, it's impossible, your metabolism just moves too fast.

TD: How do you work now?

RG: I usually get up eight hours after I go to sleep. That's very important to me. I try to keep myself in excellent condition physically, so I can have my reactions and stuff like that. For example, I'll not produce tonight. What I like best is going into the darkroom in the mornings. I go through long periods where I do that, print in the mornings, but if the weather is good, after I get up and have my breakfast, do my little things, I'll go out and shoot.

TD: How do you know what you'll shoot?

RG: I don't know what I'm going to shoot, but I know what I'm in pursuit of, what I'm working on. I never know how it's going to reveal itself or what's going to, ultimately, be the manifestation of a concern that I have. I learned that from Dorothea Lange. Always have something you're going after, you don't just stand there, you have something in mind. The point of departure theory. I'm always working on a project. Right now I'm dealing with some problems of scale and photographing up very close and finding it very disorienting, disquieting, difficult. Trying to expand, I don't want to imitate myself.

TD: Now that the trilogy is completed, you're moving in other directions?

RG: I have a lot of exhibits this year and I'm trying to develop a view, a look, a presentation for exhibits, a show for exhibit purposes. I may or may not succeed, but I'm thinking in terms of the wall. I'm thinking in terms of relating to the viewer at a different distance. Anybody looking at my book is going to do so at approximately six inches. They hold it in their hands. Scale, the size of the print, the size of the page to the distance of the viewer, were things that I had very much under control and enabled me to get certain things stated. Working on the wall is different. You have to use another kind of graphic emphasis to produce certain feelings, to make certain statements viable.

TD: You think the prints have to be bigger?

RG: I have been making some big prints, 16 x 20, thinking that would be a solution of sorts, but I've stopped doing it. I got all set up for 16 x 20, bought trays, an easel, then stopped doing it. Naturally you start on a new project or a new thing, there's a tremendous amount of ambivalence involved. But I was reading in Ingmar Bergman's book, **Bergman on Bergman,** which I highly recommend. If you want to get inspired some night, just read him. He said in making *Persona* he realized for the first time in his career that his ambivalence could be a valuable and creative tool. If you know how to use your ambivalence, if you know how to use that sense of being unable to decide—because new work always is difficult to comprehend—if you're able to use it creatively, it's a fantastic thing. So I happen to be involved in a period like that now, I'm trying to grow and change. I know when the pictures have it, that quote, "it", unquote. I know when they're good or strong or have a presence. But one of the things I don't want to do is produce work that relies on making references to previous work. I'm trying to somehow go beyond my own periphery of reference. It's absolutely the most intriguing process. This is harder than anything I've ever tried to do before. It took me fifteen years to get a signature as a photographer and it might take me fifteen years to outgrow it, but at least I know that that's the problem. In the current *Afterimage*, in the noted and received section, whoever this punk is writing that thing, saying, "**Days at Sea,** a continuity of, in the manner of, however more erotic than appears," you know, I get a chuckle, I think with a great sense of irony, fortunately I'm not highly dependent, in any sense of the word, on a good review in *Afterimage*. What the fuck does it mean either way?

TD: I didn't think that was necessarily negative?

RG: No, I don't think it was negative, but it was this incredible, arrogant encapsulation of two or three years work of somebody who has been working for eighteen years. I thought that the reviewer held himself in extraordinarily high regard. I've been very well handled by the critics, but criticism is only, as far as I'm concerned, legit when the critic tries as hard as the artist. Then there might be what we'll call creative criticism about somebody else's art. I once had an enormous debate with Alex Sweetman, he was so down on Friedlander, well, Friedlander was shooting photographs when Sweetman was shooting peas. I mean he's been at it a long, long time, and for Sweetman to just come along and blah! blah! blah! It's a bit presumptuous. So that's the sort of thing that I'm very disdainful of. Some undergraduate, who can work on the school paper, gets to slay a few dragons or something. I think it's hilarious. I want photography to mean much more. I want my images to have much more content, I want them to be harder and harder, tougher and tougher images. I want them to resonate longer and stronger and I want to pack more content into an image. How to get an image to mean more and more, this is what I'm desperately concerned with. That's why reportage is so meaningless to me. You just slide right over the surface, you just skate over the meaning, you see it and it's over with. I don't want to make photographs that are open and closed statements. I want photographs that will continue to engage my intelligence, like any good work of art does. The average photograph is about on a par with the average decorative painting. I just don't want to take those kinds of pictures. I don't want to be involved in the making of them, they don't satisfy my needs. I like to hang photographs up to see how long they last, what kind of staying power they have.

TD: At a certain point in your career, going from documentary to surrealism, was there much anguish, suddenly realizing that what you had been trying to become no longer meant anything?

RG: Yeah, a great deal. You must know this. It sounds like a loaded question. Sure, I actually thought that I was dying. I had been working twelve years and thought that I had my route pretty deeply set. I was with Bill Brandt three months ago, December, in London, and I said, "Of all the great things you've done, of the many things I want to thank you for, the one thing that is most valuable to me is that you did your nudes when you were over fifty." To make that great a change in one's art at fifty is enormously inspiring to me. He was a really very heavily-established, documentary photographer, in England, their heaviest documentarian. All through the war he had all those big commissions, his portraits were a little bit bizarre, but other than that there was no indication that he was going to take off as far as he did. So for that I'm very impressed. Remarkable.

TD: How much time do you spend working?

RG: Generally I work every day. I try to shoot every day. I like to shoot at least 360 rolls a year. I can't do anything in this kind of weather though, in this kind of weather I'm in the darkroom. I did print yesterday morning and I plan to print tonight. I didn't shoot today, oh yes, I did, I've been shooting a few things around the studio. I have that camera set up on the tripod. I shot some things yesterday. I have four rolls of film now to develop. After you go I'll do that. That's my next thing and I'll probably get one image which I will then print in an edition. If I get something I really like I'll make a few of them, then probably wind up by going to sleep about 2:30 or 3, having written in my journal about the new picture.

TD: You keep a daily journal?

RG: Pretty much. If this evening is anything like others, that's the mood I'm in, especially if I don't drink too much Beaujolais with my fish.

TD: What is the advantage of keeping a journal?

RG: It's very useful a few years later. When I do occasionally read back, I find there are certain things I can discover about myself that I trust absolutely, and could not discover any other way. There it is, take it or leave it, it's just point blank, a certain truth. I tend to work in an introspective way and the feedback, the results are often horrifying, enlightening, amazing, many different things, but at least I know that they're for real. For me the difference between an artist and just a craftsman-photographer is if their work is reflecting their deeply buried aspects, their subconscious, if they're in touch with their soul through their art. That's something that I can see very quickly in somebody's work, if their work is reflecting that aspect of them. Consequently, I have a great need for this kind of reflection, which surely would wither up without it, and all these things add up to a feeling of being more intensely alive, learning things about myself. So consequently, the journal is part of that.

TD: Is it important in the sense of posterity?

RG: No, I don't care so much about that. I got all I need already. I'm not sitting around waiting. It's a very interesting thing, as a photographer, because I have a little recognition, but it's nothing compared to a movie actor or something. It's not enough to distort my reality too much. To be a recognized photographer in our racket, in our end of the medium, doesn't mean too much. You don't have trouble going down to the grocery store to buy a roll of toilet paper. You don't get mobbed. At the same time it does give me enough that I don't worry about posterity. That particular urge or need is out of the way.

TD: When I asked the question, I was thinking, of course, of Edward Weston's Daybooks. Could you see something like that in 20 or 30 years?f

RG: I don't think much about publishing. Once I did in a magazine about **The Somnambulist** (*Camera 35*, Nov. 1970.) I was amazed how it came out. I didn't mind it. It gave me something to write about that was, at least, authentic. At least I could put some honest words down in a magazine. And I find it very soothing and relaxing, fun to do. I could just go back to a page and look at how my handwriting was, without even reading the words, just looking at the hieroglyphics.

TD: Do you illustrate it?

RG: A little bit, occasionally. I was with Lartigue in the south of France a while ago and he showed me his journal. He illustrates it with drawings of the weather and this incredible, beautiful handwriting he has, then he keeps another daybook with his photographs. He puts pictures in it every night, over 400 pictures a year. That guy's got masterpieces you wouldn't believe. It'd be easy to make another great book out of Lartigue, very easy, no shortage of work whatsoever. Everybody thinks his earlier stuff is his great stuff. He's got tons of it. He just never stopped.

TD: Would you be interested in publishing him?
RG: Under certain circumstances I would.
TD: How do you get to publish other photographer's books?
RG: I made a company, I have partners now, I used to do it all alone myself, now my partners do a lot of the work. So that's one of the ways I'm able to have more time to myself. I'm still the editor.
TD: Do you solicit work?
RG: A lot of unsolicited work comes my way. I got a letter today from someone and I usually just answer him on a postcard, write a nice note back saying I only do one or two books a year and I'm all booked up. I did one book that was unsolicited, a guy came up to me with **Young American Photography.** He had the dummy all put together. He had already taken the project on his own; he was a graduate student. He had written to everybody, got all the work in, made all the copy prints, pasted them down and showed it to me. I've never wanted to do a book that wasn't in dummy form because then you have a point of departure, you've got something you can work on and improve. But if a guy just walks in with a box of prints, it's ten times the work, ten times.
TD: You're not interested in becoming a big publisher?
RG: No. I want to do it just the way I'm doing it. The only thing I'd like out of the publishing business is to sell more books. I'd like to do bigger editions of the same books I'm doing, and sell more of the kind of books I'm doing.
TD: You work exclusively in 35mm?
RG: Yeah.
TD: I know how involved you are in technique. I can always pick your prints out, because of the contrast and the grain, I know you have worked to achieve this effect. Could you speak about the technical considerations in your work?
RG: From the very start I was interested in grain, I always liked it. I came out of the Navy where I'd been very heavily schooled in the fine grain approach. I learned photography on a 4 x 5, speed graphic and view camera. I've always liked texture, if you look at the sky, concentrate on it, you'll see those little dots popping in the air.

You had said, for example, that you can always recognize my prints. You can do that, I can do that, with any photographer who has what I call a signature. It's not only a question of how they handle their film and paper, but it's how they handle their camera, how the eye sees, it's many, many things. It's a very important thing to a photographer, to have a signature, I feel, that's another one of the major differences. Anybody who is really any good doesn't even have to sign his pictures, if you're into it as far as we are, if you're that serious about photography. In terms of my look, for many, many, many years—finally I can give you something that's interesting about my childhood—I've been trying to express certain feelings that I've had. It wasn't until recently that I began to realize that essentially I was trying to express myself as an artist, trying to express feelings that were so subtle, bizarre and peculiar that the only way they could be expressed was through an art medium. There'd been no other way. That's what's so important and significant about art. You can express things that you can't express any other way. And I happen to be riddled with those kinds of feelings. In quest of this sort of expression, through the years, I have done several things. I have continued to court grain and I have become increasingly contrasty. I can go back to early work from 1960 and the prints used to be very flat and gray, printed on Varigam, but there was an effort to get a black. I happen to have a difficult thing to do because I overexpose, overdevelop, and print on contrasty paper. Now if somebody else goes out and tries that, it'll be a disaster. People come and show me work and some admirers will occasionally try to emulate something I might have done, I can see them trying to do it, and it doesn't work, and the reason is because ultimately the thing that makes an artist's technique or look, work is that it's being created in response to a deeply-set personal need of the artist. And when somebody comes along and tries to do the same thing, you don't get the same look. There's some alchemy involved in photography and this is part of where it's at. The only way I can get my statement across, the only way I can express the kind of things that I'm still concerned with, happens to be involved in the use of certain graphic devices. I like contrast because the kind of things I'm talking about are so subtle and peculiar that the only way that I can make them evident is to wipe the slate clean in the viewer's consciousness. You couldn't look at one of my pictures, coming in out of a crowded subway with a transistor, rock and roll thing, in your ear, and walk through a crowded museum and nudge people and expect to be able to see what it was I was trying to say. I have found I have to arrest the mind in order to make the statement clear. And part of the way I have of arresting their attention is through a certain attitude. The other thing is that I change things spatially, spatial values, objects in space. That's where a lot of it takes place. It used to be more in the darkroom; now, through the years, it's become more in the eye. I only use a 50mm lens, rarely ever use anything else, and certainly for the last two years I've used nothing but the 50. I can't see an interesting picture with anything but the 50, either. Essentially all the technique does, all the camera handling, all the lenses, film, the development, all it does is reflect the eye of the beholder, the photographer. That's really where it's at. I've thought, ultimately, I'll give a workshop in photography where nobody had a camera, where we'll just discuss how to see, train the eye how to see. I might do it. I think in my workshop this summer I'll spend one day where there's no camera, where we'll go out and take pictures without a camera. That's what I like the Leica for, because you just kind of put the camera to your eye after you've seen it. Whereas with the reflex you could walk around with the camera at your eye and find pictures.

TD: Even to this day you're experimenting, trying to enhance this contrasty, grainy effect.

RG: Well, I did recently make an interesting discovery in the way I'm handling my film. I feel that if I'm not growing, I'm sliding backwards. If I'm not doing something new and fresh, I'm in fact getting stale. It's a frightening thing. I don't want to lose the good feeling that my art gives me. I try hard to sustain it.

TD: What are some of the important picture books in recent years?

RG: I can tell you the great books. Lately, I have friends who are book collectors and they've been collecting old books from the Bauhaus. Let's say the ones that have shaped me, let's just settle for those. Naturally I was very impressed with **The Decisive Moment** (Cartier-Bresson) when I saw it. It moved me in a way that the other Europeans didn't. Then there was **The Americans** (Robert Frank) and, to a lesser degree, there's that book of Aaron Siskind's back in that time. Then there was **Perspective of Nudes** (Bill Brandt). I liked **Sweet Flypaper of Life** (Roy De Carava & Langston Hughes) very much. But there aren't so many, and we all know what they are. I'm just talking about the ones I've liked. I loved **Diary of a Century** (Lartigue) very much. I think **Tulsa** (Larry Clark) was a great book. I think it will be a long time before anybody will do anything better than that, in that genre. Tony Ray Jones has a good book **(A Day Off)** now. Now there's an awful lot of books and many of them are good. I feel, to interest me now, a book has to be kind of seminal. It's got to be a little different, it's got to be something I haven't seen. I've really been looking at a lot of them for a long time. I saw an incredible Man Ray book recently that he did with Paul Eluard, (**Facile,** 13 photographs by Man Ray, poems by Paul Eluard). But its got to be more, it has to change things somehow in photography, it has to be very strong, that's what I want to see. I love all of Weston's books, I think he's great, I'd have to include him, any book of Weston's is superb. I love the new *Aperture* (Edward Weston) book. I've had it out for about six months. I just look at it continually. You can see I have a lot of books around here. I buy books every day. I manage to get them. I only see books that have a tremendous amount of authority and are different. There's an awful lot of marginal efforts. It's always been, in fact, that there were photographers who have made good books and then there are those who haven't and there's a distinct difference between those who have and those who haven't. It has always been one of the challenges in the medium. There is a certain kind of respect when you respect somebody else's book and he respects yours. That's a little inroad that you share that the other people don't share, the ones that haven't done it. Snobbish, clique. It's interesting to see the life of a book, how long it will last. Photography has been relegated to ephemera. You look at the picture, turn the page, you look at the picture, turn the page, throw it away, get a new magazine next week. Some books are really lasting, like **The Americans.** It's really holding up, continues to sell. Some books are going to last a long time and that's really the proof, that's when you know.

TD: It's a shame that The Americans **was never well-printed. Maybe it matters less for that book than for some others, but it still seems a shame.**

RG: It still might be, I'm sure it will.

TD: Were any books forerunners of your books?

RG: No, I'm not aware of them. Are you?

TD: No. One of the things I find most admirable about you is that you published your books, the first one at any rate. It must have taken a great deal of courage. You must have gone through a great deal in putting that book together. I can't imagine what it must have cost you in terms of inner turmoil.

RG: There was a great deal. It's true. If you perceived that, you're exactly right, because it was my coming of age. That's what it was. That's where I slayed my first dragon. I used to wake up in the middle of the night chewing my teeth, and stuff like that. It's when my hair started falling out, a lot of shit. At one point, I don't know who I said it to, or what I said it to, but I remember one night I made a pact to the darkness in which I said, I don't care if I die, if I can just get this book out. I would settle for that, I would make that deal, if it were possible. It was some kind of a bizarre prayer to something. We're at that extreme sometimes. It had a great deal of personal drama involved, yeah. My life had been hideous since I was seventeen, it had been wretched for as long as I can remember. Somehow this was just a symbol. I was hanging on to it, like Medusa's wrath or something. This was going to be the one thing, if there was going to be nothing else, this had to be something. I was involved in a way that I had never been involved with anything else before. It was just that. I think you're very sympathetic because I think you're going through some of those things yourself.

TD: Did you show it to anybody that you felt understood it?

RG: I was living with a girl who was starting to rep me, trying to get me jobs as a free lance and she'd carry the dummy, she'd go out one day a week, around to see art directors, and she started to go to the photo magazines, something which I would never have done. They all got very interested in running portfolios. One of the things that happened, when the book did appear, simultaneously, in the same month, there were 30 pages of photographs in magazines all over the world, which turned out to be quite fortuitous for the life of the book. I started having incredible luck like that. Things changed, the thirty year war was over. That's the way it was for me. Now I have a very good life, certainly by comparison to what I had before. I'm not saying everybody has to wait thirty years, has to eat shit for thirty years, it just happened to be the way it unfolded for me. But there's something you find out that way, I guess.

TD: How did Larry Clark's Tulsa **come about?**

RG: We were friends. We had been friends in New York and I had seen what my book did for me. He had all those pictures. **Tulsa** was nine years shooting, that's nine years of photography, a very talented guy. I said listen, man, let's do it. And Danny Seymour came along, put up the money for the project and we were in business. Off we went and did it. Larry and I worked on the dummy here. He was living here and he'd fly down to Tulsa to pick up some pieces when we'd need them. Then we went out to the coast and did Danny's (Seymour/**A Loud Song**) book and Larry's book at the same time.

TD: Are you satisfied with The Somnambulist **as it stands now?**

RG: It's totally autonomous, it's its own thing. Sure, I have since evolved so far beyond it. I'm no longer the person who made it. Each year I look at it with more and more objectivity. It continues to change, Some of the pictures still hold me locked in their spell, others seem naive. As a work it seems to have a great deal of its own presence. It lives its own life that way. It doesn't have anything to do with me now. That's what's so amazing about books. Boy, you send them out, they live their own lives.

TD: What circumstances led to the book finally being published?

RG: I got the money.

TD: That was what held it up for three years?

RG: Actually I was in and out of other publishing deals. They kept fucking me. So finally I went around to art directors, people that I knew and sold shares in the book. Once I got that idea, the money came very quickly. I was out in Hollywood doing a job, staying with a friend of mine, a graphic designer, Bob Overby, who's been involved in a lot of tasty books, and he put me next to a great printer and off we went.

TD: Do you continue to use the same printer?

RG: No, he since went out of business. Now I'm doing it all with Rapoport.

TD: How did you decide on a trilogy?

RG: One book has always pointed me. By the time I'd finish one book I was already starting to work on another. I never know how long I'm going to have to work on a book but, all of a sudden I know when I've said what I set out to say. That's when I consider a book finished, when it says what I've set out to say. But by that time I already have some photographs that didn't make it in the book which are already harbingers of things I'm trying to do, which turns out to be the next book. So I decided to make a trilogy because they do interrelate and there are cross references. But now I'm not going to work on a book for a while or if I do, I'm going to do it in secret. I'm not going to publish another book of my own for a while, certainly not in the next few years. I've been doing a book every two years and I'm not going to now. The next one will be very, very different, I hope.

TD: Why in secret?

RG: Pressure from people expecting too much too soon.

TD: Did you discuss your book with anyone as you were putting it together?

RG: Not very much. Girls. Whoever happened to be around. Once in a while I would show it to somebody I like, sure, but I never paid any attention to him.

TD: You edit as you go along?

RG: Um, hmm.

TD: Some photographers work on several projects at one time. Do you?

RG: I'd pretty much work just on one project. Lately, though, I find I have a couple of others going, but they're long-range projects that I would never work full time on. They're kind of peripheral. I only really work on one thing at a time.

TD: How do you know how long a book will be?

RG: You never know. I just don't think I can hold the kind of interest I want beyond a certain point, hold a spell, a certain kind of attention. I can't go past maybe more than fifty photographs. I don't like really long books. Certainly not of the sequential nature that I work with. If I worked with another kind of feeling or overtone, if I was interested in another set of concerns, then the length could be different. But the kind of mood that I'm involved with, I've found my form.

TD: Do you ever leave out a photograph or photographs that you wish you had included?

RG: Not so much. Maybe once or something. By the time I publish them, I don't hastily push them out, I spend a lot of time with them, I consider them perfect, as good as I can do. Now I could probably go and improve **The Somnambulist** five years later, but it wouldn't be the same thing. I'd probably ruin it. It becomes its own thing in a way that excludes me toward the end. I feel that very much. By the time they start getting finished, there's not much I can do, I'm more out of the picture, the book's its own thing.

TD: Do you work longer on projects than you originally intend to?

RG: I find the time passes quicker for me every year. I'm busier every year of my life, I have more to do, more commitments.

TD: Have you had any regrets about self-publishing?

RG: Not in the least. I have autonomy, that's the big deal, I can do what I want.

TD: Why do you think more photographers don't self-publish?

RG: A few books came out recently. Steve Kahn did **Stasis,** David Pond Smith did a book **Manself.** Sometimes they come here, like Hans Levy came, and I said no, do it yourself, and he did it himself, **Street Jesus.** I've had that happen quite a bit.

TD: Do you find you're the example for a lot of people?

RG: It has nothing to do with me, it has to do with them. I'm more interested in my work than in publishing. I am. I always talk more about the content of my pictures than the structure of my publishing company or how I make books. That's something that everybody has to solve for himself. I've got that solved, so now I can start working on other problems. You're never off the hook. It's very hard to make a good book, but then once you've made a good book, it's very hard to produce it well, and once you produce it well, I've seen a lot of titles come and go since I've done mine, they just didn't get to go too far. They got published, but they didn't seem to do anything.

TD: You do everything on your book?

RG: I do all the layout, editing and sequencing and now I have a partner who's a designer, who helps me with the type, but that's just since **Days at Sea** and the last three or four books we did. We've only done four, five books in partnership. But as long as they're in the Lustrum format, there's not a tremendous amount of design to do. We just did some limited edition portfolios where my partner had to do more as the designer, he had to design the box, and such.

TD: You feel you have achieved what you've been aiming for with your trilogy?

RG: Um, hmm.

TD: Where do you get the inspiration for your books?

RG: I just think about my life, what it is, where it's going, what it does, what it means. I don't know what else I would do.

TD: Do you feel anyone was instrumental in your success other than yourself?

RG: Ultimately it's about the work itself. In order to do something well, to have what you call success, I feel there has to be an unbroken string of right decisions pretty much. Now my projects have had a lot of thrust or momentum. In terms of my relationship to my work, I'm really desperate. I'm a cornered rat. It's not very hard for me to get my work out once I've made it. I'm not going to make something exquisite and then put it in the closet. You don't make a baby and then put it in a drawer and let it die. I have a responsibility to it. Essentially I'm a desperate man, I'm very obsessed with this. As it happened I did make a book at a time when photography was really ready for the kind of book I made. There was a great need. If I do have an audience—I think I do—I help fulfill some of their needs, because people are tired of looking at the same thing in photography. Now, all you have to do is look around at all the museums and things and you see how receptive and responsive and open everybody is to everything. We have this great need for a more sophisticated quality of input. So I think that might have contributed a little bit. For one thing I know that I have insisted on certain things. I won't have my work treated like ephemera. I won't show in just any gallery that asks me, and I won't do many things unless they're right. I think about things like that, I continually evaluate every step I take. Is it going to be good for my work? Is this going to help me make more pictures or fewer pictures in the future? I've been very fortunate at the same time. A lot of people have, too. I'm certainly not a success like, I mean there are small businessmen all up and down this street who are more successful than I am in monetary terms. You can open up any art magazine and there are hundreds, literally hundreds of painters and sculptors who are better known than I am as an artist. Minor White once said of himself, "I am a first-rate practitioner in a second-rate profession." That's a great line. Part of my obsession now is, I'm going to make photography really mean something. I'm going to win a kind of peerage for our art. Hopefully, the time will come when painters won't be looking down their noses at us. If I could use any of my recognition as any kind of a lever, it's going to be to produce a greater respect for the medium. I'm very much committed to that. That's why I publish in Lustrum. What's there in it for me to publish other people other than the fact that I am going to influence the direction things take and hopefully in a positive way.

TD: Do you have dealings with other photographers and do you count photographers among your intimates?

RG: I'm close with a few, I know them all.

TD: Do you influence each other?

RG: No, my influences now are from Balthus, Francis Bacon. There's nothing in photography that's influenced me. There were so few and I've been through them all and I'm so concerned with my own efforts now. I'm more influenced by Ingmar Bergman than I am by any living photographer. I'm certainly more influenced by painting than I am by photography. It's more interesting, there's more going on, there's more to be influenced by, if you want to hold out for a little quality. There's a lot of tremendously creative and productive experimental work going on in photography now, but there's very little work that has any real authority. Obviously the only things that would influence me would be those things that have authority and, for the most part, they've already influenced me. I've worked them out, through them.

TD: Are the prints you sell from your books?

RG: Um, hmm.

TD: And they are sold as a result of someone seeing your book?

RG: Usually they're sold from shows. In Europe I think I'm better known for my exhibits than my books.

TD: Did Deja Vu **sell as well or better than** The Somnambulist?

RG: It's almost out of print now, but it took three years. A lot of people found it difficult. **The Somnambulist** is easily the most legible of all my books, but the second book got off to a very good start and I've had more exhibits of the photographs from **Deja Vu** than I have from **The Somnambulist**; sold more prints from that book, far more.

TD: When you first published The Somnambulist, **how long before you knew it would be a success?**

RG: I knew right away, maybe two or three weeks. It very quickly became very apparent. Everyone I tried to sell it to, bought it. That's when I first started to be invited to give lectures and I couldn't carry enough of them with me, I'd just sell them for cash, they were just flying out of my hands. I got the message pretty quick.

TD: What will you do now for the next couple of years in terms of making a living?

RG: I have a lot of exhibits coming up this year. I have exhibits in Tokyo, in Arles, all over the country, Texas. I'll fulfill those obligations, and I have a bunch of workshops in the summer. I never think more than a year ahead. I know if I can live up to my obligations this year, one of the things I've discovered is, having a lot of obligations makes me do more work. Promise the moon. I've always done that. I discovered, very early in **The Somnambulist** I'd say, "Oh, yeah, it'll be out," and people would say, "Well, when's the thing coming out, man?" I'd say, "It's scheduled for the fall." And it'd be early summer and the fall would come and they'd say, "When's it coming out?" "It'll be out in the early winter list." I found out that promising and promising I would do more.

TD: Are your shows from the trilogy?

RG: They're all different kinds. That always depends on the size of the hall, if it's a museum or a gallery. If it's a gallery where there are sales expected I would put a different show together than if it was a museum show. Probably I'm not going to insist on holding my sequences together as much as I used to in the past, I seem to be more willing to break them down, to take pictures from different sequences, and combine them with new work.

TD: So the future will be devoted to exhibits?

RG: Quite probably.

TD: Will you publish other portfolios?

RG: I don't know. It's too soon to see how well this one is going to do. I just got it out, and it's a mammoth amount of work.

TD: Are you as satisfied with Days at Sea **as you were with the other two?**

RG: More. This one is harder and it's my tightest book, my most mature effort. I have a great deal of satisfaction from this recent book.

New York City
March 11, 1975

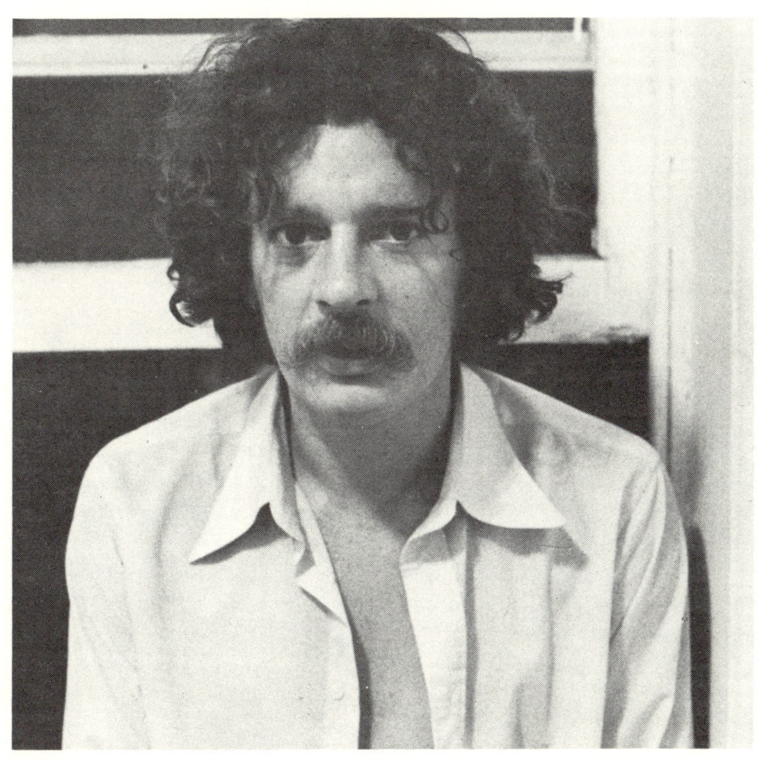

Larry Clark

Interviewer: Once you decided to do Tulsa **as a book, it didn't take long?**
Larry Clark: No. What happened is I had all these photographs and Ralph told me, "You have to make up a dummy." I didn't want to do it. Nobody wants to make a dummy of their book. They don't realize when you make that dummy, all the photographs change, it's a whole different scene. I tell people this. He forced me, he absolutely forced me, he screamed at me. I said, "I'm going down to Tulsa, I'm going to finish it, I don't need no fucking dummy, I know what my pictures look like." He forced me to do it. I put them on the wall, made stats, and put them in a book; it changed the whole world. I saw the relationship of the photographs and knew what I needed, what was missing. The last part of the book, I was laying for those pictures. Nothing is set up, all the stuff's happening. I was just very aware that when it happened, I was going to break my legs to be there. I knew that had to be included in the book. I was really cooking then. I was really working hard.

In the spring of 1975 I had made arrangements to see Larry Clark. He was coming into New York and Ralph Gibson made the plans for me to meet Larry. Unfortunately some personal difficulties surfaced and our meeting never took place. Early July, 1978, Ralph contacted me to say Larry was now living in New York and I should give him a call. On July 28, in Ralph's studio, the interview finally happened. Our conversation, which lasted two hours, was tape recorded. On a couple of subsequent visits, Larry made a few minor revisions and deletions, but mostly it appears as it was recorded. Unfortunately **Tulsa** is a difficult book to come across and to see it, one probably will have to visit an institution such as The Museum of Modern Art in New York City, or travel to Rochester to either The George Eastman House or The Visual Studies Workshop. It is a harrowing book, one of the most important social documentaries in the history of photography, an insider's first-person account of the contemporary drug scene as witnessed by a gifted artist. The book must be seen, it must be experienced.

Larry Clark, tall, rangy, is a good-natured, intense bundle of nervous energy. If he was more traditionally ambitious his work would be known far and wide and he would easily be one of our most important and famous photographers. He spends little time and energy worrying about the past, and even less time thinking about the future. Invariably he'll be photographing the seamy side of life, producing a body of work which is near impossible to publish because of all the legal ramifications involved. He doesn't worry about being published, only asking that he be allowed the freedom to take the photographs for their own sake, come what may. When asked if he'll ever photograph publishable subject matter, he laughs easily and shrugs his shoulders. Larry Clark simply wants to be a photographer, photographing his concerns; that seems enough for him.

Born: Tulsa, Oklahoma. January 19, 1943.
Attended: Layton School of Art, Milwaukee, Wisconsin. 1961-62.
Books:
  Tulsa. Lustrum Press. New York, 1971.
  Teen-Age Lusts. Unpublished manuscript.
Currently: Photographer, New York City.

Tom Dugan: How did you become a photographer?
Larry Clark: My mother started working for a photographer in Tulsa. It was a job. She was doing baby pictures with a Rolleiflex and a strobe. There's door to door photography going on; it's called kidnapping. She did that for a year and she was so good at photographing babies that my father and she went into business. They started going door to door and doing baby photography around Oklahoma and Kansas, in all the small towns. Consequently, I was fifteen or sixteen years old, selling pictures, passing proofs, knocking on doors, kidnapping, and photographing, with a Rollei, a background, and a couple of small strobes. I couldn't stand photography, I hated it. I was just a kid and I was forced to be working in it. I didn't want to be a photographer. They used to go to these conventions called Professional Photographers of America, P.P. of A., conventions and they would take me. This was back in the 50's. All photographers had little bow ties, and crew cuts, and they all looked like squirrels. I was doing a lot of drugs back then, of course. I like knew that I had to leave Tulsa. I knew I had to get out of Oklahoma. I had to do something because I was shooting dope everyday, and doing this baby photography. The way it worked was you'd go into a small town, find the minister of the town, and go up and talk to him, and be real nice, and say, "Who has new babies around." He'd tell you Mr. and

Mrs. Jones, Mrs. Brown, then you'd walk up to the door, knock on the door, and say, "Preacher Roberts told me you have a lovely little baby. I sure would like to see it." Then you'd say, "Oh, you have a beautiful little child. Her name is Deborah, I believe." They'd let you in the door, you'd see the kid, then you'd give the pitch, and bring the photographer in, and take some pictures. One of those things, a real hustle. My people got out of that. They were always honest. There were a lot of outfits that weren't honest. They got a studio, and started doing more things. Now they have a little studio in Tulsa. My mother is still photographing. She photographs babies, children, families, and does a lot of pet photography, which is big now. People come in and will spend a couple hundred bucks on their dog almost immediately. I had to get out of Tulsa. I had the opportunity to go to a school. It was decided I would go to photography school; I would be a photographer. I didn't care, I just knew I had to get out someway. There's this school in Wisconsin called Layton School of Art, so I went there, just by total accident. The photography department was in the basement, segregated from the art department. I immediately started hanging out with all the sculptors and painters. I was photographing and decided I would be a photographer. This was in '61. I snapped. You could be photographing what's around you, your life. You don't have to be photographing baby pictures door to door. I never snapped. I didn't realize you could use photography for other things. I started photographing seriously. I realized I'd just photograph what was happening around me. I said, "Wow, man, it's really happening around me." I started photographing the Tulsa thing then. I photographed my friends earlier, but in '61, I started seriously. I came home from school in the summer, and then after school, I started heavy doing the Tulsa thing, did the first big series then.

TD: How long did you stay at school?

LC: Two years. The best thing about going to school is it gives you time to do nothing but photograph. I did nothing, but photograph for two years. I did everything, I tried everything. I was very hotshot, very aggressive and I wanted to take more pictures than anybody in the class. I really wanted to go with it. I still didn't like photography very much.

TD: What were your aspirations at that point?

LC: I thought I would probably become a magazine photographer, maybe a photojournalist. I wanted to work for *Life*. I thought *Life* magazine was the God. I didn't know anything. While I was in Milwaukee going to school, there was this instructor, Walter Sheffer, who would come in one day a week. He had a portrait studio, but he was very hip and a very good artist. He did all his photography by natural light. He photographed all the actors, all the artists in town. He knew painters and sculptors. He was always trading work off. He was the first real artist that I knew who was a photographer. I got next to him right away and he gave me a job. So after school, I would work for him. We would photograph the theater at Marquette University, with all the dramatic lighting. I was very influenced by him, the way that he used light. He was a master of light. If you look at my work, you see light happening all the time. I learned that from him. I became very aware of light, shadow, space, composition, soul and feeling. I thought that coming into New York and working for *Life* was the ultimate goal. I made the rounds of the magazines and worked a little bit. I decided that I didn't want to do that. I didn't like that at all. You have no control over your photographs. You go out and shoot rolls of film. That's the way that they operate. They give you a job; you go out and shoot 20 rolls of film, give them the film and you never see it again. When it appears in the magazine you see it. They crop it, and they mess it up; they pick the wrong pictures and you have no control. I walked into this editing room at *Life*. They had all my negatives and prints. There was this woman and some more people in there and this lady screamed, "Who are you?" I said, "I'm the photographer. I did the pictures." She said, "Photographers aren't allowed in the editing room." Just like that and they threw me out. I got over working for the magazines. Since then I've just been out photographing on my own, doing my own thing.

TD: What do you remember about your childhood?

LC: I was always with my chums, kind of a gang thing. I always wanted to be just one of the gang, but I always felt a little different. It was funny. I was always aware of what was going on while I was doing things. I read a lot and figured maybe I should be the biographer of the whole scene. During the scene, it was so crazy, that everybody was always saying, "Boy, I'm going to write a book about this sometime." Back then no one was into drugs. People were into drugs, but no one knew about it, especially the kids weren't into drugs. There was no marijuana smoking in Oklahoma. We didn't even smoke it; we were into shooting speed, which wasn't called speed then, it was just amphetamine. That all started when I was thrown out of a junior high school. I had to go to another one, which was across the tracks, which was closer to where I lived. I used to go to a school that was about two miles away, but there was a school about four blocks away, but it was on the other side of the tracks. There was a circus show ground, a big field, then there was the tracks, then Lowell Junior High School. My people didn't want me to go to Lowell, so I went to Lowell anyway because I was thrown out of this other school in the eighth grade. Lowell was funkier; it was lower class people, not as much money, more people in jail, and so on. I met a lot more people that I'd known. I was hanging around with them a lot. It was a very rough school. There were a lot of things happening. Like ex-convicts and friends, who were kids, too, would come back from reform school and guys who were a little older, who would only be 20, but we were 15, 16, 14 even, they knew about drugs and stuff. Back then, in the '50's, you could buy this valo nasal inhaler for 79¢ in the drug store. Anybody could walk in and buy it over the counter, and it had 150 milligrams of pure amphetamine in it. You'd bust it open, take the cotton out, put a little water with the cotton, and all the stuff would float to the top in a grease form, and you would shoot the grease, which was pure speed, for 79¢. Everybody got into doing that. Nobody knew about it, there was only so many of us doing it, just some girls and dudes. That went on for a long time. That was a tough time; I was just a kid. I was 15 years old. I was part of this group and we used to fight, fuck, drink, shoot dope and do crazy things. Everybody else was into crime, stealing, and so on. I wasn't a thief, I was never really a thief at all. I didn't like to do burglaries and stuff, maybe a couple of times. All my friends were doing that pretty regularly. We were always getting arrested and thrown in jail. After a few years, I was close to 18, I just knew that I had to get away from it. There was something for me to do. I had a chance to go to school, and I didn't want to be a photographer, I didn't want to go to school, but I wanted to get out of Oklahoma, so I went.

TD: Was it because of the drugs that you wanted to leave?

LC: Yes, I knew I had to. I was 18, I didn't know what I was going to do, I had to get away from the whole scene. I knew I had to get away from drugs for awhile, and get on with my life. I went to Layton and I met all these kids who were artists. The guys in photography were just bullshit, a bunch of squirrels again, except one guy. A guy named Tom Zimmermann; he was older, had just gotten out of the Navy. He felt a little wierd because he was 21, but we got off and got to be real good friends. He helped me a lot. He was an influence; he turned me on to things.

TD: How did you decide to come to New York?

LC: I wanted to be a magazine photographer. Gene Smith was my big hero then, probably the biggest influence after Walter Sheffer and Tom Zimmermann was my guide. He would move me in the right direction. He taught me a lot. I was really a raw Okie. Walter Sheffer taught me what it meant to be a gentleman, how to be nice to people. I didn't even know that. He used to get very mad at me because I used to be nasty to people. Gene Smith, I thought, was the best photographer around. So I thought I would be a magazine photographer, but that was over very quickly. As soon as I got to New York and saw what was happening; I worked for a couple of magazines even. I got fired because I figured I would just do my thing.

TD: How did you live?

LC: Oh, man, that's a good one. I've never really worked hardly. I've worked for short periods of time. I've just hustled around. I don't really know how I lived, just from hand to mouth, for years and years, scuffling around.

TD: How did you meet Ralph (Gibson)?

LC: Ralph came here in about '66, from California. I got drafted into the Army in '64. I was in basic training and they kept saying, "Are you ready to go fight the communists in Vietnam?" I didn't know what Vietnam was, no one knew then. I was getting out of basic and President Johnson sent the first 50,000 troops over to Vietnam. I was in the South for a year and in Vietnam for a year. This was when all the anti-war thing was happening, so I missed the anti-war thing by a couple of months. I don't know if I would have been in it or not, but I missed it. I got out of the Army in late '66 and probably the first month of '67 I met Ralph. I've known him all these years. I met him at Phil Perkis' house. He used to have people over. We had a little clique who would hang out and talk. Now we go back; now I'm remembering. The reason I came to New York the first time was that Tom Zimmermann came first and hooked up with the Heliographers's Gallery, an old gallery on the east side. Paul Caponigro, Dave Heath, Lee Lockwood, Scott Hyde, Syl Labrot and a bunch of people were in the gallery. Tom was going to have a show there. It was a two-man show, so he wrote me. I put up the first Tulsa pictures, '61 to '63. I met Phil and a bunch of people back then. So I met Ralph over at Phil's house. I just got out of the Army and got a job for *Show* magazine. Someone connected me with them. I can't remember who. I got a job to photograph America for three months. They gave me money, and I drove around the country for three months. I was back, stopped at Phil's house, and Ralph had just come in from L.A. He came to town, he was going to be a fashion or commercial photographer, he was going to be something. He has such high energy. He would have been a very successful commercial photographer. Whatever he wanted to do, he would have made it. The thing about Ralph back then was he seemed to know what he wanted to do. Everybody else was confused. There was some animosity towards him from some people because he's smart, and he's good. He was doing a different kind of photography, and no one liked it at all. When I first met Ralph, we probably pegged each other for a day or two. I didn't like him so much, then after a couple of days, we were best friends. We've been like that, it seems, forever. I found that out through my life that when I meet someone, and I don't like him at first, usually we turn out to be very good friends. He was scuffling, and I was scuffling. Both of us did a little commercial work, and we didn't like it. We were trying to figure out what we wanted to do. We wanted to be artists.

TD: How do you work? Do you work everyday?

LC: I've been a photographer for about 17 years. So after being in the penitentiary and not being able to photograph for 19 months, getting out and coming back to it, it's new and fresh to me now. I'm also forced to be in New York, where I don't want to be, to get out of the joint, to get on parole. The easiest way, which wasn't so easy, to get out was to parole out of state, because Oklahoma knows some other state has control over you. After all that time photographing, and then not being able to photograph, it's very exciting. I'm in the street everyday. I've got a little bread, I've sold a few pictures and I've got some irons in the fire. I've sold some portfolios of future work, which I'm working on. It sounds like a shuck, but it's not. I was with a lady and we got very drunk, and I woke up yesterday morning with the worst hangover of my life, but I still got up and hit the street. I'm out there photographing no matter what condition I'm in.

TD: What do you find yourself photographing now?

LC: It's hard because it's impossible to photograph on the streets of New York; everybody's work looks the same. You can take all those peoples' work and put it together and you can't tell the difference. I'm trying to do something a little different. I'm photographing in the street but it's not like street photography per se. After **Tulsa,** I did a whole other book called **Teen-age Lust.** It wasn't published. I really didn't push to publish it.

TD: I thought it couldn't be published?

LC: That's what it has come down to. People say it can't be published. There's all kids in it, and there's all kinds of fucking.

TD: There are no releases, right?

LC: Well, no, man, you can't get releases. I've haven't ever, ever gotten a model release in my life. I'm doing something now that probably won't be published. If I get some bread I'll publish it myself, or maybe they can be published in Europe.

TD: So you would publish Teen-age Lust?

LC: Yes.

TD: Do you think Light Impressions would distribute it?

LC: If I talked to them, they might. Those guys are such good guys. We had a big fight a few years ago, but I think that's over. I think we're friends. I like them a lot.

TD: How do you edit your work? Do you develop and print as you go along?

LC: Yes. I try to do it as often as I can. You have to see what you're doing.

TD: Who do you feel was instrumental in your career?

LC: I wasn't really influenced by anybody. Maybe Gene Smith. I liked what he was doing with his space in the photographs and the way he printed them, the depth, the richness, the soul.

TD: Do you still like his work?

LC: Oh, yeah. I just saw him in Tucson. The guy is such a giant. He had a stroke about a year ago and he's not in very good health right now, but he's OK. I talked to him, he's sharp as a tack, just has some physical problems. Mentally, he's cool. As we go on through the years, a lot of people have liked my work, and encouraged me. Ralph and I got into a long thing for years, both of us were in New York, I would walk all the way over to the Chelsea Hotel, where he was staying, and borrow five dollars, and I might see him on the street some time and give him five dollars. We were always exchanging little bits of money. We were both scuffling. Ralph is so articulate. He can explain things. He told me once that he had a teacher that told him that the only thing you really understand is something that you can express in words. I can't hardly express anything in words. He used to tell me a lot of things. We would have long discussions about photography. He helped me a lot. He did his first book, **The Somnambulist,** which blew everybody's mind. People weren't doing personal photo books. That's a very autobiographical book. That book is like **Tulsa,** it's very autobiographical. I had all these photographs from Tulsa, through all the years. I never thought what I would do with them. I never thought about doing a book. I thought about a film; I thought about a lot of things. I tried a lot of different things, but I never thought about putting it all together. Finally, after Ralph did his book, I was crashing at Ralph's place, in 1971, I thought I would go down to Tulsa and finish it up. Ralph was a driving force in that. We were talking about it all the time. When I layed out the book, I did it in his studio. He went to Europe for a couple months and I stayed in his studio, and I printed it and layed it out. He showed me how to make a dummy, he showed me how to make a book. He had some ideas and I had some ideas. He helped me with that book. Also I met some people through him, so I got money to do the book. The book happened because of Danny Seymour, who did a book called, **A Loud Song.** Danny was living on the Bowery over Robert Frank; they had a couple lofts. Things happen in New York, that happen so fast. You can be screwing around for years and years and years, and nothing happens. You come to New York and things happen like snappo. There's something about New York, as much as I dislike being here, things happen here that make it very exciting. What happened, if the truth be known, I wasn't even showing my older Tulsa work. I didn't know about it, I had a bad time of it. I was trying to get completely away from it. I met Robert through Ralph, and Ralph said, "Show him the Tulsa pictures." I didn't want to show him, but Ralph forced me to show him. I dug them out, showed them to Robert and he liked them. He went and talked to Danny, and I met Danny, and Danny had some family money. Danny was interested in doing his book. Robert got us together, and Ralph got me and Robert together, so being in New York, I met all these people, and in a couple of days I met Danny and ten minutes later, he said, "Let's do the book, I got the money, we'll do it, we'll do it, we'll do it. We'll get Ralph to help us and publish it." So Ralph, Danny and I went to L.A. and published the books. Danny Seymour actually payed for my book, and payed for his book. Ralph did them for Lustrum (Press). Ralph showed us the whole printing business. Man, the guy knows everything. We went into the printing place, we met all the printers and watched every sheet come off the press. We changed things. He knows everything backwards and forwards. That's how **Tulsa** actually came about, knowing Ralph, Ralph knowing Robert, Robert knowing Danny Seymour, and all of us coming together, meeting and being pals.

TD: How many copies of Tulsa **were printed?**

LC: There's a 10% law in California, which means they can be 10% over or 10% under, so, of course, they're always 10% under, so there was 2700 copies, and that's all. What happened, you know Bill Edwards and Lionel Suntop, we made a deal for the book to be distributed. The book is all my friends, and there's family in there, too. It's as close as you can get. The book is more about me than it is about the people, even though I'm doing things with the people. I don't have any model releases, I wouldn't sign contracts, wouldn't do any of that shit. I thought that was a bad thing to do. I made a deal with Lionel and Bill, we shook hands, and I said, "OK, no one will sue you for this book. They're all my friends, don't worry about it, just don't send the book to Tulsa for awhile until I tell you to." That was our deal, we shook hands, that was our verbal contract. They sent the book to Tulsa to this guy who has a famous bookstore and also has a TV show, every Sunday morning for the last 20 years. Immediately, he goes on TV two weeks in a row, and talks about the book. All of a sudden, the book is all over Tulsa. People are running out to this guy's bookshop and buying it, then KOTV picks it up. My parents didn't know about the book. When I did the book, I sent copies to Roper and some of the people in the book, just for them, and they had it, and no one else had it. Then, all of a sudden, on TV one night, at the six o'clock and the ten o'clock news, they do a three minute special on the book. They went out and found people and interviewed them, people who knew people in the book. They didn't talk to anybody in the book. They did this incredible thing. It's on TV, and it's in the bookstores, and it's on TV again. I got very pissed off. I thought they had broken their promise by putting the book there when I told them not to. That was back then, it doesn't really make any difference now to me. Then I was really mad. What happened is the grandmother of Billy Mann's kid, Billy Mann was dead and his wife was dead, and there's a photograph in the early section of the book from '63 of Billy laying on the bed, smoking a cigarette, with his baby. The baby is like eight years old. The grandparents of the baby see all this action. There's this picture in the book of a little baby, laying on Billy, and Billy is dead, Diana is dead, and the baby has been living with the grandparents all these years, so they got a lawyer, and they sued for the baby. They said the baby was now subject to ridicule because of this picture. The baby was three months old in the picture, so it was just a money thing. There was a law suit. I promised that no one in the book would sue, so I kept my promise, except who knows a baby is going to sue. They sued and I probably could have cooled that suit. No one else in the book sued, none of my people, none of my friends. I probably could have cooled that, but I was crazy then. I was mad at Light Impressions and I was very little help to them. I was very nasty. They're such nice guys that we worked it out. They ended up giving a small settlement. They cooled that suit out, it was very easy to do. But it was months of frustration. They were suing them for millions of dollars. They didn't sue me, they didn't sue anybody else. They sued a company they thought might have some money. If they sued me, what are they going to get? I think that I handled that badly. I handled it the only way that I could handle it, the way I thought it should be handled back then. If it happened now, I would cool it very quickly, I would stop it. But then I was pissed at them. I thought they had broken a promise to me. I didn't understand about business so much. Then I thought if someone told you they'd do something, they did it. If they didn't do it, you hit them in the head. It's just the way it is. I like those guys a lot, and I'm sorry that that happened. That killed a lot of things for awhile with them. I think it fucked them up a bit. They were starting a business and had this big law suit. I wasn't being much help to them. I was being a kind of prick about the whole thing. I was really mad at them.

The Tulsa book caused such a sensation in Tulsa and all over. It sold out in a matter of a few months. It didn't last very long.

TD: Could Tulsa **be reissued?**

LC: That's the question now. Because of the baby's law suit, people would be afraid that someone else might sue now, even my friends, even though I would say that they wouldn't, and they wouldn't. The book hit Tulsa, everybody knew about it and it put some heat on some people. That's why I didn't want it in Tulsa. We're fighting the police every day there, I mean it's war. There's nothing in the book that can get anybody busted. There's not a goddamned thing that can get anyone arrested for anything. I left out all the sawed-off shotguns. That's 10 years Federal rap. In the Federal joint, if you get 10 years Federal time, it's very hard to get parole. In the Federal joint, you know how much time you're going to do. On a 10 year sentence, you're going to do 6, 7 years. If you go in a State Penitentiary, and get 10 years, you can get out on parole in a couple years, maybe sooner if you got money. I left out all the sawed-off shotguns, I left out all the Federal offenses, I left out a bunch of stuff.

TD: Did your friends mind that you were photographing them?

LC: No. I was photographing them all my life. If I didn't have my camera, they'd say, "Where's your camera?" It was another part of me.

TD: Did they get off on the pictures?

LC: Oh, yeah. Through the years I printed and gave them pictures, and the police would come in and take them. The police burned my camera one day. They came in and one guy put a gun in my stomach, the other guy put a gun in my mouth because I was yelling at him, and they took my camera. I took a picture of them as they came in the door just to mess with them. They took my camera and burned it on the stove. They were trying to get the film out, they finally got it open and they threw it on the stove and the shutter burned. I almost got shot over that. I was really mad.

When I did the early photographs, when I first was starting, I was in the scene. We were there every day and I had my camera. I got to the point very quickly, where I was photographing everything. When you shoot (dope), someone ties you off and somebody would have a shot ready and say, "Larry, tie me off. Never mind, you got your camera." I mean it got to that point because I was photographing everything. We knew each other since we were little kids. We grew up together, we were friends all our lives, from the cradle. There was never any problem, and if there ever was a problem, I'd just say, "Screw you man, I'm doing what I'm doing." Once in a while, when the shit was coming down, when there would be something that was really dangerous, maybe someone really getting hurt bad, maybe someone getting killed, maybe someone showing a bunch of guns they'd stolen, one guy might say, "You shouldn't be taking pictures of this." I'd say, "You do what you do, I do what I do." I just did it. That's the way you photograph. You know that. Everybody trusted me and they still do.

Tulsa had such an impact. People have changed. Some have changed their lifestyles, some are doing other things, some of the girls are married with kids and new husbands. I won't put the book out, even if I could, in the States. I don't want to bring all that heat back. It's 7, 8 years old now. It's no use bringing it up. Let's let it lay back and be whatever it is. I meet people who tell me about **Tulsa** and they've never even seen the book. The book is so obscure now that it's fun. I enjoy that. People know about it, but they haven't seen it. The only way that it'll get published is I might wait 20 years, or if it can be done in Europe, that would be OK. Right after I did **Tulsa** I went immediately back to Tulsa. I got a crib and I moved in. I said, "If there is any heat, I'm here to take it." Everybody knew the photographs, and they knew what I was doing, but no one knew what form it would take. No one realized it was going to be a book, and it wasn't a book until the end. A couple of people said when they first saw it, they were a little upset, but then they realized that it was a classic—they said that, I'm not saying that. Everybody wanted to record the scene, to write a book about it, so I did it, and there it is. The thing about the book is they are good pictures. That's what makes it. You could photograph that and make everybody look terrible. My thing is: they're my friends. I'm not making anybody look bad. I make everybody look as good as I can. I want to say what I want to say, but I'm not going to hurt or make fun of nobody. Some people can't even look at the book; they start shaking. Some people like it from a Hell's Angels standpoint. Chicks in black leather jackets come up and want to fuck me because of the book. Other people are scared of me.

Tulsa starts when Roper, Billy and me and everybody is young. And it ends with young people again, and the kids, at the end of the book, are the younger brothers, neighborhood friends, and younger sisters of the people in the book. So when I was back in Tulsa after the book was published, I continued photographing. I did a thing in '72, '73, I photographed a lot more in Tulsa. I photographed a lot of the younger brothers and sisters, which started the second book, **Teen-age Lust**. I photographed things that happen when you're in your early teens, and you're stupid, you don't have a camera and don't know what's going on. Ever since I became a photographer, I always wanted to turn back the years and wish that I was photographing back then. I talked to these friends, the younger brothers and sisters. I told them I always wanted to photograph what was happening back then. I actually said, "When something happens, tell me, I want to come." I photographed gang bangs. I got the most beautiful series with this beautiful little girl, and all kinds of teen-age lust stuff. That's part of the second book, then I put a lot of other stuff with it from all over the country. It's lots of sex and drugs.

TD: Will you ever do anything that is publishable?

LC: That's the hard thing. I think that it can all be published. That's the problem. For some reason, I'm doing the type of thing that can't be published right now; legally it can't. If you got all these incredibly beautiful teen-agers and everybody is fucking, how are you going to go and say, "Will you stop and sign a model release." They're kids, too, so it makes no difference. People tell me I should get model releases, but I can't. I'll publish it on my own if I want it out.

TD: Once you decided to do Tulsa **as a book, it didn't take long?**

LC: No. What happened is, I had all these photographs and Ralph told me, "You have to make up a dummy." I didn't want to do it. Nobody wants to make a dummy of their book. They don't realize when you make that dummy, all the photographs change, it's a whole different scene. I tell people this. He forced me, he absolutely forced me, he screamed at me. I said, "I'm going down to Tulsa, I'm going to finish it, I don't need no fucking dummy, I know what my pictures look like." He forced me to do it. I put them on the wall, made stats, and put them in a book; it changed the whole world. I saw the relationship of the photographs and knew what I needed, what was missing. The last part of the book, I was laying for those pictures. Nothing is set up, all that stuff's happening. I was just very aware that when it happened, I was going to break my legs to be there. I knew that had to be included in the book. I was really cooking then. I was really working hard.

TD: Why did you want to publish that book?

LC: I didn't want to publish it. It was finished, I didn't know what to do with it, and a guy gave me money to publish it. It was just moving. Ralph was going to be the publisher, the money was there, I just felt I'd do it. I figured I could do it, and if I left anything out that would get anyone arrested, it would be OK. All my friends told me I could do anything I want to with the pictures, but no one realized that I was going to put them together like I did. I didn't realize that. I was in Frisco, and we were going to Los Angeles the next day to print the book, and I wanted to kill myself, burn all the pictures, and leave no trace. I really didn't think anyone would give a damn about the book. I didn't think anyone would care. It's so personal. You're really telling everything, you're revealing an awful lot about yourself. But I just did it. Take your chances, run with the ball, that's the thing, run with the ball. Someone throws you a pass, man, run with the ball. That's why I did it.

TD: If you did it today, would you change anything?

LC: No. I wouldn't know how to change it. I didn't even know what it was. I liked it, I thought it was good, but it freaked me out, too. I'm looking at my life here and saying, "Oh, my God." Besides close personal friends, there's some family in the book. I wanted to do it, I wanted everybody to see it, but I didn't really want it to hit in Oklahoma so hard. When Oklahoma got the book, which they would have got it later, they would have gotten it anyway, it would have happened later, maybe in a year. Light Impressions, by sending it out when they said they wouldn't, I was ready to shoot the guys. Now, I'm older, and I realize it would have been in Tulsa maybe in a few more months anyway. It wouldn't have made any difference. But when it actually came out, I wanted it to slip out, slide in. Then it hit, and everybody wrote about it, and everybody liked it. None of us thought anything like that would happen. It was amazing. It's good to have a few copies of the book out. I like that. This next book you'll like, if we can get it out. We'll publish it. People want to do it. I even had a contract with Michael Hoffman, for a while, at *Aperture.* He was going to publish the second book. I don't quite understand our scene, Mike's scene and my scene. We were friendly, but the book didn't happen, I don't really think that he could have published it. I don't think that he was ever going to publish it. I don't understand why he gave me a little money, and we signed a contract. He liked the work and maybe he thought he could publish it, but, of course, he couldn't. It'll be published. I guarantee you that it will be published. Someone will do it. Probably just like **Tulsa. Tulsa** went from all those years and no one would touch it. It was never in any magazines, it was never anywhere. No one would touch those photographs with a ten-foot pole. I got private money. Danny Seymour paid for that book. Maybe I'll get a grant and publish it myself.

TD: Did you like Vagabond?

LC: I don't know that book. Who's it by?

TD: Gaylord Herron.

LC: I know Gaylord. I forgot the name of the book. I didn't know it was called **Vagabond.** Is it really called **Vagabond?** It must be printed so it looks like a European word. I have that book. I know Gaylord. We were in the 7th grade together and in a glee club together. Gaylord works for a TV station. Gaylord did that thing on TV, as a matter of fact, about **Tulsa.** I haven't seen Gaylord in years. I saw him about '73 in Tulsa. He's been working for the TV station for years, and he photographs. He's a good guy. It's a very good book, I think. A lot of people like that book a lot. I don't know how that book is selling. People should have that book.

TD: How do events in your personal life affect the way you work?

LC: I'm living it, whatever it is that I'm doing, I'm living it. I'm just one of those guys, I'm lucky. I'm no one special, I just have a camera and I can photograph because I had good training. I have all that background and experience behind me. I can do anything because of all the years. All the brain cells that have been lost, I can still remember all the little tricks.

TD: You don't use a light meter?

LC: No, I use Tri-X. There's only 6 or 7 different light situations. There are only so many f-stops, so many shutter speeds. It's very easy to learn light. There are 6 or 7 different kinds of light, so you know immediately. I use Acufine and Tri-X.

TD: What does success mean to you?

LC: To me, success is: I visualize a lot of photographs and if I can get a good photograph, that's success. That's all I want.

TD: Do you think about the future?

LC: Unfortunately I haven't, no. We all look back and think what we could have done, if we had done things a little differently. I'm sure I could have been very successful. No, I'm just out there.

TD: Are you showing the work you're doing now to anybody?

LC: I haven't shown anything since I got out of the joint, but soon I will. It's just starting to happen. It's very hard for me. I'm forced to be in New York, and I'm forced to photograph. I want to, and I'm out there doing it everyday. It's very, very difficult for me, but it's starting to happen. There are some breakthroughs coming. I want to do something good.

TD: Who will you show the work to, anybody special?

LC: I'll show it to Ralph (Gibson) first, he's my pal. If I want to sell it, there are a lot of people I can show it to. I'll show it to Lee Witkin, a pretty good guy.

TD: Are you with any gallery?

LC: Witkin has had some of my work for a long time. He has some great work. He's got some of the **Teen-age Lust**; he's got a series that I sold him, eight or nine pictures of the gang bang scene and then some more things. Sam Wagstaff, I'd like to show him stuff. He's bought work since I got back. I just met him.

TD: Is feedback important as you're working? Do you care what other people think?

LC: Yes, I care, but I find that it really doesn't mean anything. All through the years, for years and years and years and years, people have liked my work, but I couldn't do anything with it. I just kept working. That's all I do is work. Feedback is important. I had a wife for awhile, and she gave me some really tough feedback. "What the hell are you doing?" I'm at the point where I know why I'm doing it.

TD: Do you ever work in color?

LC: No. I'm not interested in it. For the kind of thing that I do, black and white is much more dramatic. You can do much more, it's much more powerful. I'm just an old-time black and white photographer.

TD: What do you read, newspapers, magazines, books?

LC: I read everything. There's this German author named Bemelman, a very well-known German writer back in the '40's. Lately somebody turned me on to him, and I've read a bunch of his books. **The Eye of God; Blue Danube,** which is about Nazis during the war. I've read about six books in a row by him. You should read him, you'll like him. Dynamite. I read everybody. I like biography and autobiography. I like that mostly. I read everybody's autobiography that I can find. I'm really interested in how people write about themselves.

TD: Do you watch TV?

LC: Sometimes, I watch a little TV, but I try to stay away from it. I don't sleep well, I have this incredible insomnia sometimes.

TD: What are your plans for the future?

LC: I'm on the street everyday and I'm photographing. I want to get some work out, I want to show some work pretty quickly. I want to publish something fairly quickly, if I can.

TD: Did you make any money from Tulsa?

LC: I got a grant, I got a National Endowment (of the Arts) grant from it, so I got some bread there. As far as the book goes, no, I didn't make any money. The book was done, as much of a shock as it sounds, I didn't feel I should make anything off that book. It was such a personal thing; it was like a purge. I was purging myself of something and I didn't want to make a dime off of it. We sold the book for five bucks.

TD: Did Danny Seymour get his investment back?

LC: No, he didn't. As a matter of fact, nobody made any money off the book. That's a tough one, man, you really caught me now. You caught me cold. What happened, OK, I'll tell you the truth. Danny paid for the book and there were some bucks coming back. There was a few grand coming back in profit and Danny let me have it. I took that money, so I guess I did make some money off of it. He just let me have the bread. I gave him a print; he wanted a picture. There were some profits,

Light Impressions funnelled me quite a few checks. The book sold out; whatever the profits were, I got all that. There was just a few thousand dollars. It was set up to sell cheaply, so no one would make any bread. If Danny got four grand back, he's still losing half his money. He paid expenses in L.A., and we rented cars, and we partied. We spent 10, 11 thousand dollars. The book cost about 7, 8 thousand to do. We spent a lot of money having fun. The money that came back, he let me have it. Who am I to turn down the bread? I took it. I went back to Oklahoma and kept photographing. Danny Seymour was one of the finest guys I've ever known. He was a good artist and had some family money. He liked to help other artists that he liked. He liked to help people. He was a wonderful, wonderful guy. He was a real good friend of Robert Frank. Robert knew him the best.

New York City
July 28, 1978

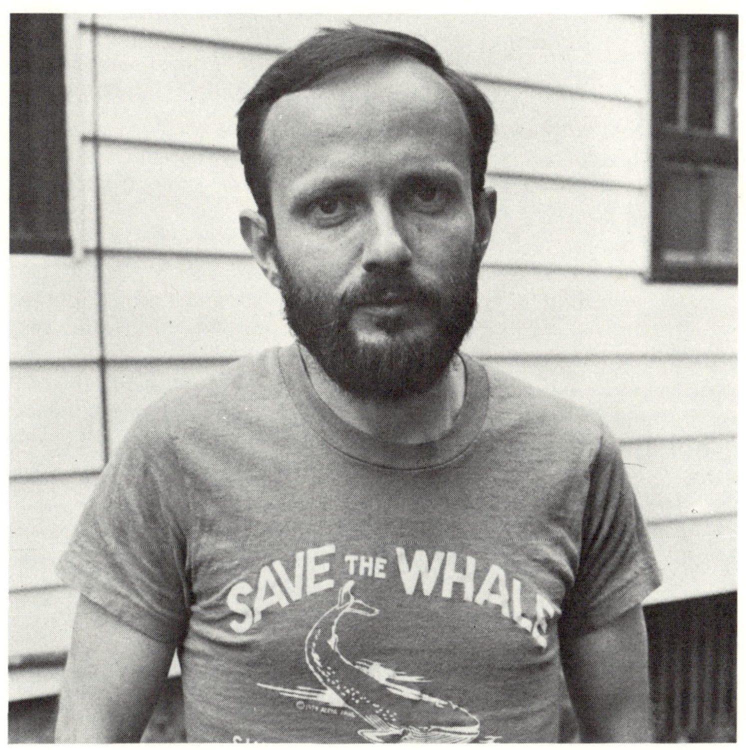

Keith Smith

Interviewer: And that experience got you to do books?

Keith Smith: There were several things. I had done one book previous to that, which was a lot of etchings, but when I got done with it, it was nothing more than a bunch of etchings held together by the binding. It wasn't a book. A book is more than the sum of its parts. That's the most important thing in a book. The etchings were just equal to the sum of the parts, they weren't more, and the order meant nothing. A book has to be conceived and designed for the totality of it. There was nothing in that, it wasn't a book. I wanted to figure out: How can I make a book? Also I wanted to get to know Nathan Lyons better, at that particular time. I knew he was interested in books. I don't use words much, so I talk through my pictures.

In 1973 Nathan Lyons showed me two unique books made by Keith Smith, and I saw another at Light Gallery in New York City. When I started doing these interviews Nathan suggested I talk to Keith. When I called Keith he invited me over to see more of his books and I spent a fascinating afternoon looking at a selection of them. In a letter dated 15 April 1968 to Nathan Lyons he described several of his books. He writes, "... four (of them) are using film positives as pages in the book. I used the transparent photograph as a transition from one side of an opaque paper page to the other (placing the film positive between the two paper pages). In the process of turning the page, the transparency is seen with one side of the paper page as a background, and then the paper page on the other side of the center of the book is the background for the transparency. By drawing or adding color to one or the other paper page, the transparency is thus seen with variation. That book, Book 2, had a film positive, 11 x 14, between each two pages of paper. I used the transparency to relate one side of the page with the other."

"I am interested in transition through a book. I liked this solution. I achieved even more a physical transition with Book 3 by using several sheets of film positives in succession before ending that number of pictures with an opaque paper page. Even then, I would cut holes in the paper page to continue the flow of the transparent pictures to the next section past the dividing paper page. I used as many as 10 transparencies in succession before terminating with a paper page. These groups of successive transparencies are seen individually in the process of turning the page, or go to make up a total picture by the sum of the parts, or variations in between when some of the transparencies have been turned to the other side and only part of the group are seen together. I try to make use of the picture diminishing on the right hand side of the page, and building up on the left as the pages of the group of transparencies are turned in the process of turning the pages, looking through the book. This book has about as many pages as the previous, but only about 1/6 as many total pictures. That is, there are 30 pages, but only 4 complete or total pictures as each group of transparencies go to make up a compound picture. By Book 5, I have reduced the number of compound pictures to one, eliminating all paper pages. (The 20-11 x 14 film positives collectively make one picture.) And I have, by using the characteristic of the transparency more fully, achieved an ultimate transition in this book. A very physical transition. This book is made up of transparencies which are mounted with 3-inch paper borders. The cover of the book has a window so that you can see the entire book without/before opening it. Actually, the glass windows in the covers are for viewing the book on a light table, if I want to...."

In a review of a Keith Smith show A. D. Coleman has written, "... 'Number 10,' is a photographic version of some of the book techniques originated by Vasarely — overlays of transparencies creating a continual image shift in both directions as the pages are turned. In Smith's case, it is perfectly suited to the self-portrait which is his theme, and would make a remarkable volume for some enterprising publisher to produce in larger quantities. 'Up,' another of the books, uses a similar approach without as much impact, but 'Out' — on the theme of insanity — creativity — is harrowing." Recently, Keith Smith, in addition to doing unique books, has been making multiples by offset and will undoubtedly gain a following.

On July 19, 1976, I interviewed Keith Smith at his home on a quiet, tree-lined street in Rochester, N.Y. The tape-recorded conversation lasted almost three hours, and appears as it was recorded, with only a few minor changes and revisions. As we talked Keith would, from time to time, bring out another unique book to show me.

Keith Smith seems possessed with the need to express himself through his art much the way we've come to think of Vincent Van Gogh. He's dedicated, severely disciplined, a prolific and gifted bookmaker, and perhaps the consummate book-maker of our time. Certainly no other artist has devoted himself to the book with such zeal and drive.

Born: Tipton, Indiana. May 20, 1938.
B.A.E.: School of the Art Institute of Chicago, 1967.
M.S.: Institute of Design, Illinois Institute of Technology, 1968.
Books:
68 one-of-a-kind books (as of June 1978).
A Bee Sees. Visual Studies Workshop Press. Rochester, N.Y. 1976.
Masturbation Meditation. Visual Studies Workshop Press. Rochester, N.Y., 1976.
When I Was Two. Visual Studies Workshop Press. Rochester, N.Y., 1977.
Currently: Faculty member, Visual Studies Workshop; Photographer, Rochester, N.Y.

Tom Dugan: Could you talk about your beginning as a picture maker?

Keith Smith: I drew pictures ever since I was about two and I started college when I was twenty-five. I never heard of etchings. I had never taken any photographs in my life until I was about twenty-three. I started school at The Art Institute of Chicago in '63. I had never been in a museum. A lot of things were new to me starting in 1963. I got interested in printmaking and photography. In '68 I got my master's at the Institute of Design when (Aaron) Siskind was there.

TD: Why did it take you so long to decide you wanted to be an artist?

KS: Well, I'd always drawn pictures, even up until I started college. It's just that I started several things to see what I was interested in. I bought an older plane; I learned to fly. I went into a monastery when I was religious. That lasted a year and then I joined the army, went to Viet Nam before it was Viet Nam. While I was over there I remembered my fourth grade art teacher said, "Someday you'll go to The Art Institute in Chicago." That's the only art school I knew of by name so I wrote them while I was over there and when I came back I started.

TD: What was working with Siskind like?

KS: I met him when I was an undergraduate and I'd go over to his house and show him my pictures. We'd never talk about them, we'd just talk about other things. He wanted me to go out there to get my master's to influence some of his students, because they were all straight photographers and my work was photoetchings. He arranged to get me a scholarship because they didn't have any there. I just went for a year.

TD: I don't see any Siskind influence in your work.

KS: Not an influence that I copied from him, no. I wouldn't want to do that. When I went there I said, "Do you want me to work on technique and learn the Zone System?" He said, "No, no continue what you're doing." And different things he'd say like, "A Nikon has ruined as many photographers as it's made." I'd see him on the beach with his little dollar Diana camera. I realized we weren't so much different and I really appreciated his approach and that he understood my approach. When I met Nathan (Lyons) I was afraid. I heard he changed the developer between every print. I figured he wouldn't understand my work at all. I was an undergraduate student, and I said something and he said, "I'm not interested in photographs, I'm interested in pictures." So right then I knew he understood. And that's what's important — pictures. It doesn't matter if they're photographs. When I was a student, one day I went to two critiques. I went to my etching critique and my etching teacher said, "These aren't etchings, these are photographs that you made on the etching plate." Then I went to my photography teacher and he said, "These aren't photographs. You're a printmaker who uses photography." They both said the same identical thing. They were still worrying about means and categories, and I wasn't interested in that.

TD: Who would you say influenced you in your picture making?

KS: DeChirico. I love him. Matisse and Picasso. My etching teacher, Vera Berdick. I didn't realize until two or three years after I was out of college how much of an influence she was. I've changed my ideas about aesthetics a lot, mostly because of her. Within her work was a lot of dichotomy. She'd have something extremely beautiful and something extremely ugly, or something tranquil and something unnerving. She played those against each other. One would be extremely beautiful with just a little bit of shit in it. I liked the extremes in her work. I used to be interested in just real beautiful and pretty pictures. Then I realized there is no beauty and there is no ugly, there's just intensity. That's what's important. Besides, if I'm expressing myself, beauty is a small part of my life compared to other things. It doesn't matter if it's beautiful, unworldly or even boring, like Warhol's movies. They did a lot for me. They were quiet and profound. I don't care what a picture is as long as it's intense.

TD: How did you make your first book?

KS: For two years I was making film positives for etchings and one day I was checking the film positive after the fix to see if it was dense enough. I got a little disturbed because I could hardly see it as my fingers were in the way and I realized then that my fingers were part of the picture. The transparency is not complete in itself, it's whatever else is seen behind it, plus it. It took me two years to see that. Perception is so hard. Artists are so blind in their seeing. Turns of habit. It's so hard to see fresh. I was so excited that that transparency was just part of the picture instead of like an opaque print. I ran around the room looking at the window through it, looking at my teeth through it, everywhere, just trying to see what I could see with it. I said, "What can I do with this now that I understand it?" If I could make room-sized transparencies then anything that passes by will be part of the picture; I couldn't afford that. I thought I could put them in mats and have color behind them, but then there's not the movement and change that a transparency has, so you might as well just have a paper print. I thought, "What's a good way of using it?" I came up with books.

TD: And that experience got you to do books?

KS: There were several things. I had done one book previous to that, which was a lot of etchings, but when I got done with it, it was nothing more than a bunch of etchings, held together by the bindings. It wasn't a book. A book is more than the sum of its parts. That's the most important thing in a book. The etchings were just equal to the sum of the parts, they weren't more, and the order meant nothing. A book has to be conceived and designed for the totality of it. There was nothing in that — it wasn't a book. I wanted to figure out: How can I make a book? Also I wanted to get to know Nathan Lyons better, at that particular time. I knew he was interested in books. I don't use words much, so I talk through my pictures.

TD: Why did you want to get to know Nathan Lyons better?

KS: I realized that he understood work very well and I had admiration for him. I think there's few picture makers and when I run across one I want to get to know him/her. It's a desert out there.

TD: What kind of a childhood did you have? Why do you think you became an artist?

KS: As I said, I've been drawing pictures since I was two, since I was old enough to hold a pencil. I don't know if it started before then.

TD: How do events in your life affect your work?

KS: Oh, they are my work. My work is a diary. Anything that happens — if I eat fried eggs, they're in that book. If I have a friendship or love affair that doesn't turn out right or does turn out right, that comes into my book. If I don't have any friends for awhile, I'm lonely, that's in the book. Everything is in my work. Sonia Sheridan said, "Put everything in your work and your work into everything." There's nothing that I don't try to put into my book, if it affects me, whether it's political, socially profound or just some little thing around the house.

TD: How would you describe yourself as a picture maker?

KS: Look at my pictures. Why say a few words and try to put me in a category? That's what my book is there for, to look at.

TD: But your books are one-of-a-kind books?

KS: You've seen it. I make single pictures, too. I make drawings, etchings, photographs. I think it's silly for me to try to put in a few words what I spent my whole life doing visually. I don't use words, I use pictures.

TD: Do you do any writing?

KS: Very little. Sometimes I try to combine or play off words with pictures, but out of the first forty-eight books there's probably only three or four that have writing in them, except for titles.

TD: How did you get into making handmade books?

KS: I started as a student. I couldn't very well afford to have Dover publish one of my books. I was unknown; also at the time I was dealing a lot, since 1964, with cloth pictures, so that involves stitching and sewing. I'm interested in tactile things, so I want the book to be sensual, tactile, so naturally the sewing connected into the pictures in the book. I'm interested in light and shadows and how these kinds of things are fleeting and are not solid, so they are very appropriate to the book format because turning a page creates a shadow and creates the focus. It just fits in, not that I'm designing it, it's just very appropriate to the book format.

TD: How did you decide that your books should be read with a light three feet away and at a 45 degree angle?

KS: If I wanted shadows I wouldn't make the books with an indirect light. Whenever I was working I always had a light about three feet away, at a 45 degree angle and that cast some shadows. In some of the books it's important that the shadows go across the other page and cross a figure or a form and cut it out, or a shadow hand will go across a page and touch something so that's part of the picture. That's as important, the shadow hand going over and touching someone's face, as the two different individual pictures are. I always set the light up the same way so that certain things will happen that happen. At the same time, I was making individual pictures, but books satisfy a certain need that individual pictures don't. I spend about half of the time on books, even though I knew I would never be able to sell any. If I sold them at $1000 a book, who is going to work for ten cents an hour? So it's just something I love to do, and I thought that I was doing certain things where no one else had been working, so that was important to me, that I was seeing in a new way. I always try to see in a slightly new way. Single pictures, you resolve it and it's over, you resolve another and it's over. A book is growing, building to a huge climax, so there's so much more pleasure, it's growing and evolving. It's really a high to work on a book. You really get involved. You talk to the pictures and then change them around just like they're old friends. I spent three months on one book and even though I knew it was coming to an end although I had stretched it out a little more than I needed to work on it, and the last day I was working on it. I cried the whole day. I often get very depressed after I finish a book unless I get started on something.

After a book is done, it's dead. It exists for someone else then — but, for me, it's dead because it's no longer evolving. Anything that is living is growing and changing.

TD: Do you sell many of the books?

KS: I don't sell any.

TD: I saw one at Light Gallery with a price on it.

KS: It's not for sale, just for people to look at. If they sell it I'll tell them to get it back. Actually when I was a student I sold my third book to Arnold Crane because I needed money for supplies. I was using sheet film in those early books and I was spending $70 a month on sheet film and living on $100 a month, so I just needed some money. I've given a few books away to friends, and I gave Arnold a big book, Number 41, last year. Harold Jones is now at the University of Arizona, and we're dealing back and forth. He wants to buy several books, so I sent him slides. I'm thinking about selling them because I want to place some of them somewhere. If I die I'd like to have them around certain places where they won't just get lost. I'm going to give up some of them if his price is right. I took slides of all of them and he sent me a list of the ones he wants me to send. As for just selling them in a gallery, no. I've never sold one of them, they've never been for sale. I made a children's book last spring that has 150 copies. I hope to sell some of those, and I'm buying an A.B. Dick and will make books, with ideas related to these (the one-of-a-kind books) except it won't be that many hours, and I hope to sell those. I am interested in disseminating books. These (the one-of-a-kind books) are all like 15th century volumes which were chained to a desk and very few people get to see them. I don't want to be snobbish and there are certain ideas I want to get out and disseminate, so it's good to make books that I can sell. These you couldn't sell — you couldn't even exhibit them in a museum. If they were put there for a month people would rip through them and they'd be destroyed. When people look at books like *Time* magazine, this is the 20th century where you flip through it and toss it down. They're not careful, 500 or 1000 hours and they don't know how to look at them. You just couldn't have something like that with my books.

TD: Do you get nervous when people start handling your books?

KS: Sure, because they look at them like *Time* magazine.

TD: Light Gallery had me wash my hands before I looked at your book.

KS: Good. When you go to Arnold Crane's house and look at any book you wash your hands. You have oil in your skin. A book can't be replaced, they get mutilated very quickly.

TD: When you begin making books on the A.B. Dick, what kind of a run do you expect to do?

KS: It depends on how much hand work is involved. If there's a lot of hand coloring, if there's a lot of stitching, or cutting holes in the pages, then they'll be limited to 10, 20, 50. If there's not, then 100 or 200, which is very optimistic. I doubt that I'd sell them. I made 150 of the children's book and they've been at the (Visual Studies) Workshop gallery for two months and I've sold one. It's a little optimistic to make too many. Nathan (Lyons) likes the idea of disseminating books very cheaply. I'd like to keep all my books I make on the A.B. Dick under $10, very accessible to anybody who wanted it.

TD: Any books you see now impress you?

KS: I don't look at many pictures. I spend all my time making pictures. I'm not involved in the history of art too much, contemporary or past, I never go to galleries, I never buy *Artform* or *Aperture*. I'm involved in making pictures and I'm fairly illiterate when it comes to looking at pictures, that's a bit tongue-in-cheek because I have a lot of pictures around my house that I've traded with different people. If I like certain people's work I follow them, but I really don't know a lot about what's going on.

TD: Whose work do you like?

KS: DeChirico. He's a great friend of mine. Picasso. Matisse. Vera Berdick's etchings. Robert Frank. He and Vera Berdick are my two idols. I like certain other contemporary work, maybe a lot because I know the people, maybe it's because I like them. I don't know how much it's them I like or the picture or book I like. Lucas Samaras. I like his books. I think the things he did with Polaroid are something a photographer couldn't do or wouldn't do. It took someone in the "art" field to do that. Once he did it, lots of people do it. To take a Polaroid and make something out of it, and, of course, his subject matter, too. Too many art schools turn out certain kinds of picture makers, and all the same.

TD: Is that one reason you court illiteracy?

KS: I don't know. I don't read at all. I can't stand galleries, they depress me. I try just to mail things to mine and not go there. I don't like crowds and strangers, so I don't go to museums or galleries. It's pretty hard to see work then, except when you get to know different people, and you can see their work, or send things to each other through the mail. Teaching is very hard when you're uneasy with people. When I have people over for dinner it's rarely more than two. I don't like crowds. The first time I started teaching at the Workshop, in 1970, I lasted about eight weeks and then left. I gave Nathan about a two-day notice. I'm very happy there now because it's not teaching, it's just an apprentice kind of thing where I just do my work and they look on and maybe ask me some questions, but I'm not a teacher.

TD: Do you teach primarily photo etching?

KS: I teach printmaking which is silkscreen, etching, cyanotype and drawing. I teach different workshops in books, bookmaking, book ideas. The only photography I do is applied color. Then there is copy machine pictures, various machines I use as copy machines, but no straight photography.

TD: Do you do any straight photography?

KS: Some, but most of it either has some applied color in it or some collage, or it's messed up one way or another. Very little of it is just a picture, just a negative printed, not because I don't like or appreciate that, it's just my ideas run in a different way.

TD: So obviously, for you, isolation is necessary.

KS: Yeah, I've always lived alone. It took me a while to know myself. I think most artists, partly because they just can't get along with others, and partly because the work goes better, prefer to be alone. I just couldn't concentrate on the work if someone else was around. I often listen to music, I play it all the time while I'm nearby making etchings or coloring or making drawings. I usually spend twelve-fourteen hours a day on my work. I work most of the time. Then I teach at the Workshop. I go there and for groceries, then back here and work, and that's about it.

TD: You don't have much of a social life?

KS: No, I see people when I'm at the Workshop. I have a few close friends, two in Pennsylvania who come up about every month or I go down for a couple of days. And a group of people I write to, like Robert Frank. I rarely see him. I used to write a lot of letters — 20-30 letters a day, but they were mostly postcards of my pictures, collages or drawings. I did a lot of postcard art in the 60s. Now I rarely write, it takes too much time.

TD: Why do you admire Robert Frank?

KS: He's a wonderful guy. Of course, I like his pictures but we never talk about his pictures. His pictures — this is one of his pictures here that I'd never seen. It has applied color and is a collage. He sends me things like that. I don't have any of his straight work, all I have are collages or he'll send a Polaroid with a drawing on it, but mostly, he is just a wonderful, warm person. Either he has his hands in his pockets or smiles and looks like a little boy. And he has helped me a lot, too.

TD: How did you meet Frank?

KS: In 1970 when I started here he was going through the Workshop and he saw a print I was working on and liked it. I said, "Why don't you come over to my house and I'll show you more." He didn't have time, but then the next day he missed his plane so thought he'd kill some time, and came over. I showed him pictures and books of mine. He liked them, and we started corresponding.

TD: Have you been up to Nova Scotia?

KS: No, he told me to come up. I asked him when was the best time and he said winter. Most people go up there in the spring. He lives right on the ocean so you can see whales from his front door. It's a long way up and I can't go too long without making a picture.

TD: You don't seem to be commercially oriented.

KS: I'm not against selling. Any money I can get for my pictures helps me buy equipment and make more pictures.

TD: How well does your work sell?

KS: It sold better when Harold Jones was there because he understood it better. I don't think the people there now understand my work as well and they're pushing more straight work. When Harold was there I had a show in Italy and the whole show sold out. He'd get my work around different places where they're now handling Ansel Adams. They're more understanding in knowing straight work. I don't really think they understand my work, whereas he did.

TD: How do you decide on the size of a book?

KS: Certain things are determined by the sheets that I'm using. If it's 11 x 14, pictures go all the way to the edge, certain other books, 11 x 14 photographs, but I use paper borders, so that determines it. A great deal of them are square or nearly square because a vertical or horizontal works well in it. The process often determines it.

TD: How did you learn bookbinding?

KS: I haven't. They're just simple case bindings, I don't know how to bind books.

TD: How do you decide on the materials you use (for the covers)?

KS: That's a shirt I was wearing, the blue one was the edge of my bed sheet, the very bright, flowered one I found in Woolworth's at 29¢ a yard. I used the back side of the cloth because it was so bright. The striped one I picked out because it had rainbows and I'm dealing with auras and prismatic light and certain hallucinations in that book. Either it's something I had around or I picked out.

TD: With the A.B. Dick you'll continue to do everything yourself?

KS: Most of them will probably just be folded and stapled with a very simple cover. They won't be elaborately bound. If I get some money I'll buy an industrial sewing machine and stitch them.

TD: Do you work every day?

KS: It's an exception when I don't.

TD: When do you usually work?

KS: I start in the morning and work all day, unless I have to go out for an errand.

TD: How much sleep do you get?

KS: I get lots of sleep, at least eight hours. I remember reading about Darwin. He slept eight hours a night, he worked two hours in his lab in the morning, and he'd take a nap. His wife would read to him, he'd go for a walk, and in the afternoon he'd work two hours in his lab, then take a nap. He worked four hours a day and look at all the books he wrote and all he did. I need a lot of sleep, I always take at least one nap, usually about a half hour. I have to have eight hours sleep or I just can't do anything. Plus I like to dream. I try to pay attention to my dreams.

TD: For your work?

KS: They usually don't fit into my work because it's a different kind of vision that's very quickly evolving and metamorphosing, it just doesn't fit into single pictures. If I were a moviemaker they might fit in, but that's just something I don't enjoy.

TD: Do you use drugs?

KS: I had an acid trip in '67 because they came out with that. I don't smoke grass and I don't use drugs, but I do hallucinate. Sometimes I do exercises, something like yoga, only I make them up myself and I feel like I'm suspended, floating in the room, and start seeing different things. Sometimes I can do that or if I'm working long hours I'll start seeing some things. Usually I have no control. Once in a while I can control them a little bit. I can see certain things, now and then, but not with drugs.

TD: Do you meditate?

KS: Not in the sense of Zen where you blank everything out of your mind to try to see something. I try to concentrate on different approaches to a certain form of subject matter and I start seeing different things sometimes. If that's called meditation then I do it.

TD: How much does an A. B. Dick cost?

KS: A new one is $6000. I'm looking for a new one or a rebuilt one with a guarantee. I'm hoping to get a CAPS grant which is $5000. I haven't heard yet, so I may not get it.

TD: How many grants have you received?

KS: The only two I've ever applied for were the CAPS and Guggenheim, which I received in 1972. I'm going to start applying for NEA because they give out so many. Everyone I know has received at least one.

TD: In what direction do you see your work going?

KS: If I knew that I'd do it now instead of then. In a certain way it's always evolving, unless you just copy yourself, but in other ways it's like a signature. It's very much you and the same. That's true of anyone's work.

TD: Are you afraid you'll repeat yourself?

KS: No. I'm not afraid of my work at all. A lot of Siskind's work is very similar. When I was a student he told me, "Never repeat yourself. You have to resolve each picture in a new way." He deals on a very subtle level.

TD: Where do you get the inspiration to continue working?

KS: A lot of my work is just intuitive and I don't think too much about it. For about four years I worked on cloth pieces, making quilts, pillows and such. I once asked myself what in hell I was doing. I didn't know. I figured that was where my head was at, maybe later I'd understand it. A lot of the time I don't know why I'm doing certain things, I'm just doing them. They just come out of me and I work on them. Other things are preconceived and I know more what's going on; whatever is concerning me I bring down to my work.

TD: Mostly you do etchings?

KS: Of my single prints I certainly do more etchings than silkscreens, and more etchings than drawings because drawings take too long. I guess there are more because they don't take so long. I don't do any more copy machine pictures. I did a lot of that for years. Etching has such beautiful quality that it really attracts me and it's a good way of combining drawing and photography into one picture. In the last couple of years it's been more important and I'm dropping off other things, except etchings and drawings, and photographs because I take photographs for the etchings.

TD: Do you do many silkscreens?

KS: No, because I look on screening as crude compared to etchings and it's a very dangerous process with all the clean-up and fumes. It's not good for my system to breathe all of that, so I don't want to be around that several hours a day. Photoetching is dangerous because you have chemicals with a lot of potent things in them and the acids, of course, but I spend most of the time printing the etchings or drawing on the plate, so most of the time I'm not around toxic things.

TD: Do you have a background in the history of photography?

KS: I sat through Hugh Edwards' course twice, mostly just listening to him talk.

TD: Do you have a sense of yourself within that context?

KS: I do consider myself a photographer. Everything I've done, whether it's with copy machines, they're photo-related, or whether it's with cloth pieces, a gum print on cloth, or a blueprint on cloth or copy machine on cloth. If I do etchings, again they have photos in them, I'm using photography in various ways. I'm not worried about it, someone else, later on, can look back and see what I've done.

TD: Do you do any color photography?

KS: I did as a student. Most of it was flashing and solarizing with different color lights to alter the picture from a black and white negative. Then I got into cliche verre on color paper.

TD: How much time do you spend on silver printing?

KS: It depends, if they're hand-colored, some might take four or five hours. At one time I was elaborately dating everything down to the minute. For instance, this print (holds up a print) says 9 PM to 1:06 AM, 6 February. That's how long it took to do that. Some of them take a long time, and during this time period I was working very slowly. I work much faster now, there's a different result. Certain years, depending on the way I'm working, I might do pictures very quickly, like my copy machine pictures I crank them out one right after the other, and other times I'm working very slowly on a process.

TD: How did you come to sew in your pictures?

KS: In the early 60's I was sewing photo silkscreen quilts so it just came over into the prints. It's probably influenced by Japanese wall hangings. I like combinations of paper, acetate, cloth.

TD: How often do you photograph?

KS: It's usually in spurts. I might photograph someone and take 20-30 rolls and I might work off them for months, or there might be a period where I photograph several times in a year, but not too often because once I get the negatives I'm doing various things with them, etchings and such, so I usually don't have a need to go back and photograph. It's not the kind of photography where you are constantly imaging with a camera, besides I can take an old negative, add drawing to it and make a totally different picture out of it, and later on use some other aspect of that negative, print it, add something else, and have another picture.

TD: How often do you draw?

KS: Every day.

TD: Do you think it's necessary to draw everyday?

KS: It is for me. It depends on the person. You can't make any rules for anything.

TD: When I mentioned to Syl Labrot that I was going to talk to you, he smiled and said, "That should be about a one-page piece."

KS: I'm very wordy compared to the way I used to be. I didn't talk to people, I didn't speak much.

TD: Were you quiet as a child?

KS: I was very withdrawn. I didn't like to be around people.

TD: Do you have any idea why?

KS: Once, in kindergarten, something happened to me and I never wanted to be around people after that. That was one thing, I don't know if there was anything before that. I'm talking much more in the last couple of years. I'm settled down, I'm not moving around a lot, I enjoy my job. I'm more stable.

TD: Your life didn't have stability before?

KS: I moved a lot and I hated teaching. I quit a couple of times. I didn't know how I was going to earn a living. Now I realize I'm not a teacher and I don't pretend to be.

TD: How did you make a living before teaching?

KS: That's it. After I got out of college I started teaching. I taught at UCLA for a couple of quarters, then I came here and quit and went to work in a grocery store for awhile. Then I was asked to teach in Chicago, then came here for the second time.

TD: How did you make a living before college?

KS: I was in the army for three years.

TD: What about after high school?

KS: I was in the seminary. I became a Catholic right after I graduated from high school, then went in the seminary for a year. That was the extent of my religion — it lasted two years. I wasn't anything before then and I wasn't anything after. I'm glad I got it out of my life, and I'm past that. I've tried a lot of things. My work keeps me going, otherwise I'd have been dead a long time ago. Since I started art and making pictures I felt something was worthwhile. My work was respected, people appreciated it and that made me feel good. I'm actually doing pictures for very few people and they recognize something they've gone through and it was a great comfort to me. That makes me very happy. Like I have a great friendship with DeChirico just by looking at his pictures. I used to talk a lot to Van Gogh, too.

TD: What kind of student were you in high school?

KS: I made very good grades, even though I didn't read.

TD: You have no interest in reading?

KS: If I read something I listen to the way the words sound or I repeat it over and over, I love repetition. It will take me forever to get anywhere and I forget what I'm reading. Also I don't want to ruin my eyes by reading. I think you can be very intelligent without being too literate. You can gain a lot of things without books, they aren't that necessary, although I know I'm missing a whole different aspect, just like I don't go to the movies. They take three hours out of your life. I haven't got three hours to waste away at a movie.

TD: Do you use found photographs?

KS: I used to a lot, not too much anymore.

TD: Any of the contemporary workers impress you?

KS: Sure, in different ways, to different degrees. I trade them pictures and put them up on the walls to look at, so that must mean something.

TD: Do you like any of the books that have appeared lately?

KS: I like Nathan's (Lyons - **Notations in Passing**); I saw a handmade book by (Lucas) Samaras, hands, cut out shapes on cardboard that pulled out; I liked that.

Syl's (Labrot) is nice, too, because it's created as a book. Mostly the books I look at are children's books. Sometimes people say they are just gimmicks, sometimes they *are* just gimmicks. One of my favorite picture makers is Maurice Sendak, visually he does a lot. He does children's books and the drawing is nice. I think he's a fine bookmaker. I have about all of his books.

TD: So you're not quite as illiterate as you pretend.

KS: Yeah, I read children's books. (laughs)

TD: Probably they're more interesting than many of the so-called adult books.

KS: They're novel. I was going to do a round book because I was interested, in 1969, in a man on the moon. I did an Up book. I did it because Nixon said, "We're going up to the moon," and (Walter) Cronkite pointed out that's a 15th-century idea, there's only out, there is no up. I wanted a round book so I could use it all the way around, there would be no up or down, but when you fold it closed, that axis would create an up and down, so you destroy the idea. I found a children's book with cardboard circular pages with an eccentric grommet, so I found the idea already resolved.

TD: You buy a lot of children's books?

KS: No, just when I find either one that is unique in transition or unique because of some kind of gadget or gimmick. I like to find different books or well-done books.

TD: Do your books have any relationship, one to another?

KS: Not directly that I know of. Some of them go back and use certain ideas, or certain moods I was working with that I try to handle in a different way. They are only related indirectly.

TD: Do you ever take vacations?

KS: Dutifully, once in a while — maybe at Christmas, I go to see my mother in Florida. I try to stay about two days and then return. I don't travel, but I'd love to go to Europe. For me, a vacation is being able to do my work constantly. All my phones are plug-ins. Sometimes it's nice to unplug them, have enough food for a week, and not go out for a week, nor speak for a week, and do my work. That's so nice.

TD: Do you collect old photographs?

KS: I used to collect postcards, I have a few thousand, but I haven't bought any in four or five years.

TD: Do you collect anything now?

KS: I trade a lot of pictures. I have an awful lot of other people's work. I don't collect anything else.

TD: Whose work in particular do you collect?

KS: I have about twelve of Vera Berdick's etchings. That's the most of anyone's work I've collected.

Rochester, New York
July 19, 1976

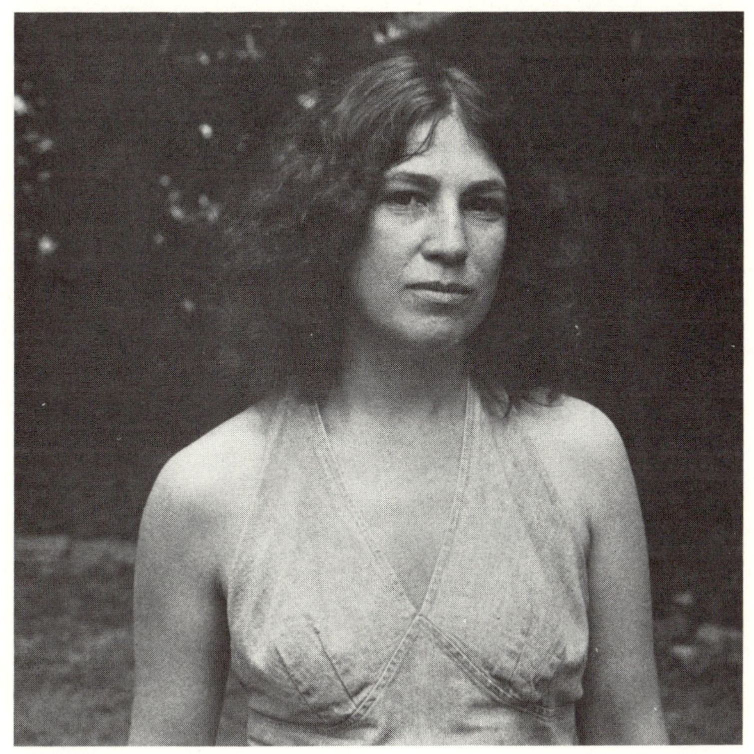

Joan Lyons

Interviewer: How do you find the time to do your own work?

Joan Lyons: That's another reason I do books. I don't have a lot of time to do my own work and there is a certain kind of work you can do in public, with people present, and there is a certain kind you can't. It's difficult to do a press run when people are around, but little printing kinds of things, and little experimental things I can do where there are other people working, or students interrupting to ask questions, and it's good for them to see that kind of work going on. The only way I know to teach is to think of myself as a worker in a shop with apprentices, and they will learn more watching me work, even peripherally than all the talking I might do about working. These kinds of little printing things often I can work on piecemeal, while doing other things, whereas I can't sit down and make drawings, if I don't have a good spread of time. A lot of the way I do work is governed by the time I have. This last book (**Abby Rogers to her Grand-Daughter**) I printed when I had a week with nobody in the shop. It went very quickly.

Whenever I have a conversation with Joan Lyons, she'll invariably get quite animated discussing a book project she plans to do, a recent book she has seen, and is excited about, and, as often as not, the books will more likely be by other people. On a hot, muggy, Rochester-summer day, July 19, 1976, I interviewed Joan in her home studio. I soon got the impression she would rather have been off working on one of her projects. By the conclusion, she was somewhat more relaxed, still protesting, however, that she had very little to say. The conversation lasted just under two hours and appears mostly as it was recorded.

Joan Lyons is a dynamic, independent, hard-working artist, consumed with a passion for books as a form "for the transmission of visual ideas." Amazingly, she is as involved in other people's book projects as she is in her own, and sometimes, it seems, more involved. Her energy and selflessness is continually directed toward books, and the possibilities inherent in that medium.

Born: New York City, March 6, 1937.
B.F.A.: Alfred University, Alfred, New York, 1957.
M.F.A.: State University of New York at Buffalo, 1973.
Books:
> **Self Impressions.** Visual Studies Workshop Press/the artist. Rochester, New York, 1972.
>
> **In Hand.** Visual Studies Workshop Press. Rochester, New York, 1973.
>
> **Busform Shadows.** Visual Studies Workshop. Rochester, New York, 1973.
>
> **Bride Book.** Visual Studies Workshop Press/the artist. Rochester, New York, 1975.
>
> **Abby Rogers to her Grand-Daughter.** Visual Studies Workshop Press/the artist. Rochester, New York, 1976.

Currently: Faculty member, Visual Studies Workshop (coordinates the print shop which is, in addition to being a teaching facility, a production shop for limited edition books: artists' books, poetry and photographic research and reprints.); Artist, Rochester, New York.

Tom Dugan: What is your background? How did you get involved in making books?

Joan Lyons: I was a ceramics major and I always had an interest in printmaking as one of the primary forms, particularly lithography. Over the years I had a whole range of little isolated experiences that seemed to fit together into what I'm doing now in a bizarre, but interesting way. I'd always hoped to have a print shop accessible to me someday and it just came about that I've had that opportunity. It's really great, it's a great big playpen. I'm still not qualified as a printing technician to run a production shop, but, in a way, amateurs do things in a good sense sometimes. You learn as you go along and don't regard the machinery in a fixed way. I'm uncomfortable being called a printmaker because printmakers don't see what I do that way. I don't think about it much. I think you use any means you have at your disposal. If it's a pencil or an offset press you want to investigate that and see how you can interact with it and what it's going to do. I don't see a vast difference between hand printing and printing with automatic machinery. All those tools do different things, but I can't separate that out of my head and say that one is printmaking and one is photographing, they're all imaging.

TD: You're very interested in doing something with a machine?

JL: I don't know. I've tried to isolate my interests in machines and find out what they are. I'm not interested intrinsically in machines or machinery. There's a little perverse factor in there, too. I enjoy taking a machine which was designed for a set purpose, or is used commonly by industry in a particular kind of way, and find very obvious and natural ways to use that piece of equipment besides the accepted way. A process camera is used commercially to photograph copy and photograph type on to graphic arts negatives. I look at a copy camera as being a large format view camera. As soon as you make that transition, what is this thing? It's not a copy anything, it's a camera, which is very simple and very obvious. I always have to plough through lots of complexities until all of a sudden I get down to something that is pretty simple and obvious. That's always exciting.

TD: How about more about your background. How you got where you are?

JL: It's hard. It's really circumstances. I probably just as easily could have been a potter. I really think it's a matter of where you are at a given time. As an undergraduate I was a ceramic design major at Alfred University, which means I was studying pottery, but, along with that, I was doing a lot of work in painting and graphics. I became very interested in graphics, design and printmaking, probably because John Wood was teaching there and he and his work interested me a great deal and therefore influenced me. I think John is a big influence and has been over all the years. Probably, if he wasn't at Alfred at that time, I probably would not have developed an interest in printmaking at that time. I went to graduate school very briefly at Mills College in California on a fellowship in ceramics. Again I was doing ceramics, I was painting and I was doing printmaking, and they got a little freaked out because they felt I should specialize and I was getting a little tired of being in school, so I left there. I needed to go to New York for awhile because of some family problems, so I decided it's time to see what the real world was like, which meant going out and getting a job. Beginning design jobs were difficult to come by and difficult to live with once you got them. My first job was with Tiffany and company; I was hired to work on their catalog. This exquisite company had a catalog that looked like the worst direct mail drugstore schlock you'd ever seen in your life and that's the way they wanted to keep it. That was a very strange job. They wanted me to do things like design silver, although I had never worked with the material in my entire life. They told me that was fine, none of the other designers had either, just draw the picture and the guys at the factory will take care of it. And because I had essentially a craft background I couldn't deal with that kind of attitude. Within a period of a year and a half I had a whole bunch of little design jobs in New York and what I began to realize more and more was that all of these designers and art directors just didn't know very much about production. They were drawing pictures, layouts on a piece of paper and sending them off. I felt that the way to get at something was real hands-on, craft approach to it, that there was something about the experience of handling ink and handling type and handling the materials you were working with that was invaluable. The few good graphic designers in New York knew production very well. They knew exactly what the means they were employing would do, and how to use it. Anything short of that seemed absurd to me, so I decided if I was going to continue working as a designer, it didn't make much sense to work for studios and agencies; I had to get jobs working for printers, and so I did. I had several jobs working for printers. Of course I was non-union and unskilled, so I didn't get to do anything like presswork, but I did a lot of mechanicals and stripping, and observed a lot of the rest of the operations. They were not creative jobs, but they were incredibly interesting because I was finally getting to learn a craft, and what was involved in production. I felt more comfortable with that. Then I married Nathan and moved to Rochester, and I didn't have access to a kiln and didn't have access to printmaking facilities. I continued working for printers and doing freelance design work. I did a lot of posters for galleries here. But since I didn't have any other facilities I started painting and drawing a lot and remaining a frustrated printmaker. It was a lot of years, ten or so, until I got back to printmaking and that happened because I was doing certain kinds of drawings that suggested that the next step would be to start doing some stencil prints, so I started doing silkscreens. I had always photographed a little bit all along, but to avoid conflict with a photographing husband, I tried to avoid it as much as possible. In about 1967 I did my first photo silkscreen portfolio, employing very crude means, washing out screens in the bathtub and that kind of thing, and, at that point, a lot really came together. I had been living with a community of photographers all these years, although I was not a photographer, and I started to suspect that the influence was deeper than I had realized. I put up a drawing show, maybe forty or fifty drawings, and I realized it was a sequence of images and it had to be in this order and things related in ways, I mean, most people did not make drawings that way, that was a photographer's way of working, sequencing images and making extended statements and dealing with more than a single image. Then we started the Workshop and more toys appeared and inadvertently I got more and more involved with that development. I had been, by this time, raising lots of babies and doing lots of painting and drawing and odd jobs on the side, freelancing, teaching some at the local museum. I got involved with the workshop very slowly. I was interested in printmaking and other people came along who were interested in that, so I set up a silkscreen thing, then Syl (Labrot) appeared and taught silkscreen, and Keith Smith spent a semester involved in printmaking. I then began working with and teaching non-silver processes, like blueprint, brown print, gum print. It was very difficult to learn these processes, at that time, because there was no information. We acquired an old press and I learned how to run it. We made a lot of mistakes, but it became apparent that it would be very nice to have a little print shop. Both Nathan and I had always been interested in printing and books, so little by little that grew. It was really pretty difficult, not knowing much about equipment or commercial production. Now I'm up to my neck in printmaking, printing, copy machine images, and it all feels very comfortable and very right.

TD: How did you come to do books?

JL: I talked about books and thought about books long before I ever did any. I did several little one-of-a-kind books back when I was a student, even as long ago as that I had been thinking about visual book possibilities, which again probably had a lot to do with input from John Wood. Books were always very special things, almost sacred objects in my childhood.

TD: How did the first book come about?

JL: That's very hard to deal with in the kind of books I do because you almost slide into it. It's impossible to say when your first book came about.

TD: How do you slide into a book?

JL: It's not like getting together four hundred photographs and going out and looking for a publisher to do The Book. I've done a number of funky little one-of-a-kind things that might be on the sketchbook level, but I was thinking about as sequences and book pages. The first book edition that I did of my own was **Self-Impressions** in 1972. That came about because Sonia Sheridan persuaded 3M Corporation to bring a color machine to the Workshop and there was this frantic thing going on for a week with people practically killing each other to have access to this machine which generated huge amounts of waste as well as images. There are intermediates which are waste products, and I ran around and gathered up all the waste stuff to work with later and realized that that machine produced image sequences. Those things individually didn't quite satisfy me as prints; the machine did them. There were some preliminery responses, but there was something about a series of those responses that seemed interesting, so I started working toward a book idea. The book is about twenty images and I think of it as being a print in book form. It's not that different for me from printmaking. It's just a kind of print that belongs in book form instead of a frame on a wall. It's a multiple kind of thing. You have to go back and relate ideas about multiple images that may be on one sheet of paper. I had been doing those kinds of things. That and a little book idea are all part of the same thing in a way. Obviously once I had access to a printing press that's what I was thinking about, making books. One of the things I like about making books as a finished product is that it is so nice and unprecious. I also make prints that are rather precious objects, that have to be viewed in frames on walls, although some of my things I like better as portfolios. I stopped painting about ten years ago, it was no great loss to the art world, I was not a very good painter, but every so often, even though I preferred graphics and drawing and photography, I'd feel to be a "real" artist, I have to make canvasses, big ones, paintings, "real" art. I'd stretch a bunch of big canvasses and go at it, and besides the fact that I wasn't terribly committed to painting I started feeling very funny about having these large objects that needed large wall spaces, which meant galleries, museums and being that much a part of this institutional system that was beginning to look kind of funny to me. Painters painted large so galleries and museums built bigger walls and because of bigger walls, that dictated what the artist would make to fill them up and it seemed funny. At that time books and prints started looking better and better and feeling better and better. There's something really wonderful about a book. The first book I made, a minimal little thing, I made fifty copies or so and I got forty-five mailing envelopes and sent them out to people I knew or people I didn't know so well, but whose work I like a lot. I thought that was just a wonderful kind of thing to do. Books are expendable, they're not a burden on anybody. You buy a book, you enjoy it and you tuck it away on a bookshelf. It's not a commanding object that you have to deal with and make this great committment and live with out in the open. I like work that you just take out and look at when you want to look at it, then put it away. When I stopped painting I started doing large pieces on fabric because there were still some kinds of things I wanted to do large, but I preferred the idea that they could be folded up and put away in a closet. I guess that relates to my feelings about books, too. They're really nice, they're not precious.

TD: That's interesting. I don't think people generally think of books as being expendable, but the relationship of a book to a large painting certainly sets that sort of an attitude up. I don't think photographers think about books in that sense.

JL: Well, they do think about distribution, that it is a way of getting the work out easily. Maybe the difference is that a photographer generally thinks he's done this series of photographs, he's done this work, and he's going to put it in book form to get it out, and that's one kind of photographic book. There have been other kinds of books that are more than that, where the work has to exist in book form, like Nathan's book **(Notations in Passing)** and Robert Frank's **(The Americans)**. The kind of books I do, that work just doesn't exist until it's on the printed page. There are two attitudes you can have about printing. Most printing that goes on in this country is a reproduction of some copy. Most photographic books are trying to be as close as they can to being a facsimile of the original photograph. That's one kind of marvelous and very valid attitude about printing and the other is a kind of printmaking approach and that's the area of printing I'm interested in. In other words, there's no original copy that's reproduced, the image evolves out of the process itself and the first time it's evident is on the printed page, so the books are, in every sense, original prints. They're primary material, and that to me is incredibly exciting, and what is infinite and endless about printing. Syl (Labrot) is very involved in that kind of idea, and takes it even further to structure that in such a way that it can be printed by any careful printer. I'm interested in all kinds of alternatives. I'm very excited about the idea of something being produced commercially which is an original print. I can draw on a plate, a direct lithograph, and put it on the production press. One of the things I'd like to do someday is to illustrate a book that way, where the illustrations are original prints and theoretically I can run thousands, actually I may go into a run of ten. There's still a discrepancy between the possiblilities and the need. That's a pretty exciting idea.

TD: Where do your ideas for books come from? For instance, the Wonder Woman **book.**

JL: I was approached by Juliet McGrath, a poet who teaches at the University of Rochester, and we were just talking about books and things one day and I said I was interested in doing collaborations with poets and she said that was wonderful, she would just love to do something with me sometime, so our first experience we got together and played with the copy machine one day. She was doing some spontaneous writing and it was through relating back and forth. Then we thought we'd do something in an edition. We didn't have enough time to pursue the idea of the immediacy of an active collaboration, which interests me, I'm very excited about that possibility, but that might be a long term thing. You might have to work together for a month, a year, and hone it down. So I looked through her work and found a Wonder Woman poem and thought, well, I'm an old Wonder Woman fan. It's sort of a feminist macho poem and I liked something of that response, and thought of relating a little sequence of images to it, that don't illustrate it, but somehow plays with the spirit of it, in a parallel kind of way. I'm interested in non-literal relationships between poetry and illustration. I think the next book I do will be illustrated poetry, but drawing on traditional book form. Books that use words, images and decoration. I'm very interested in book decoration, symmetry, borders, all the systems but to develop those systems photographically, instead of by hand. That's something I spend a lot of time with, and the results are not too fantastic yet, but the right means will come along. So that's an idea I've been kicking around probably ten or fifteen years. The other day—Sonia Sheridan was doing a workshop here—and she brought this crazy little machine with her, a little wax lettering machine, and I started playing with it when they were all off on a field trip and my office now is deluged with thousands and thousands of images from the strip printer. I have to admit that I'm timid about the idea of books. Because I do printing myself I realize how incredibly involved the process is. Usually a person does a book and spends this incredible amount of time planning it and putting it together, writing it, editing it, laying it out, but then it goes off. Well, at that stage, I've just started and I still have to put in incredible amounts of time and energy physically putting the thing together, usually down to folding the pages, collating it and binding it myself. Because it's a little intimidating I've started with very simple things and also I'm always trying to feed those ideas to students. I keep saying, "If I do a real simple book that I can do in a couple days, they're going to see how easy it is, so everybody is going to want to do books." So there's a didactic function to them in a way. Most of the books I've done are very quick and easy. They're printed rapidly, the ideas just occur to me almost as little conceptual ideas and are executed quickly. They're simple as ideas. Now I'm gradually beginning to get into slightly more complex books, more traditional kinds of books, although I still like books as these little print ideas.

TD: How did the new book come about (Abby Rogers to her Grand-Daughter)?

JL: Several things came together. Elsa Voelker, one of our students, found a letter from a relative describing her childhood in a small town in the late nineteenth century. I thought it was a lovely letter and an important one to publish, as a women's document. I thought I could give a voice to this woman who ostensibly would never have a voice at all. I was moved by the letter; it's well-written and I thought I wanted to publish it. Elsa wasn't interested in using it herself. The other thing is I've been doing fabric prints for awhile, and I thought it would be fun to carry that idea to a production situation and use that bit of technology. The occasion of the letter is the handing over of the family quilt to the granddaughter, and the making of the quilt is the thread woven through the idea of the reminiscence of her life, so it was appropriate to illustrate the letter with quilt fragments. It was a document I was moved by and it coincided with some visual material that I had at hand, and was interested in, and was working with, and the two came together.

TD: Why did you go with a large edition for this book?

JL: The others are my own personal prints and there's probably not much of a market for that. In the interim the Workshop has started a marketing service, The Book Bus, for small edition books. This book is a test to see if I can sell 500 of something and I think the content will interest people. Probably a fair number will be sold because of the content as well as the quality and the look of the thing, it's not purely a visual book, and the economics of printing 500 was good.

TD: How did you select the paper you used?

JL: This book is printed on Mohawk Superfine which is one of the few neutral pH and, therefore, fairly archival papers made. That interested me, but what interested me more is it's an off white paper, which I prefer for something like this. I consider it more appropriate than stark white paper, and it's a beautiful sheet. It runs very well through this minimal press we have. I have trouble running harder paper. It's expensive paper, but worth the difference in price. Small run books should be done on good paper. You're going to all that trouble to make a book and paper costs aren't that great. I do not intend to get rich making books.

TD: How do you find the time to do your own work?

JL: That's another reason I do books. I don't have a lot of time to do my own work and there is a certain kind of work you can do in public, with people present, and there is a certain kind you can't. It's difficult to do a press run when people are around, but little printing kinds of things, and little experimental things I can do where there are other people working, or students interrupting to ask questions, and it's good for them to see that kind of work going on. The only way I know to teach is to think of myself as a worker in a shop with apprentices, and they will learn more watching me work, even peripherally than by all the talking I might do about working. These kinds of little printing things often I can work on piecemeal, while doing other things, whereas I can't sit down and make drawings, if I don't have a good spread of time. A lot of the way I do work is governed by the time I have. This last book **(Abby Rogers to her Grand-daughter)** I printed when I had a week with nobody in the shop. It went very quickly.

TD: You did everything yourself?

JL: Yes, but that's only necessity. I don't want to do more than I have to, and this one I was able to get to a bindery to staple and trim, I didn't have to do that at least. I don't see any intrinsic virtue in handmade. The Siskind book we did we hand set the type and it's hand-bound, but that came about because we couldn't afford to do it any other way.

TD: Do you think you'll get into doing larger editions?

JL: I don't think so, as long as I regard books as printmaking kinds of things and deal with poetry or something that doesn't have a vast market. I'm not terribly interested in making commercial books.

TD: Could you discuss the concept of success for yourself?

JL: I don't think I would want to have to earn a living making pictures. It would make it into something else. It's the one thing I do that's a very private thing. I do it for myself. I have some ego and I like an audience, but the audience could be two people I really care about, and past that it's nice to have a broader audience. It's nice, but not essential. If you make books it's a real problem. If you make five hundred books there has to be five hundred people who want to receive them. There must be five hundred of us who like these kinds of little personal books and are willing to collect them. **Abby Rogers To Her Granddaughter** is quite frankly, sentimental, reminiscent, and it does have an audience. People really like that book. My next door neighbor likes it. She bought a copy for her 82 year old sister, a nun. This is a different audience than I've ever reached. I spent the first part of my life trying to reach an audience of men. I didn't even realize that women were an audience. That's the kind of awareness that's come to a lot of women lately. My work over the last eight or nine years has dealt very heavily and almost exclusively with women's issues. It's either been about fabrics, self-portraits, the books are **Wonder Woman,** a bride self-portrait, and a grandmother's letter about a quilt. I really don't consider them feminist. I think I've finally gotten brave enough to make work about the things that are closest to me and most a part of my life. But I don't have the same attitude as a man about making it in the real world out there. I'm not terribly competitive as an artist. Success, in terms of the outside world, has not been terribly important. Selling work to earn a lot of money has not been terribly important. It's only been important to sell enough work to make more work, which is more or less the cycle of the books. If I put some seed money into a book and I sell enough of that to make another book, that's fine. I'm content with that. If there's a little money left over as well and I show a little profit, I feel pretty good about that.

TD: How did the Bride Book **come about?**

JL: That book is based very simply on a little production thing. If you turn the ink off the press each sheet gets successively lighter, so it's based on an idea about that and an idea about the law of simultaneous contrast where two complementary colors of equal value kind of vibrate and the boundaries disappear, so in the middle the image disappears. At the time I was thinking about that kind of possibility I found a bunch of glass plates and there was this silly traditional forties bride portrait which I thought would be good to use.

TD: It's interesting that so much of your work is based on found images, and yet they come out as a form of autoimagery or autobiography.

JL: I don't really mean those things to be autobiographical. I have to make that comment. There's a difference between autobiographical and personal and ideas that seem to be universal and common, and I think that's what I'm after. Experiences that will be understood. For instance, I did a series of self-portraits on the Xerox machine. I don't consider them self-portraits. The machine does funny things and I could make portraits of myself on that machine that make me look sixteen years old or make me look eighty-three. It's a different person each time. I thought I wanted at that point, for some reason, to do a series of portraits of women, but not portraits of individual women, but a cumulative kind of portrait of some aspect of women. Mostly I didn't know what they would be, I was just curious. Most of the portraits, the whole art history of women images, are mostly done by men and I thought, "How would a woman describe a woman differently than a man describes a woman." If I started photographing nudes, how would they be different? And there were some men who were very upset with my nude self-portraits because they don't relate to the stereotype of what nudes are supposed to be. They're matter of fact and direct and a little distorted and maybe grotesque. They're not models. They're there, they're lifesized, they're a confrontation. They're self-portraits because of the medium used. They relate to this first book I did, that self-portrait and copy machine. It's a funny thing about copy machines. Everybody intuitively sticks their face down on the copy machine, then they start undressing and sticking their body down on the copy machine, and this whole thing relates, in my mind, to that mark that Man made on the cave wall with his hand, "I'm here," The most direct kind of mark making and it translates to these sophisticated machines. The impulse is to make that same kind of mark and that fascinates me. Everybody's copy machine pictures look alike. How do you work with that impulse and take it somewhere else? I like the idea of just having the machine and myself. Then the machine is just acting upon itself and with the operator. There's something kind of pure about that. If I was dealing with another person as model I would start feeling uncomfortable because it takes a very, very long time to put together one of those images. They're pieces and it might take a whole day to do one and to impose upon another person for a whole day is awkward. A lot of my ideas come about, not only what I find, but what relates to what the machines do, what they dictate. How they can be played with and manipulated.

TD: What do you think the future will hold for you?

JL: I've got a lot of work to do. Now I'm pretty happy with lithography, both hand lithography and offset lithography and books and prints. My involvement with books is I help other people make books, too. Part of my involvement with books is didactic. I want other people to become excited about book possibilities and that's all combined. I want a book that can't be anything else, but book. If that idea could exist another way, as a portfolio or a bunch of single prints, I would do it that way. A book is related to film. It's a kind of experience where your movement through it is governed to an extent by the sequence, turning pages and something has to occur on the page to stop you or start you or hold you back or slow you down or speed you up or force you to refer ahead twelve pages or back six pages. There's an intimacy about the experience of a book. You hold it close to you. It's a tactile experience, the book is an object. The feeling of the paper, the feeling of the binding, a book is an object. There's no reason why a book has to be a traditional codex. I'm experimenting some with venetian blind books and scrolls. A scroll is a very interesting form. It's something you unravel in time and a book is just in time. I like playing with time in books. I like playing with the real time of a copy machine book where the time it takes you to go through that book is about the time it took me to make the images. I think there is a real regeneration of interest in the picture book. Five years ago there probably weren't any visual books, except children's and standard photographic books.

Rochester, New York
July 19, 1976

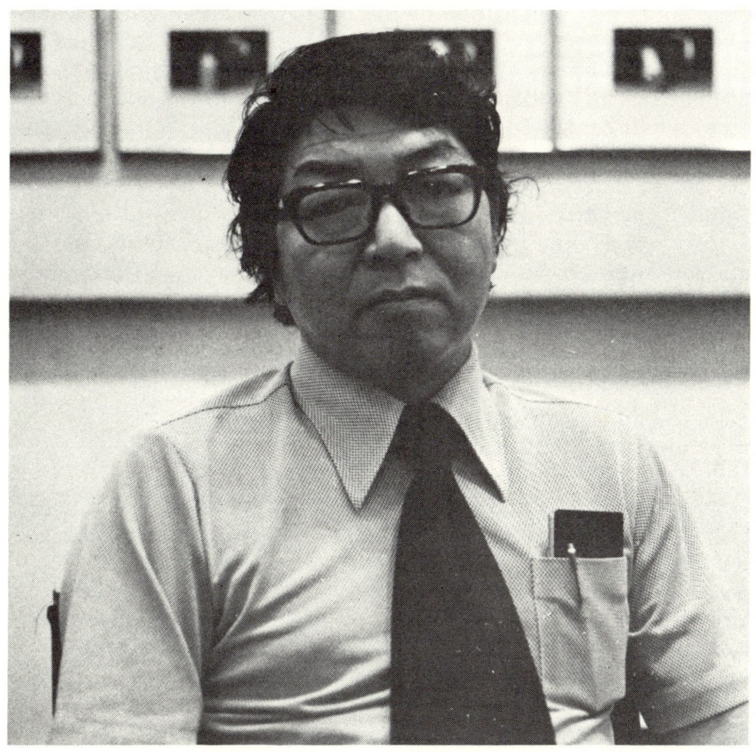

Eikoh Hosoe

Interviewer: Is there such a thing as a Kamaitachi (literally translated means chilblain or weasel's slash)?

Eikoh Hosoe: Right. Anytime I wrote about **Kamaitachi,** I wrote it as a record of my memory. My photographs are an explanation of myself. Sometimes it looks very objective, but it's very subjective. That is why it is a little bit difficult for other people to understand them, but they can feel something. I don't mind other people's reactions. I really want to record my past days. In photography you cannot describe your past when you photograph the contemporary, present thing. But the photography is made by the man who has complexes about many things. And even in the medium of photography you are allowed to do it. In **Kamaitachi** the dancer is my catalyst, but photography shows the person or the thing as it is. It is free for you to interpret, it is quite free. My motives come from my experiences, my remembrances of days.

My introduction to the work of Eikoh Hosoe was his book, **Kamaitachi,** which appeared in its entirety in *Camera* magazine (October 1970), and later in *Photo World* magazine (March 1974) when a portfolio from **Ordeal by Roses** was published. I was completely enchanted by the man's vision and imagination.

I read in *The New York Times* that Eikoh Hosoe would be in New York for the opening of his latest work, "Simon: a Private Landscape", at Light Gallery. On a whim I stopped by and Hosoe was in the gallery. Larry Miller pointed him out, and I introduced myself, explained my mission, and he agreed to be interviewed. The following day, May 30, 1975, we talked in the back room of the gallery. Business as usual went on around us. Victor Schrager served us coffee, and everybody was quite gracious and cooperative.

Eikoh Hosoe, of slightly less than average height, compact in build, is quietly serious and intensely self-contained. Unfortunately, his work is still too little known in the West. To see his books one would have to visit such places as The Museum of Modern Art in New York City, or the research library at The Visual Studies Workshop in Rochester, N.Y.

Born: Tokyo, Japan. March 18, 1933.
Attended: Tokyo College of Photography, 1954.
Books:
>**Man and Woman.** Camerart. Tokyo, Japan, 1961.
>**Killed by Roses.** Sheisha Co. Ltd. Tokyo, Japan, 1963.
>**Ondine.** Genkosha. Tokyo, Japan, 1964.
>**Kamaitachi.** Gendaishichosha. Tokyo, Japan, 1969.
>**Ordeal by Roses.** Shueisha Co. Ltd. Tokyo, Japan, 1971.
>**Embrace.** Shashin Hyoronsha Publishing House. Tokyo, Japan, 1971.

Currently: Teacher, Tokyo College of Photography; Photographer, Tokyo, Japan.

Tom Dugan: How did you choose photography as your life's work?
Eikoh Hosoe: This is the only medium that I could do a little bit better than others, so I chose it.
TD: At what point did you decide it would be your career?
EH: It's a long story. One picture changed me. I was a high school boy, second grade, sixteen years old (1951), and I submitted a photo to a big photo contest, the Fuji Photo Contest. I got first prize. I was given plenty of money from the company and could afford to buy enlargers, new cameras, and so on. I was a very serious student, but photography was more interesting, more attractive than studying. I wanted to enter Tokyo University to study law, but the photography made me a lazy student in the sense of academic study, so I really fell. I thought it was my fate to go to this career, although I did not know anything about photography, maybe photography had some magic power to attract me, so I went to the Tokyo College of Photography. After graduation I wanted to be employed by a newspaper because I was very much interested in photojournalism. I failed the examination, there was a very good reason, but I failed. Then I decided myself to stand independently as a photographer by studying photographs.

I went to a barber shop to sell my prints. I thought, at the time, a barber shop would need something to show. The barber said no, he didn't want photographs. Then I went to magazines with my portfolio and one of the magazines published my pictures, and the publisher asked me to write a book. I wrote a small book in one month, a handbook about 35mm technique, it was published and sold well. I was given a royalty, but felt that I was not a writer, but a photographer. My decision was to become a photographer, not a writer, so I decided not to write anymore, but with the money I made a trip to the Kansai area of Japan, and spent all the money in two months.

I was very much concerned with American children at that time. The picture I won the photo contest with was a portrait of a very cute American girl. I was very enthusiastic in learning English, so I used to go to the American camp to be taught conversational English by Mr. King, a lawyer of the Tokyo trials. He had a son, sixteen years old; we became friends. Nearby his house there were many apartments for the soldiers and civilians. There were many kids playing around. At that time, soon after the war, although our daily lives were healthy, we were miserable in many ways. All the houses, everything, were wrecked by American bombers. I felt that seeing these very happy children did something bright for me. I photographed those children, and the next time I went I would bring snapshots to give them, and that helped me very much in making many friends. Two years later, after I graduated Tokyo College of Photography, I wrote a scenario for a photo story entitled, "An American Girl in Tokyo." It was a photo story like Rene Burri's "The Eye of Love" and the photo stories Leonard McCombe, the *Life* magazine photographer, did in that magazine. This was about the relationship between an American girl, living in Tokyo, and me, my camera. Through this friendship some warm relationships occurred. This is not a love story, but a very pure, warm story between us.

I held my first one-man show in 1956 in Tokyo and this exhibition was warmly welcomed, but no pictures were sold. The story was bought by a broadcasting company for a radio drama. Story based on Eikoh Hosoe's "American Girl in Tokyo," or something like that. I felt that my concern about American children was over then, and in 1957, 1958, 1959, we had a group called "The Eyes of Ten Photographers," all serious photographers. We had work-shows once a year and through the photographers' relationships to each other I cultivated myself, I made myself stronger in many ways. I acquired more knowledge, including techniques in photography. In 1959 I founded a group called VIVO. This group was ended in 1962 because some of the photographers desired to go to other countries for a long period. Ikko was one of them, my very good friend. He went to France. Akira Soto came to live in New York, and others wanted to do many other things independently. In 1960 when VIVO was most active I did the series **Man and Woman.** There I changed completely, I feel I became a man, before that I was a small kid.

TD: Why did you change?

EH: I don't know. That was the time for me to become an adult. There are many reasons, physically, mentally. It is something like this: if you go to the military service, you become a man, suddenly, through the relationships between your friends. This is something like that. And in 1961 I met Mr. Mishima. Before I met Mr. Mishima I read his novels and suddenly I was asked by Mr. Mishima to take some pictures of him for his coming book. I went to his place and photographed him. He said to me, "Mr. Hosoe, you can photograph any kind of my activities, so please do so." I said, "OK, may I wrap you with a cloth?" He said, "OK, if you like." He asked why. I said, "I want to destroy you, destroy a symbol." He said, "I'm not a symbol, I'm just one of the novelists." But to me he was a giant. I had a feeling that if I saw something strong, I had to break it, to destroy it. I had a strong image of him, to his work. His behavior was a little bit childish. Mischievous. But two, three months later I had a very strong feeling to take more pictures of him. I could not forget the strong reactions I felt in my finger, in my camera. It was a strong response. So I asked him this time to be my model. He said OK. He really liked the pictures I took for the book.

I did the book design and layout for him with my pictures, and he really liked it. Then I began taking pictures of him. I had the feeling that it was my very subjective documentary on him, my very subjective interpretation of him, so some change was necessary in taking pictures of him. It was a straight approach, but my concept was different. It's the first subjective interpretation of him, so I used all of his belongings for my photographs, even neckties, even caps. The owner's spirit exists, so his choices, his selections, are him. I photographed him in his house, in his garden and I superimposed Renaissance paintings from his books. The Renaissance paintings are not his, but from his books. He really liked Renaissance paintings and had much knowledge about the Italian Renaissance, especially he was interested in paintings of St. Sebastian, so I made a double exposure with Renaissance paintings. The Baroque chairs and desk are his. You can find those in his garden. He had a very Japanese spirit, but his house was in the western style. Western, classic and very modern, all mixed up. It was the fall of 1961 when I began and the last time was 1962. It took 1½ years. When it was completed I wanted a title for the series. I had a strong desire to have the series published in book form. He hesitated first very much, he was a little bit shy about pictures with him as the subject matter. He really liked the word hishatai, subject matter, in Japanese, so we called him, hishatai. He finally accepted my offer on book publication and a year later I published it. I asked him to make any proper title about it. My title was just Mishima. He said, "It might be good, but maybe I might give you some ideas." The next day he gave me a post card on which I found nine titles and, **Barakei, Ordeal by Roses,** was one of them. I made a telephone call to him that I liked **Barakei.** I felt that title had everything, everything that was contained in the series. "OK, Mr. Mishima, I love this title. I'm going to use it." "OK, it's yours" and he gave it to me. And I asked him also, in the book, since he is a writer, to write something. He said, "OK, I'll write a preface." And he did.

TD: The book was first called Kill by Roses?

EH: Actually, it was a mis-translation. There are two reasons why it was changed. At the beginning **Kill by Roses** was very good, I liked that title, too, and he really liked it also, but it was a slight mis-translation. From Japanese **Ordeal by Roses** is the correct translation. We did not think the English title was so important at that time, we felt it was just a kind of decoration, but five years later, when I planned to revise **Kill by Roses** he asked me to change the title.

TD: What was the reason for an English title if it was only published in Japan?

EH: I must tell you the story behind that. In 1970, I planned the second edition because we received many letters and responses from other countries. From America, France, Germany, Italy, Spain, even from Portugal, so we thought the book should have some text written in another language and we thought English would be the most international. Actually, it is. We call it an international edition, so it starts from left to right, but in the original, first edition, **Kill by Roses** starts from the right to left, Japanese-style. Books start from right to left because the Japanese writing is ordered from right to left. It's his rule that his writings should not be placed like western literature, horizontal. In Japan we have two, vertical and horizontal. His writings have never appeared in a horizontal way. **Ordeal by Roses** is an exception because it's an international edition. English should come first, with Japanese next. If the book is opened from left to right Japanese words cannot be placed so that it starts from right to left. Mr. Mishima accepted it. It was supposed to be published in November 1970, the time he killed himself. It was the timing. In the process I found many, many places I did not like in the reproduction quality, in the printing quality. I went to the printing company quite often to say no, no, no, no. I don't like this, I don't like that. Then the publication was delayed, so it was not in time for November publication. So before the realization of the publication, he committed suicide but he knew the concept of the design, the book layout and everything. It was a great coincidence. So after he died the publisher came to me to rush publication. I said no, I do not want to have this book published anymore, so it was postponed. But when I met Mrs. Mishima she asked me not to postpone the publication, but publish it as soon as possible, because Mr. Mishima himself was looking forward to seeing the publication. I said, "Yes, Mrs. Mishima, if you say so, OK." I did not want to get money from his death; it was apparent that the book would sell well. So many publications had featured him, and they made lots of money, which I did not like. The next year the book came out, and sold out in a very short time.

TD: How many photographs make up the book?

EH: About 50 or so.

TD: Are most of your books in that range?

EH: Um hmm.

TD: How large was the edition?

EH: Two thousand. It was very lucky for him and me that the book was published at that moment, because the economy was good that time. If it were now, it would not be possible for such books to be published for $100. It would be $200 or so because of the cost of paper, binding and printing cost. Moreover, the publisher loses his willingness to do experimental things. The time when the book was published, the publisher gave me all rights to do anything.

TD: Were all of your books that expensive?

EH: No, that is an exception. It was such a luxurious book, using painted velvet, an original metal photograph, using Japanese woodblock print paper for offset printing in seven color offset, three times printing black and white, so everything was deluxe.

TD: How did all that come about? Did you insist on that?

EH: A friend of mine, a designer, Tadanori Yokoo. This book has three parts. This book is consisting of three characters. The subject matter, Mishima, the photographer who photographed the subject matter, and the book designer, Yokoo. It's well-balanced, I believe. In Japan, the book design has a high social status; book design is considered one of the fine arts. It is our Japanese tradition.

And also I will tell you why I do many series. Not only me, but other Japanese photographers like to do series, narratives or stories. It comes out of the Japanese tradition. Even the scrolls, it's a story, even one single woodblock print is a story. You can find many characters written and the descriptions.

TD: When you first started working, you were dealing with the single photograph?

EH: I did know the conception of a story at the time.

TD: Were your earlier essays shorter than the books?

EH: An American Girl in Tokyo was 60 or so.

TD: I just saw Gene Smith's Minamata show and I felt his essays were much more effective than the book-length Minamata series. Other photographers seem to have made the transition much more easily. Was it difficult for you to make the transition into the book length series?

EH: I think when I make photographs, book will be my best medium. For instance, in this series ("Simon," his show at Light Gallery), if it were a book, it would be better.

TD: Will it be a book?

EH: I'm thinking so.

TD: Is this the whole series?

EH: This will be the length. I think it will make a more effective development in the book.

TD: Is this done with 35mm and 4 x 5?

EH: Right, you are right. 35 and 4 x 5. You may find which are 4 x 5 and which are 35. I use more 35 than large format cameras. I have all kinds of cameras though; I love cameras. I have all formats. I use one or two cameras mostly, the Nikon F and one larger.

TD: Is the Linhof the 4 x 5 you use mostly?

EH: I have four 4 x 5 cameras. Sinar, Linhof Technica, Deardorf, and a handmade 4 x 5, with a 75mm Schneider Super Angulon lens and a Horseman press back.

TD: You made that yourself?

EH: No, I had it made by an expert.

TD: Why? What's special about that 4 x 5?

EH: I can hand-hold it. I'm an expert at using a 35mm camera, so if I photograph with a 4 x 5 camera I lose a sense of shooting the action. I don't want to lose my sense, I want to have the same feeling as when I use 35. A speed graphic would be good, but it's too heavy, so this hand-made 4 x 5 is very light, very handy.

TD: Can you focus with it?

EH: Yes.

TD: With a rangefinder?

EH: No rangefinder. I zone focus it, pre-focus it. It is very sharp as you can see.

TD: And it has a pistol grip?

EH: Um, hmm.

TD: How heavy is it?

EH: Not heavy, about the same as a Nikon F, maybe two pounds. And I use a monopod, and Tri-X film pack.

TD: Do you do commercial work?

EH: I used to, but these days, no. They don't come to me to ask. Actually I'm not so much interested in those.

TD: You just teach and do your own work?

EH: Right.

TD: Is success important to you?

EH: Success? In what way?

TD: That your work be published and exhibited. Do you seek that out?

EH: Yes, of course. I want to be a successful photographer in that way.

TD: At any time did you reject material success?

EH: Generally speaking, I have had many opportunities to have my photographs published, so I don't think much about that. What I'm very much concerned about is that my photographs should be published in a very right way.

TD: Even in magazines?

EH: Even in magazines. Interpretations of my photographs are quite often dependent on printing quality. I care, but it's quite free. Magazine publishers should be more careful about the printing quality and the layout, because the printing quality shows the photographer's whole vocabulary. For instance, if Edward Weston's prints were printed very badly, what he wants to say will be lost.

TD: I was comparing the quality of your portfolio in Modern Photography, **with the** Kamaitachi **portfolio in** Camera. Camera **is so beautifully printed.**

EH: Yes, so beautiful. It interprets my series very well, cleverly, smartly.

TD: Did you approve the layout in Camera?

EH: Yeah.

TD: It was very effective, I thought. Did they decide which pictures would be full

page?

EH: That was up to his interpretation.

TD: You sent him the whole series?

EH: Yeah, then he sent it back to me.

TD: How did that portfolio come to be published?

EH: He asked me for it.

TD: They did a really nice job.

EH: I really think so.

TD: How do your moods affect your work?

EH: When I'm headachy, I can't do anything. But spiritual headache will be OK.

TD: Are you ambitious? Do you work every day?

EH: Not every day.

TD: Are you always working on a project?

EH: No, not always, I'm always thinking about it, but it takes time to start it. I have a long-term preparation, of thinking. Once I start, it's very rapid. In my book, **Embrace,** my preparation took ten years. I had three times shooting, that's all.

TD: How about "Simon"?

EH: It took five years thinking, and maybe one year shooting. The landscape pictures I needed the change of time, so I waited for the right time. It started in 1971, four years, start to finish.

TD: And you shot on a few different occasions.

EH: Um hmm.

TD: How do you select the models for your series?

EH: It's a happening. I meet the right person. I don't say, well, what I want to do is this. No. This is not the same job as you do in selection of fashion models. If I see him, and if I feel some impact, it touches somewhere, I'll ask him.

TD: Who was your model for "Simon"?

EH: He's a doll-maker, and he was a part-time actor for underground theater, and he's a poet. He calls himself Simon.

TD: When you plan your series, is there any writing involved?

EH: No, in that case, no writing.

TD: Do you write your ideas down at all?

EH: I do. I write memos. I write memos everyday, what I feel, what I might forget, just to clarify my ideas I write memos, even in the nighttime. I wake up suddenly and write memos. So I always have memos beside my bed.

TD: What is the source of your ideas? Do you read a lot of fiction, folk tales?

EH: I'm a lazy photographer, but I make it a rule to read novels, religious writings and books.

TD: On mysticism?

EH: No, Buddhism. I was interested in the Old Testament stories, especially Genesis. It's a great story. One word describing the reason for Man and Woman, why Men were created. You remember that Woman was created from the rib of man, that was a symbol, that was the paragraph that symbolized my **Man and Woman** series. I'm a curious man, I don't have any Christian background, but maybe I'm a very religious man. Maybe it stems from my family background.

TD: What is that background?

EH: My father is a Shinto priest, and I was raised in a shrine. My father had a shrine, and beside the shrine we had a house and I knew everything, the ceremonies. That religious atmosphere gave me something, not apparent, but some unconscious background.

TD: Who were some of your early influences?
EH: There are many, but a conscious influence is Edward Weston.
TD: In what sense did he influence you?
EH: I don't know. Impact. How can you tell? I also don't have his subjects, forms, in my photographs, but his photographs affected me very much.
TD: How old were you when you first saw his work?
EH: In 1954 or '55 when I was twenty one or two I saw a show in Tokyo.
TD: Were you influenced at all by western photography as you evolved? Had you seen American and French photography?
EH: Yeah. I was still a student when I saw Cartier-Bresson's **The Decisive Moment.**
TD: Did that influence you?
EH: The work is the evidence of the time. It's his testimony of the instant. I have a great regard for his work, but I thought his testimony was not mine.
TD: Did you change Ordeal by Roses **when it was published the second time?**
EH: Yes, I wanted to change.
TD: Did you go back and shoot Mishima after the publication of the first edition?
EH: I have a feeling that the first edition, **Kill by Roses,** published in 1963, was original. I wanted to get another original by changing the book's design. So I just left one-third to the designer's interpretation, the book design. And the book design is not simple work. Book design is the realization of the content of the book. It's not simple, even in monographs. He made a new layout and he used materials for the design such as cloth and such which relates to the content of the photograph.
TD: Did he get involved in sequencing?
EH: No, I did; I did it myself. That was my statement.
TD: Did you use a script when you're working?
EH: Memo.
TD: The memos are your script.
EH: Um, hmm and my head.
TD: When you set out you have everything arranged?
EH: No, I'm quite often responding to a coincidence, or happening. Sometimes it comes from here (points to head), sometimes it comes from the subject matter. Then I take plenty of time to keep looking at my photographs every day, under many psychological situations. In the morning, in the afternoon, when I'm tired, when I'm not tired, I look at my pictures. Then I decide.
TD: So how much shooting do you do? Do you shoot a lot, then edit it down?
EH: Sometimes many shootings, sometimes no. It depends.
TD: Do you look at your work immediately following a shooting?
EH: Yeah, of course.
TD: How long would that process take, from when you start shooting, and the story starts to evolve, until you're satisfied with what you have?
EH: Sometimes one hour later, sometimes one day, one year. It depends. I can't say simply.
TD: Were there any photographs of Mr. Mishima that he censored?
EH: He didn't say so.
TD: He went along with anything you suggested?
EH: Yes, but next time, I'd bring the results of the pictures I'd take, contact sheets, and show him. He really loved those results.
TD: You were photographing his life. Did he agree that that was his life?
EH: I don't know, maybe yes, maybe no.
TD: Did he understand what you were doing?

EH: Yes, very much.

TD: It's interesting because Mishima was seemingly a very strong man, and yet he allowed you to mold him like clay.

EH: Maybe he enjoyed his own metamorphosis. Everybody has such a desire.

TD: When you begin working on a series, you always see a book as the final form?

EH: I always have a hope. I always plan someday maybe.

TD: That's your medium, books.

EH: Yeah, right.

TD: Is a series usually an exhibition, then a book? Is that the process for you?

EH: A book is more effective. An exhibition is an exhibition. It's O.K., but when you open a page you have a new experience. You can consider the dimension of time.

TD: You don't feel you have that in an exhibition?

EH: I feel exhibitions don't have the psychology I want to see in books; they are different, like radio and television. An exhibition is television, a book is a radio, more personal. I'm a radio man, not a television man.

TD: As a series evolves, do you show it to anybody?

EH: No.

TD: Do you do all your own processing?

EH: Yes.

TD: Is it difficult to get published in Japan?

EH: More easy, I think, there are many publications, magazines and books.

TD: How have your books affected your reputation?

EH: I don't know. Books will help your reputation and sometimes they will give you a bad reputation. (Laughs)

TD: Has anybody been instrumental in your career?

EH: There are many people who have come to me and I show them my pictures and I enjoy their reaction, their interpretation. Sometimes I enjoy their misinterpretation.

TD: Do you have many friends who are photographers?

EH: Yes, I have many, in Japan, in America too, and in Europe. I like people who do their individual work and respect their originality, individuality, so I respect those.

TD: Whose work do you appreciate now?

EH: Of contemporary photographers?

TD: Yes.

EH: In this country, Duane Michals, Ralph Gibson, Michael Bishop, Jack Welpott, Judy Dater, there are many. I really respect what Nathan Lyons has been doing.

TD: Who are some of the Europeans you admire?

EH: Bill Brandt; above all, I very much like Atget.

TD: How about Japanese?

EH: Ken Domon, Tomatsu, Ikko, there are many, many.

TD: There seem to be many Japanese photographers working in series. Is this because of the culture?

EH: We have been doing it that way unconsciously. You make me aware of that.

TD: Is this true of the Orient in general, China for example?

EH: I have never seen Chinese photography, except some reportage photographs published in the China Graphic or something.

TD: What about Korean photographers?

EH: No. In Korea it is difficult for photographers to have their photographs published. Photography has quite a limitation, technically and psychologically.

TD: Is this because Japan is so modern and prosperous?

EH: In Korea the society is restrictive because they are under war conditions. They can't go out after twelve o'clock. You see many soldiers walking around in the street and high school students' uniforms are camouflage and so on. You can't imagine it. It's a war. You have a 45-minute drive from the center of Seoul to the 38th parallel. You see missile sites pointing to the north. These conditions are not normal. On the other hand, Japan is quite open and our economy is quite good.

TD: Do you now make your living from print sales and teaching?

EH: Selling photographs, teaching, and editorial work for magazines. In general, I sell few prints.

TD: You don't do assignments for magazines, only your personal work?

EH: No, assignments, yes. I'm a very good photographer.

TD: How much editorial work do you do?

EH: Five, six a year, eight pages, twenty pages sometimes, 50 pages of color for a magazine.

TD: What kind of assignments?

EH: For instance, the recent work which I did for a magazine called *Taiyo*, was a special issue on Zen. I traveled all over Japan, and photographed old temples, exteriors, interiors, landscapes.

TD: When you get an assignment, is it very general and you interpret it?

EH: The assignment I am given—they know my work—so I'm doing my own work. I have been doing a regular assignment for *Economy* magazine. I take top-class businessmen who are over eighty years old and I shoot an inside report. A different, very interesting assignment, because I can ask them many questions. It is really hard for us to meet such people, over eighty years old.

TD: Mostly it's just portraits?

EH: It's sort of their daily work routine.

TD: So you keep pretty busy doing editorial assignments?

EH: Yeah, I do many things all the time.

TD: You are ambitious?

EH: Ambitious in my living, in my life.

TD: Do you think you will leave Japan?

EH: No, I will never live any other place. My permanent residence is in Tokyo; it is easy to travel these days. I don't feel New York is a long distance place, or Paris or anywhere.

TD: How important are the technical aspects of your work? The camera? Film? Paper?

EH: If I know the standard level of technique then everything is OK. But I pay a great attention, careful deliberation to the finishing of prints, making prints, developing. I make quite sure in each step. If it were called a technique, it will be a technique. I am not aware of techniques, because my technique is very simple.

TD: Do you always use the same materials?

EH: No, I use always the same film, the same developer, but I use all kinds of papers. For instance, in this show I used (Ilford) Ilfomar III.

TD: What are some of the current books you like?

EH: I don't have much opportunity to see many books.

TD: What are you working on now?

EH: I'm thinking of photographing Tokyo, the city as she is.

TD: Are you familiar with William Klein's Tokyo?

EH: Yes, but not that way. More calm, more honesty, more depth.

TD: You did not think much of Klein's book?

EH: It's Klein's interpretation, its's Klein's thing, very strong, very good, in that way. But Tokyo is the city where I live, where I was born, so it will not be Tokyo as he did it; that was his eye.

TD: When will your books be published in the U.S.?

EH: I don't know. I wish I knew.

TD: What do you think of self-publishing?

EH: Wonderful, very good.

TD: Would you consider that alternative?

EH: Here, in this country, in the future.

TD: In Japan?

EH: Not now.

TD: Is it too much trouble?

EH: No. I bring my work to publishers and they are happy to publish it. Distribution is the problem. It is easy for me to produce a book. I like to go to the printer and I like the smell of ink. It gives me great pleasure. I like it very much. But if I think of distribution I lose my interest. Book making is easy as far as you have the material and some money. Distribution is business, so I cannot solve that. So far I have published some books in Japan, and most of them have sold out. So to the used bookstores, prices go higher, higher and higher. For instance, **Kill by Roses,** when it was published in 1963, the original price was about $15. Now you have to pay more than $200.

TD: How do you feel about that?

EH: I have two feelings about it. Fortunate and unfortunate. Fortunate to know that my books are sold for higher prices, but if I really want it I have to pay that price. You understand? **Kamaitachi** was mostly purchased at the first stage by the book-sellers; they keep them, they know that those kinds of books will go up year by year.

TD: Is that true of all picture books in Japan?

EH: Not all, but in my case.

TD: Is that because they are published in such a limited edition?

EH: Well, yes, it is one of the biggest reasons, and the second is the content. I don't know why, but they know, collectors, speculators.

TD: Where did you get the idea for Kamaitachi?

EH: It comes from my boyhood during the wartime.

TD: Is there such a thing as a Kamaitachi?

EH: Right. Anytime I wrote about **Kamaitachi,** I wrote it as a record of my memory. My photographs are an explanation of myself. Sometimes it looks very objective, but it's very subjective. That's why it is a little bit difficult for other people to understand them, but they can feel something. I don't mind other people's reactions. I really want to record my past days. In photography you cannot describe your past when you photograph the contemporary, present thing. But the photography is made by the man who has complexes about many things. And even in the medium of photography you are allowed to do it. In **Kamaitachi** the dancer is my catalyst, but photography shows the person or the thing as it is. It is free for you to interpret, it is quite free. My motives come from my experiences, my remembrances of days.

TD: At what point did you move away from photojournalism and into a more personal vision?

EH: I have such characteristics by nature. I'm quite natural, you know. In photojournalism you cannot be too subjective. My pictures are filled with plenty of prejudices, but in photojournalism you can't. Any art is based on the prejudices of the artist, in a good sense.

TD: Do you do photojournalism?

EH: My editorial work is full of prejudices, but they know.

TD: So your editorial work is very personal as well?

EH: Yeah, to some extent. I cannot be Eisenstaedt.

TD: Did you feel the show "New Japanese Photography" at the Museum of Modern Art helped your reputation?

EH: I really do not know.

TD: How did your work first come to notice here?

EH: Nathan Lyons, when he was curator at the George Eastman House, wrote me a letter and showed my pictures in an exhibition called "Contemporary Photographs" in 1963.

**New York City
May 30, 1975**

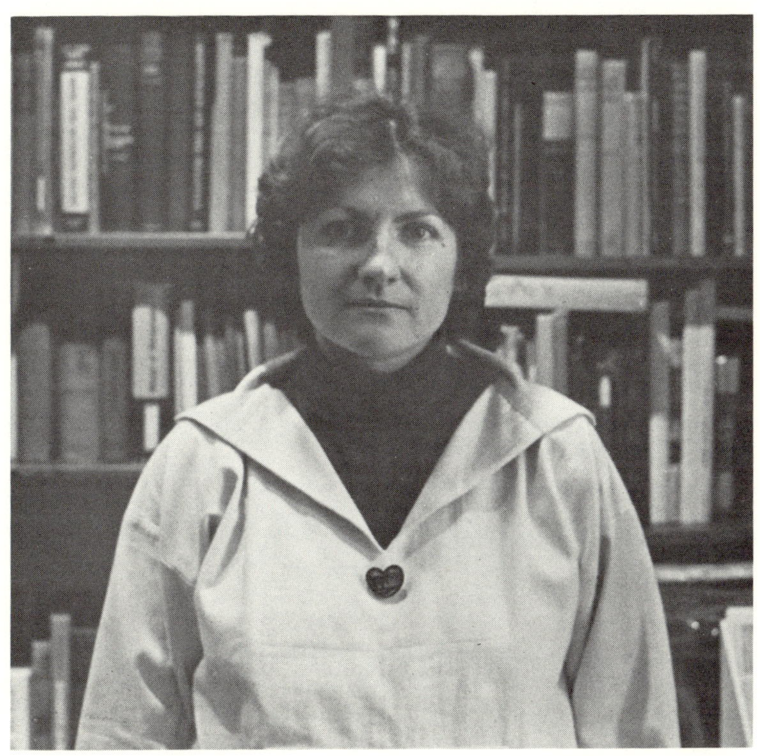

Bea Nettles

Interviewer: Do you think you've had to struggle less than most people?

Bea Nettles: My work was exhibited early in my career, but I wouldn't say it was accepted quickly. I've had negative reviews and still get some. My work has always been on the borderline and challenges a lot of people's preconceptions about photography and art. I guess it depends what you think struggling is. I certainly haven't had to scrounge around to find shows. I've always seemed to have the work and been in the right place at the right time. It's certainly important that you have some significant work. If you don't have the work, no matter how much hustling you do, it just won't get you anywhere. In that sense, I've worked very hard to have that backup of work. That can be very lonely, at times a real struggle.

For a year and a half or longer, I tried to see Bea Nettles, but somehow we kept missing each other. Finally, in January, 1978, we arranged a meeting and the interview took place at the Witkin Gallery on East 57th Street in New York City.

Our tape recorded conversation lasted an hour and a half, one of the shortest in the series. Previously Bea had read several of the earlier interviews and was familiar with my concept. The interview, allowing for changes for clarification, appears basically as it was recorded.

Bea Nettles projects an image of a woman aware of her destiny and in charge of her life. She's warm, gentle, considerate and obviously intensely involved with her work. I related a story Scott Hyde told me of her need to always be working and her inability to be idle. She thought for a moment, laughed, and agreed. This degree of commitment is apparent in her manner. We sat in a corner of Lee's gallery and the talk went smoothly from one question and response to the next, with a bare minimum of distractive chatter.

Born: Gainesville, Florida, 1946.
B.F.A. Degree: University of Florida, Gainesville, 1968.
M.F.A. Degree: University of Illinois, Champaign, 1970.
Books:
   Events in the Water. Privately Published, 1973.
   Events in the Sky. Privately Published, 1973.
   The Imaginary Blowtorch. With poetry by Grace N. Nettles. Privately Published, 1973.
   The Elsewhere Bird. With poetry by Grace N. Nettles. Privately Published, 1974.
   A is for Applebiting Alligators. Private Published, 1974.
   The Nymph of the Highlands. With text by Connie Nettles. Privately Published, 1974.
   Dream Pages. Privately Published, 1975.
   Of Loss and Love. With poetry by Grace N. Nettles. Privately Published, 1975.
   Breaking the Rules: A Photo Media Cookbook. Privately Published, 1977.
Currently: Photographer, Rochester, N.Y.; Photography Instructor, Rochester Institute of Technology, Rochester, N.Y.

Tom Dugan: How did your involvement with photography come about?
Bea Nettles: I was an art major at the University of Florida in Gainesville and photography was a required course. I took it as a senior. Robert Fichter was my first teacher, and I had him for one trimester. I enjoyed it right away, but wanted to take some other electives. Robert encouraged me and said, "When Jerry Uelsmann comes back from his leave of absence you should study with him." I said I couldn't afford it, but Robert wouldn't take no for an answer. He came back to me several days later and said he'd talked to Jerry and I could be an assistant to him. He needed someone to run the labs in the evening. That settled it, that would pay for the expense of doing the course. I worked for the last two trimesters of my senior year as Uelsmann's assistant. This was when the department was very small, 1967-68. I had already decided to go on to graduate school in painting at the University of Illinois in Champaign. Both of my degrees are in painting and printmaking; most of my photography was done on my own. I really give Robert Fichter a lot of credit as a very good teacher. He would say, "Bea, what you are doing in your drawing and painting? You know, your photography can relate to those ideas." Not only Robert, however. This attitude was common at Gainesville, to interrelate the different things that you were doing. Fichter actively encouraged it, and that is apparent in my work now. It's a real blend of all the things that I've learned using photographic imagery with a painterly approach.

Throughout graduate school I was incorporating photographic remnants or collage techniques in drawings, paintings and printmaking. My thesis show was two-thirds photographic imagery. At that point I was stitching photographs on the sewing machine, hand coloring and doing a lot of mixed media work. A lot of people still associate me with that work. It takes a long time for information to get out. That's one thing I like very much about books. They can be fairly current work. An exhibition doesn't reach quite the audience that a book can.

TD: How did the major emphasis in your art come to involve photographic imagery?

BN: It was fairly gradual. It happened during the years of '68 through '70 when I was in graduate school. The photographic image was very believable and I was doing quite a bit of self-portraiture at that time. Of course, the photographic self-portrait is much more recognizable and believable than anything you can draw or paint, so I began incorporating them into my work. At the time, I was attempting to put photographic imagery onto canvases and drawing papers. I didn't know very much at all about nonsilver processes and that was painfully learned. It was very difficult to find anyone who knew about these techniques. If they knew, it seemed that they would always leave out a step, so it would be guaranteed not to work. In 1970 Robert (Fichter) was responsible for a very significant break for me. I had continued to send slides of what I was doing to him, and he mentioned it to Peter Bunnell, at The Museum of Modern Art, who was organizing a show called Photography into Sculpture. That show opened in the Spring of '70 when I was still a graduate student. Peter Bunnell had flown to Illinois, looked through my work and selected pieces for that exhibition. Almost all the work was either from New York City, California, a few things from Canada, and then there was my work from Illinois, which was really funny. He would have never known the work if it hadn't been for the contact I had with Robert.

TD: Did you completely give up painting?

BN: Yes, I pretty much did. When I left graduate school in '70, my first teaching job was in Rochester at a small liberal arts college. I taught several courses: painting, drawing, design and photography. At that point, I was doing mostly mixed media photographic work. In December, 1970, Harold Jones gave me a show at the Eastman House in one of the small rooms on the main floor. It was all photographic mixed media, hand coloring, cut photo paper, photo linen, Rockland Emulsion and blueprint on canvas. Some people at RIT (Rochester Institute of Technology) saw it and offered me a job teaching photography. So in my teaching involvement I became more a part of the photographic community, and lost touch with painting and printmaking. I tried painting briefly, in 1972, and just didn't feel in the mood to do it. I continued with the mixed media work for a couple of years until May, 1972 when I had a major show at Light Gallery. It was a natural stopping point for that work, and I knew it. It was a culmination, a very large show, about sixty pieces, plastic quilts, mirror topped tables, a whole range of sculpture, and collages. I left knowing that that era of my work was over. I then went to Aspen, Colorado, to teach a workshop for a month and started playing with the instamatic camera. That came about because the camera I had borrowed jammed and I had this instamatic and just started playing with it. That was the first time that I felt content to leave a photo alone and just print it straight. I began doing little sequences of black and white photographs, and that's what was in my first two books. I wasn't thinking in terms of the book when I was first doing them, but it didn't take long to come up with that idea.

TD: How did you come to work with sequential ideas?

BN: I was very influenced by the developments in the photographic book, particularly sequencing of the photo image. I had met Lionel Suntop of Light Impressions, at that point, and we discussed contemporary photo books often. I was very impressed by Raph Gibson's **The Somnambulist.** That was one of my favorite sequences. I responded to the archetypal symbolism that was used throughout that book. I had seen Duane Michals' work, but I never approached sequencing in that literal or dramatic a sense. Mine was much closer to Gibson's approach.

TD: Was that when you first worked sequentially?

BN: No. I had made a series of unique photo notebooks in 1970-71. Some were collections of images that could be shown in any order (B and the Birds, Ghosts and Stitched Shadows, Bruises and Other Collections). But I did do at least one narrative sequence of photocollages called The Neptune Series.

It was with the snapshots that I became most seriously involved with sequencing. At first I was satisfied with the snapshot as a single image, but that waned in less than a month or two. I didn't feel that single images were enough, and I began putting images together. The very first series I gave a name to was **Western July,** a sequence of ten images from that period in Aspen (Colorado). I made five copies of that book in silver print form. In the fall of '72, I visited Gainesville (Florida), where I grew up. I took a lot of instamatic photographs and did a twenty-five print sequence called **Florida Fantasy.** I printed it up in silver print form and made five or six copies. That book was at Light Gallery and Anne Tucker saw it while she was looking for the tenth woman for **The Woman's Eye.** She was interested because it was sequential, it was black and white, and I used shapshots. Eventually another followed which I called **Escape,** and that appeared in **The Woman's Eye.**

TD: What was your first offset project?

BN: I was living in Philadelphia in the Fall of '72, teaching at Tyler School of Art and went to an offset printer with a very ambitious project in mind. I wanted to print my photographic Tarot deck in offset form. I showed them the images and I realized I was in over my head financially and technically, so I decided instead to do something very simple. I picked one of my twelve print sequences, **Events in the Water,** and got an estimate. I made the halftones, stripped them up and went to the printer's and he printed the sheets. I took them, folded and collated them, made the cover by photo silkscreen, and trimmed them. Right from the very start I did as much of the work as I could to save money and to get a sense of what was involved. With that printer I did two snapshot books (**Events in the Water** and **Events in the Sky**) within three or four months. That was really a good introductory experience. I think it's good to do something simple and relatively inexpensive just to get the vocabulary.

TD: What was the size of the editions?

BN: 100 copies. It's really a joke for most printers to do that few, but this was not a large press. I learned quite a bit from them. I was allowed to be in the room while the press was running, and that was the first time I really paid attention to an offset press. I then decided the third book would be a poetry book using my mother's poems. **The Imaginary Blowtorch** was quite a dramatic change from the first two, which were one simple black and white image to a page. This was quite a commitment of time and money, but at least at that point I knew how to make and strip halftones. I went with a color sample book and picked out several colors. I was not allowed to be at the press during the run in this particular printshop. It was a lot closer to where I lived and cheaper, so I went along with that, and went back later and picked up the press sheets. They did fairly well on the print quality. There were pages that I felt I either wanted to hand color or silkscreen over the offset printed image. In addition, I did photosilkscreen on mylar and began sandwiching the books together with pages of tissue papers and fabrics. This was also done in an edition of a hundred. **The Imaginary Blowtorch** and **The Elsewhere Bird** constituted a whole year's work for me, six months on each book. That was all I was doing in addition to teaching. I wasn't doing any wall imagery at all.

TD: That marks a radical change in making books, from simple to quite complex...

BN: Yes, it was quite a jump. I had had models for **The Imaginary Blowtorch.** In graduate school, four years earlier, I made unique books with overlays and transparencies. I was very interested in that sort of book and people would say, "It's too bad you can't make more than one copy." So with the technical knowledge from the snapshot books and the pattern image in my mind of a more complex sort of book, I was able to solve most of the problems, and make mixed media limited edition books. They have probably been the most memorable and successful of the handmade books. The poetry was my mother's.

TD: Is that why these books came about?

BN: Yes. She's been sending me poetry since about 1970 and I felt it was so strong, I always wanted to do something with it. It was an interesting challenge, to do a visual book that wouldn't overpower the poetry and vice versa.

TD: Had she been doing poetry long?

BN: She had been doing some and had not really been showing it to anyone; she teaches English at a junior college in Florida. She wrote a few poems as gifts to me and I was so taken with them that I gave her a lot of encouragement, so she started writing more and sending them to me. This has been ongoing for about seven years. I have a lot of her work that I haven't done anything with and I suppose someday I'll do another book of poetry.

TD: Has she done anything else to get it published?

BN: No. She really has no desire to publish it. She likes what I do with it. I would certainly like it to reach a larger audience, I think it is very fine stuff. I know the few people who own these books really think they're very special.

TD: Have you ever tried to get these books published by a commercial publisher?

BN: No, I really haven't.

TD: How does it feel when you meet people who know you through your books?

BN: I meet people who have collected the books occasionally and it's nice. When I give lectures sometimes, it's amazing to me. You have to separate yourself from this fictional character that is created. I remember I gave a lecture in Louisville, Kentucky and there were about four hundred people there from all over five states. This girl came up afterwards and said, "Oh, I thought you'd be taller." It seemed like such a strange thing to say. It doesn't make me uncomfortable, and I have learned to deal with it. People think they know me from my body of work but, of course, I'm more complex.

TF: So you're really not interested in going commercial?

BN: Well, my largest edition is **Breaking the Rules,** and I hope that will always be in print. The earlier books are limited editions. I just don't have the energy or desire to go back and do them again, so anyone who has them has made a good investment. They are unique; there won't be anymore.

TD: You'll continue working in books?

BN: I don't know. I never dare commit myself more than maybe a year or two at a time.

TD: And you're not working on a book now?

BN: No, I'm not.

TD: After the poetry books you did the children's books. Why did you decide on them?

BN: Mostly for a break. The poetry books are very serious and artistically very challenging. They fit together like a puzzle. In other words, as I put a part in I'd have to make sure it would work and it was always a risk. The children's books were relatively fast and could be fairly spontaneous. **A is for Applebiting Alligators** (1974) was the first I did. I did two hundred of those because it was a small book and I could afford the paper and it was easy to do. This was the first book I did in Rochester (New York), when I moved back from Philadelphia. It was just refreshing, really fun. Quick, maybe a month-long project. Then **The Nymph of the Highlands** was my second children's book and a bit more complicated. It was an attempt to incorporate some of the overlays and things that were surprising and tactile in the adult books. I used a story that my sister, Connie, wrote when she was thirteen, a creation myth. I had always wanted to do something with it. That was maybe two or three months' work.

In Summer, 1975, I finished **Dream Pages,** which was the first time I had ever done anything with my own writing. I had kept a dream journal and still do, for maybe three years before **Dream Pages.** I went through it and took dreams directly from the journal, ones that were most vivid in my memory, or most interesting, and incorporated them into this book. It is probably the most esoteric and personal of all the books, but it's been one of my favorites. The imagery is derived from xeroxed photos and collages which I drew into, made halftones and offset printed, then photo silkscreened over. It was done in an edition of a hundred. There are still a few copies of **The Nymph of the Highlands** and **Dream Pages,** but everything before that is out of print.

TD: Then you did the Tarot deck?

BN: No. It was in the works from Summer '74 until January '75 and was a monumental job. It was very complicated. I had hoped to make a thousand decks, but there were really only eight hundred when I finished collating. There are seventy-eight cards and it required going to a good-sized commercial printer in Rochester. They shot the halftones, did the stripping and made the plates. I went in for practically a month, checking each step along the way, and when they printed it, I was there all day for four or five days at the press. This was very important to oversee the quality of the job. I was provided cut cards, in stacks, and I had to collate them, which took me several months. I could do about twenty decks an hour, so it was really a torturous job. Once they were collated, I cut round corners on a little foot treadle die-cutting machine. I had had the boxes made, glued labels on the boxes and did all the assembly work. That's how I kept the price down to $10 a deck. The expense of commercial collating would have been out of sight. It was an interesting project; I learned a lot.

TD: Will you keep that in print?

BN: I probably will put that back in print. There are less than a hundred left, it's getting very close to being gone. It will never look quite the same, and there are a few changes I'll make. I think that this project will be, in retrospect, one of the most significant things that I've done, because it's the first photographic Tarot deck in history. Tarot decks have been around for five hundred years, and they've reflected the history of the graphic arts. There have been hand painted decks, woodcuts, water-colored decks, etc. As each printing process developed, Tarot card decks were made by that method. It's surprising to me but, somehow, a photographic one had not been made until mine in the 1970's. Even the modern ones were illustrative or hand drawn. It's historically significant for that reason.

TD: How did you come to do it?

BN: It came to me in a dream, actually. That's why it's called **Mountain Dream Tarot.** Somebody had shown me a book of Tarot drawings; I had never even seen a deck. At that point, the star was a little symbol of mine, so I did some self-portraits of myself as Queen of Stars. In the summer of '70, I was in the mountains of North Carolina, at Penland School of Crafts. I woke up one morning and contacted several people and asked them to model for this photographic Tarot deck that I was going to do. It was about lunch time when I started questioning myself, "How did I get started on this?" It must have occurred to me in my sleep, that it would be a good idea, and I was thoroughly committed to it. The shooting took two to three years. To find these different people, get the costumes, locations and props, was a very elaborate project. The deck was one thing that I wanted to see printed, and originally, what I was going to a printer with at the very first. So you see, it took me from 1973 to nearly 1975 to feel confident enough to attempt it. Of course, throughout this whole time, it's been really critical to me that Light Impressions would distribute these books. Otherwise nothing would have happened with them, I'm certain of that. The very first book that I did, **Events in the Water,** was bought outright by Light Gallery, when I was with them. I believe they had copies around for a few years, or maybe they still have copies. People weren't looking to buy books when they went into Light Gallery. The books just sat there, and I didn't feel that that was the reason for making them. I wanted them to get out fairly rapidly, so when the second book was done, I started dealing with Light Impressions, and they sold them through the mail. There were a variety of things that started happening in my career that gave people enough faith to buy something sight unseen. The hard thing with limited edition books is to sell them to someone who has never seen them. It's fairly slow, but they do sell out eventually, and I sell them when I travel to give lectures. They do get out; it's amazing, they're all over the country. Sometimes people will start to collect them, and then they'll buy each book that I do.

After the Tarot deck, I did **Dream Pages** and then the children's card deck, **Swamp Lady** (a deck designed for a show called "Colors" in 1974). This was sort of an experiment for me. I actually ran the press. By this point I had learned to run an offset press, and the deck was printed in four colors, so it was a pretty good printing job. Each sheet went through the press seven times. There were four colors, two coats of varnish on the front, stars and a coat of varnish on the back. I did a hundred and fifty decks. I followed the same process as in the Tarot deck. I cut them up, rounded the corners, collated and boxed them. They sold for five dollars a deck and are sold out. It's really a charming game for children. It's a verson of Old Maid.

TD: Will you reprint it?

BN: I rather doubt it. I tend to put energy into new things rather than go backwards. I also feel committed to the people who have bought them. They have made a unique investment, and it's not something that is going to be constantly available. If I were to do something again, I would probably change the format somewhat. I'd just go nuts doing the same thing over and over again.

After I did **The Swamp Lady** deck, the last limited edition offset book that I did was **Of Loss and Love,** again with my mother's poetry. It's my first hardbound book and I printed it completely. I did it on a Davidson 500, which is a fairly small press, but a very tough one, in that it holds register, and it's a very good press to run. In a lot of ways, it's more conservative than some of the earlier books, in terms of texture and mixed media, but it was one chance where I could really thoroughly control the color. In other books I'd have to choose something out of a sample book and get the printer to print it. For this one I mixed the colors right on the press. It was finished in 1975 and it was just about that time that I began to do some wall work again, some large blueprints and brownprints. With those I received a CAPS (Creative Artists Public Service Program) grant in New York. I began to work with Kwik Print, which is a commercial graphic arts product. I dropped my book concern to work on my grant ideas. For the last two years ('76-'78), I've been working exclusively in Kwik Print. That's why I'm here at Witkin Gallery today, with the work of that two year period. I tend to work in two year cycles. I don't see this involvement ending right away, but it could. Usually I know it's ending and there's maybe a six-month transition when I know I'm getting tired of something; I'm imitating myself, or something should change. Generally it's a fairly natural shift into doing something else. That's why I don't commit myself to what I'll be doing in the long run.

TD: How did Breaking the Rules **come about?**

BN: That was done this summer, '77, but I've been collecting the information for about seven years. I've been teaching workshops, and have a lot of the information in handout sheets. I decided I'd like to get it all written out in some kind of nice form. I started writing in May, traveled some, then came back and really concentrated in August on finishing the writing. I got the type set, did all the paste-up myself and started going to the printer's. It was done by Mohawk Printing in Rochester and they're very used to me by now. They're the people who did the Tarot deck as well. When the book was being printed I was there the whole time the sheets were coming off the press. They are very good printers, but I still caught a few things that I didn't think they were doing as carefully as they could. A pressman will try harder if he knows you care, so it's a good idea to be there.

TD: Do events in your life affect your work?

BN: Sure. Physically if I'm not well, or traveling, my work gets interrupted. Sometimes I find that if I'm going through an emotionally rough period, I work better, because it's a release or I work out problems. Sometimes if I'm too happy, it's harder to work but definitely, my work is very autobiographical and it's all tied together. Very often the work will predict things that are going to happen, that I subconsciously knew were going to happen, but I wouldn't admit to myself consciously. I've seen this occur quite a few times. For example, I'll have a series of images of myself in a very vulnerable role and later I'll find out I was that way, but I wouldn't admit it to myself.

TD: Did you work as much with the self portrait when you were painting?

BN: Not quite so much, no, because I really didn't have the drawing skills. I was never really good at figure drawing, but my work has always been literal. It always had something to do with a recognizable object, place or event. It wasn't abstract at all, and almost all my work is storytelling, in some way or another. There are symbolic and literal kinds of objects in the work.

TD: And it's all involved with you, your family and your personal landscape?

BN: A lot of it is very personal, but I think a lot of it's universal. I'm quite familiar with, and fascinated by, mythology and archetypal imagery, so there are images that fall into that kind of realm which are much more universal than my particular family or friends, who are my models.

TD: You don't have a need to go out and find images?

BN: No, I don't. There are long stretches when I don't photograph at all, because I construct things out of a set of stock images that I have all stored up. In my studio for the Kwik Print work that I do, there are several hundred ortho film images that I keep recombining. The tree, the landscape, the water negative, whatever it takes to make new images. That's a challenge, to see how many variations I can come up with, with a lot of the same elements. I'm very close to the work. For instance, there's an image in **Breaking the Rules** of my sister with the full moon ("Connie in the Moonlight," page 34). The moon has the face of my sister in it, and I had a very vivid dream about her while I was working on that image. She was wearing the same dress and that photo of her was in my dream. At that point she was going through a rough period, and so a lot of my thinking and work evolved around her. I wouldn't be doing images of her quite like that now because she's changed, but for about six months or so I was working with her, sympathizing with her. Then there are certain themes that are found in the work like moonlight, the moon, water, and those, of course, are very feminine things. I'm much more attracted to the moon and the water than I am the sun and fire. I just have a natural inclination towards those kinds of places and that kind of light.

TD: Is isolation necessary for you to do work?

BN: Yes, it's really helpful. One thing that I have found though is that if I don't teach, or have something to do in addition to my work, I waste time. There was a very brief period between teaching jobs, when I had seven days a week at my disposal and because I was not under pressure I found that I'd waste time. I got a part-time job and found that if I just had three or four free days, I'd do much more work than if I had seven days. Now I teach three days a week and have three days in the studio, and Sundays free. I pretty much stick to that routine, and it works quite well.

TD: You usually work the three days you're in the studio?

BN: Yes, pretty much. Sometimes I have to do errands, but I don't feel comfortable if I fritter the whole day away. I always have to at least clean the studio, or do some kind of busy work there each day to feel happy. I'm a compulsive worker. I have the work ethic drilled into me and I feel best when I'm working. Occasionally I do let things sit around. With Kwik Print, I can leave an image for weeks at a time and not resolve it, whereas if I'm printing a silver print I've got to resolve it. The Kwik Print images might hang around while I really think about how I want to finish them up. This goes back to my painting of ten years before, when I could let an unfinished canvas sit around for a while. But there is a midway point where I have to take something before I can rest, otherwise I feel like it's naked or something; it's embarrassing. I can't remember what I wanted to do if I don't get something taken to a certain point before I stop.

TD: Of what influences are you most conscious?

BN: I look at a lot of visual things. I'm very fond of antiques, illustrated books and quilts, for instance. I've always been fond of fabric and that influenced the whole sewing-stitching collage aspect of my work, that need to patch things together. I look at many of the new books, but I'd say, in terms of real influences, there are very rare photographs that I see that strike me in a way that would influence me. One of the most exciting bodies of work that I saw recently was the **Disfarmer: The Heber Springs Portraits.** I can't see how that work would directly relate to my work, but when I see a strong body of work like that, I'm very excited by it. I do read a lot. I read novels. I like to read fairly exotic writers like South American, European, Japanese and African writers, and I get a lot of visual imagery out of reading those sorts of books. One of my recent favorites was **A**

Hundred Years of Solitude by Marquez. I also read about five of Yukio Mishima's novels recently. Also my dreams are a real source for me, of course that's a personal source fed by everything I take in.

TD: You always write them down?

BN: I don't always, I'm getting kind of lazy about it, but I do remember them often, and I try to make myself write things down. They're pretty interesting, too, the combinations of things that happen when your body is resting.

TD: Do you try to interpret them?

BN: No, not really. Some are obvious, like when my teaching was very frustrating, I dreamed of trying to do a demonstration on a three-legged table. But I've had other dreams and maybe told them to my husband and they're often obvious. As I mentioned when I was working on the images of my sister I would be dreaming things where she would be involved.

TD: Do you talk to her about them?

BN: Yes, I actually told her one of those dreams. She wrote me for advice and I wrote her that the night before I had had this dream which told me that I was going to hurt her with whatever it was that I tried to do to help her. It was amazing to me that I'd had that dream the night before she wrote and asked for advice. But other influences? I love film when it's really good. Not too many good ones come to Rochester unfortunately, so I don't get to see as many as I'd like.

TD: Mostly do you prefer European films?

BN: European, Japanese and sometimes American films if they're really good. I'm still a child at heart and I loved the imagery in **Star Wars,** though it certainly wasn't a serious film. I'd say probably the imagery more than the meaning of films strikes me first. A powerful film has a combination of both. I get bored with pretty films before they're over.

TD: What do you remember about your childhood? Were you visually oriented?

BN: Yes. I always wanted to be an artist. My mother says that when I was three or four, I used to draw on the walls. I had this very serious look on my face, and she felt she shouldn't scold me. I was really serious, it wasn't mischief, it was serious business. She encouraged me to draw on paper, and suspected I'd be an artist, way, way back. As a young child, I always felt that's what I wanted to do. The first camera that I had was a little red plastic camera that my grandmother got when she bought a sewing machine; I was about eleven or twelve. I remember taking photos with it, and actually two of them appear in **Events in the Water,** the first and last images. The reason they're so memorable was there was so little money for film that I really cherished each shot. I loved taking those pictures. I'd take the rolls of film down to the Florida Pharmacy to be processed. It was quite exciting, but the money was used for other things. Then I won a Kodak Brownie as a door prize, and didn't do too much with that. Throughout high school I didn't do any photographs to speak of at all, but I was involved in art, so I always had some creative outlet. Through college I was completely involved with painting and drawing. My father bought a Yashica D 2¼ camera because he knew I would be taking photography eventually. He was using it for about a year or so, and it looked so hard. When I took that course I really enjoyed it. I don't think I ever had the magic feeling that I had about photography until I started doing the instamatic snapshots again. The sheer spontaneity and surprise of it wasn't present quite so much in my first black and white photos as an art student, because I was very self-conscious and the equipment was clumsy to me. Of course, the magic of printing was really marvelous, but I wasn't doing much straight printing, even at the very start.

TD: While in college, what were your aspirations?

BN: I was going to be a fine artist. That was a decision made during my sophomore year. I had to decide whether to major in art education or fine arts. At that point most everyone expected the women to major in art ed. I didn't want to take education courses, I wanted to take the fine arts courses, even though it meant going to graduate school, and who knew what would happen after that? I felt it was very important, and I discussed this with my mother, who said, "You should do what you want to, not what you think you ought to." It was wonderful advice. That's really what I hoped she'd say, and that's what I did. So far it hasn't been a mistake. Most everyone said, "You'll find it hard getting into graduate school," but I did. While I was in graduate school on a fellowship, everyone said, "You'll never get a teaching job because you don't have any teaching experience." But I got a job for the next year. I've been quite fortunate. Mainly that's because I had a lot of interesting work at the right time to show people. If I didn't have that work I wouldn't have gotten anywhere, that's for sure.

TD: How did your relationship with Light Gallery come about?

BN: When Harold Jones left the Eastman House to start Light, he invited thirteen people to be under contract with them for two years. I had started doing books, about the time to renew the contract. I felt uncomfortable because I wasn't doing wall work and didn't want to have the pressure on me to meet artificial needs, so I said I didn't feel I could renew the contract. It was a fairly stringent contract at any rate. It had a lot to say about distribution and publishing, and I felt I was working out a better deal with Light Impressions on my own. I stayed with Light for another two years, not on contract, just in the drawers. That whole period was a difficult one for both parties. It was hard for Light to handle my work because it went for two, almost three years exclusively to books, so the relationship just died a natural death. It was a mutual agreement. I didn't have any recent work, so I didn't send them anymore. Eventually, when I did start doing wall work again, I asked Lee Witkin whether he would be interested in handling it and he said, "Yes." I've known Lee since my first show at Light in 1972 or maybe a little longer. It is a different working relationship. Lee is not as restricting with his artists. He, in turn, doesn't promise to do quite the same kinds of things, such as sending out exhibitions or promotional things, although he's been very helpful when I've asked him. I found in the long run, I end up doing almost all that work myself. It's masochistic, but I think, in a lot of cases, I do it best. I like to know where my work is being sent and in what context it's being shown. Arranging shows takes a tremendous amout of time and effort.

TD: Are they worth all the effort?

BN: Increasingly less. I don't do as many. I just had a large show in San Francisco, at Focus Gallery, and felt like that was very worthwhile. I hadn't shown much on the west coast, and there were good reviews, and a lot of people got to see the work. Something like that is worth it. To show at some small, isolated place is usually not worth the risk of damage to the work. Most of the work is unique. Occasionally I send out shows of my offset books. That's a lot less strain on everybody. I don't mind doing that, but when it's unique and the work gets tied up, or damaged, and it usually doesn't sell, it isn't really worth it, financially anyway.

TD: Does Lee Witkin handle all your work in the United States?

BN: Lee handles it in New York City really. If someone wants to, they can contact me directly, and I sell directly. I don't have any other galleries. I could. It's just a case of not having gotten back into that routine. I've only been doing this sort of work again since '75. He can handle almost everything I can produce.

TD: What was your childhood like? Were you a joiner or more a loner?

BN: I come from a large family. I was very close to my brothers particularly. There were five children, and we still are very close. I'd say they were my peer group really. I had some friends, but I did most of my playing and growing up with my family, most significantly with my older and younger brother, two years older, two years younger. This was a very good thing, because I felt I could do almost anything they could do. I could. In terms of sports and certain activities, I could keep up with them and it just never occurred to me that there'd be any reason why I couldn't do anything I wanted to because I was a girl. There were a few restrictions that my mother placed on me. Certain places I couldn't go by myself, that sort of thing, but I could always do as much work, or physically excel as well as they, so it never really affected my attitude. I worked with tools, I did gardening, I did carpentry.

TD: Which contemporary photographers do you particularly admire?

BN: That's one question I have to think about. There are so many. I do have a lot of admiration for so many, especially those who persevere. Emmet Gowin I'm very fond of. A lot of these people I know personally, too. Then it gets complicated because you start admiring them as people. There are people whose work I admire, and maybe I don't admire them as people. It's a complicated question. I've always admired Robert Frank, Diane Arbus, Dave Heath, Linda Connor, the work in Europe in the '30s. I'm bound to leave out people.

TD: Do you collect anybody?

BN: I collect by trading. I'm not an avid art collector because I've filled so much space with my own stuff. I do love antiques and quilts, and I have a small collection of prints.

TD: Do you show your work to anybody as you work along?

BN: I don't get much opportunity to get feedback. I've become fairly independent, so that I listen to myself mostly. I think that's something that an artist has to develop. You just can't survive if you really, really depend on constant feedback. It's not like when I was in school, when I was surrounded by peers, and that kind of pressure which makes one produce. I have to be able to sustain myself for long periods of time between any kind of critical response or review. My husband doesn't speak very much about my work, which is probably just as well. That might make it difficult for me. I might feel intimidated somehow, that there was some kind of imminent judgment. He's very good about that. Our tastes are often different about photographs anyway, so it works out.

TD: How often do you bring work down to Lee Witkin?

BN: Not that often, maybe twice a year I might get to New York, and usually I'll bring him some new work and take home some old work.

TD: Does he comment on it?

BN: He's a great collector of mine. He's one of my major collectors. I guess that's how I first knew Lee. He bought work of mine quite a few years ago. He's very supportive and recognizes my best work.

TD: How would you describe yourself in terms of your photography?

BN: I would say, if you can divide art into classic, romantic and fantastic traditions, I'm in the fantastic. I'm in the tradition of surrealism, fantasy, and those who work from the heart. Sometimes I'm made to feel guilty that I'm not out there making images that will change conditions, and that sort of thing. I think that my work, at its best, really touches people in a very strong, very good, very positive way, and I think that that's important, too. If you can put together a body of work that's very memorable to people, very inspiring, I think that's a significant thing to do as well.

TD: Primarily you make your living from teaching?

BN: Yes. With the books and the other projects that I have going, I certainly support my work and still have some money left over, but I couldn't be living on my photography alone. If I were not teaching full time I could arrange enough workshops and lectures so that I could at least survive. It's a rare photographer who can totally support himself, his work, and a family with "Art" photography. But I'm able to support my habit. I can finance almost anything I want to do.

TD: Do you foresee a day when you'll be able to generate enough work to live entirely from the work?

BN: No, I don't really. I don't sell that much work. The Kwik Prints have been selling gradually. Also because I do unique pieces, I'm just not able to turn out quantity. Let's say if I had a moonrise image that everyone liked, I can't produce that many of them. Because of the nature of the process, it's layers of color applied over many, many exposures, I may make a second version, but I could never make exactly the same image. It doesn't bother me. It's not in my nature. Occasionally I'll do an edition that I can give away, like the poster for the Witkin show. That's a really nice thing and I'll be able to give that out, but that's not considered an art collector's piece.

TD: How long does it take you to make a Kwik Print image?

BN: It can vary. It can be a day, five hours, or I can work on some of the larger images for four days, maybe eight hours a day. I get a certain amount of mileage from an image in forms other than the original, like in book form, or in slide sets for teaching. My images can live on in different forms and they still produce a certain amount of income.

TD: How important is success to you and how do you define it?

BN: Success is being able to do what you want to do, without having to worry about finding the time or the money. At least to date I've been able to do that, so I feel that I'm successful. It's quite important. If I was feeling very frustrated, it would be rather hard to keep a positive outlook. I do see people who get bitter at a certain age. I think there's a difference between success and fame, and fame has never really interested me particularly. I've wanted mostly to have the respect of people whom I respect. I don't care what the general public thinks of me, but people who I really respect, I hope will respect me and understand my work, and basically that's enough satisfaction.

TD: Do you think you've had to struggle less than most people?

BN: My work was exhibited early in my career, but I wouldn't say it was accepted quickly. I've had negative reviews and still get some. My work has always been on the borderline and challenges a lot of people's preconceptions about photography and art. I guess it depends what you think struggling is. I certainly haven't had to scrounge around to find shows. I've always seemed to have the work and been in the right place at the right time. It's critically important that you have some significant work. If you don't have the work, no matter how much hustling you do, it just won't get you anywhere. In that sense, I've worked very hard to have that backup of work. That can be very lonely — at times a real struggle.

TD: Do you read reviews?

BN: Sure. They can upset me. It's a very frustrating feeling when maybe two years of my work is hanging somewhere and someone, in twenty minutes, can poison so many people's attitudes towards it. I'm very defenseless really, in terms of answering back. It's only human to be pleased when they're good reviews and upset when they're bad. A lot does depend on who's writing them, too, and whether I have that much respect for the writer. Certain people I would expect to dislike my work, and if they didn't, I'd worry.

TD: How do you edit your work?

BN: That's a real hard thing to explain. That does get down to aesthetics. I can give you some idea of my working ratio; at least one, sometimes two, weak images for every good image. The weaker images I'd call seconds. I keep them around because I learn from them, but they just don't quite make it. Occasionally an image will be revived out of that group of work. I'll realize I misjudged it, and there really was something there. But how one judges images, it's really hard to say. I will listen to other people's responses occasionally, and see if maybe I've missed something or misjudged a piece. Usually I have to go by my feelings about how effective that image is, in terms of what I was trying to convey or what it conveys without my even trying.

TD: You just leave something up and look at it?

BN: Yes. I have an upstairs and a downstairs studio. When an image is good enough to get from downstairs to upstairs, and it gets signed and finished, then I tack it on the wall and live with it. Then I put it away, sometimes I take it back out to look at it. It's good to have a period of time before you exhibit to get a sense of how you feel about new work.

TD: How often do you take new pictures now?

BN: I find I don't photograph in the winter in Rochester, outside. I'll do some interior things. To get to the Kwik Print stage, things go through so many steps. I can work with certain stock images for months at a time. I probably shoot two or three rolls of film a month, but when I travel, that might be six to eight in a few days. It averages out probably to a roll a week.

TD: Do you usually have a concept in mind?

BN: Sometimes I will have something in mind ahead of time and actually set it up or look for it. Other times, I'm playing with things. Occasionally I'll realize I need certain images, say myself as a landscape prop. There are several in the Witkin show of myself as a moonrise. I'll just set aside an afternoon, get in costume and rig those things up. It works both ways.

TD: Do you only shoot black and white?

BN: Yes, pretty much. I've done color, just rarely, sometimes as a tourist, but that's it.

TD: What kind of camera do you use these days?

BN: I have a 35mm Canon with two lenses. I'm not equipment oriented, and it serves quite well for the sorts of things that I'm doing now. Before that I had used a 2¼ and the instamatic, basically. Sometimes I've used a view camera for direct Autoscreen images, and sometimes pinhole cameras. I don't really know that much about other things. I'm open to learning, but camera stores are probably my least favorite places. They give me the creeps actually.

TD: Do you ever shoot with the instamatic anymore?

BN: Not very much, no. For a long time I carried one in my purse all the time. I felt very uncomfortable, unarmed, without one, like I definitely would miss something. Eventually, after carrying it for months and months and realizing I wasn't using it, I quit, and noticed I didn't have to do it, and felt alright. I think that came about for the practical reason that the instamatic negative doesn't work as well with the film I'm using for Kwik Prints.

TD: What's the difference in the negatives?

BN: I'm using high speed duplicating film and it duplicates the grain of the negative and the grain in the instamatic negatives is very mushy, generally, very soft, so Tri-X works a whole lot better.

TD: Why not just get 126 Tri-X?

BN: That's a good idea, but the lenses on instamatics are so cheap, I think that's part of the problem. The whole image, by the time you blow it up to 16 x 20 or 20 x 24, just looks like mush.

TD: You do all of your own processing?

BN: Yes. I don't make silver prints any longer, I haven't done one of those in years. I never was highly involved with the silver print, ever. I almost immediately started hand coloring photographs. The only period when I made "straight" prints was when I did instamatic prints. Even then I felt that the life of those was in the book form, and not in the print form. They were conceptual series of images, and the prints themselves were not that important.

TD: Could you use the Kwik Print images to do another book?

BN: Yes. I hope someday to do something like that. I don't know that it will be sequential, but at least a catalog of color images. I did reproduce some in **Breaking the Rules** and they do reproduce beautifully.

TD: Kwik Print is your current favorite?

BN: Yes. That's really what I'm sold on right now. It's a synthesis for me of all the things I've been involved in up to now: multiple negatives, color built up in a painterly way, and it lets me do almost everything I always wanted to do, but didn't know how.

TD: You like to work big?

BN: Yes, if I can.

TD: Do you ever make small Kwik Prints?

BN: I haven't made any smaller than 15 x 18. Scale is important and you should really be aware of the scale that you select and not be influenced by Kodak. There's no reason, just because it comes out of the box that size, that that's what you have to use. I do like working large. When I painted, I used to paint six foot canvases. That was a great feeling. I had to stand up on something to reach the top while I worked.

TD: How large can you go in Kwik Print?

BN: The largest sheets are 54 x 75. I've got two in the show that are 30 x 52, and wouldn't mind working larger. The main problem is exposure, development and getting negatives that big. It gets to be pretty clumsy, but it can be done.

TD: This is strictly a contact printing process?

BN: Right. I'm working in a fairly realistic fashion in that everything's connected, but if someone was doing splashy things, they could easily work that size, just by developing different areas of the image. The style I'm working in now, things are fairly perfect and uniform. You may see where my negatives join or overlap, but it's pretty controlled.

TD: Do you feel that your books are most important in terms of your reputation?

BN: I really don't know. I would say probably more people have seen **The Woman's Eye,** and soon, hopefully, **Breaking the Rules** will reach a large audience. Probably the number of people who have actually seen a lot of my original work is small. Most have heard about it or they've seen reproductions or a few originals. I've shown the books in exhibitions where I've just sent book pages to five or six large shows around the country, so if people haven't held the books, they've at least seen the pages.

TD: How well do individual prints sell?

BN: It's not that common for me to sell work. I rarely sell work in shows outside New York City. Most of my work is sold to institutional collections, rather than private collectors. The books sell well, and the slide sets, so eventually — let me age another thirty, forty years, then ask me again.

TD: Is your work known in Europe and Japan?

BN: Probably not in Japan, but in Europe, I've had color portfolios in a French, a Czech and a Russian magazine, and had smaller things in Italian magazines. I've had shows in Paris, in London, and work has traveled around different European countries, so I would say it's beginning to be known there. That's a very hard thing to follow up on. You really have to work at it. There are 10 pieces in a show that will open in Holland and will travel until 1980, all over Europe, so I expect that may help.

TD: Have you received grants other than the CAPS?

BN: No, that's the only one so far.

TD: Have you applied for them?

BN: Yes, I have. When you speak about not having to struggle, my problem is that I'm right on the borderline of media. A lot of photographers reject my work, as well as the painters who would reject the work, so that's my struggle. I'm right there on the edge, so it really depends on the jury. My work is very offensive to some photographers. It's just a question of trying to keep at it until I hit enough people who see things my way. That's probably the major difficulty of working the way that I do. I'm in between both camps. I don't care what I'm classified as. I seem to have become a photographer. I think that was because I started teaching specifically photography, and mainly meeting photographers. I would think that my work could be equally at home in an art gallery.

TD: Do you like teaching?

BN: Yes, I do. Sometimes I really like it and there are some bad aspects of it. If students are working and I can see that they're developing, and they're interested, I enjoy it.

TD: You mentioned before that you read novels. Do you read newspapers and magazines?

BN: No, I'm terrible about current events. My husband reads the newspapers, I don't. I read magazines in doctors' offices, on airplanes and such, but I would never go out of my way to buy a magazine or newspaper. I'm much more likely to go to the library and look at books or bring home novels.

TD: Do you read nonfiction?

BN: Yes, I do. I like to read all sorts of things. I want to read **The Ascent of Man,** and books like that are interesting to me. I just finished a very large book on the archetype of the great mother, and **The Hero with a Thousand Faces,** which is another mythology book. I read books like that, which feed directly into the work.

TD: Do you watch TV?

BN: Yes, mostly public television. I don't watch cop shows or situation comedies. I'd rather read.

TD: Do you have dealings with other photographers?

BN: Yes, I do. Of course, we see quite a few who pass through Rochester. I know quite a few people in the field and have enjoyed meeting a lot of them. Several of my friends have moved away. I was close friends with Betty Hahn while she lived in Rochester. Mostly, I keep up by correspondence, and trying to see people a couple of times a year. People get scattered, end up teaching all over. I keep in touch with quite a few of the photographers who have been friends of mine, and other people I've taught or taught with. I try to see people once a year at the S.P.E. (Society of

Photographic Education) conference. I enjoy that. I keep in touch with Robert Fichter and Robert Heinecken, who are also friends of mine.

TD: What are your immediate plans for the future?

BN: I'm having a baby so that's going to really change my immediate plans, I would imagine. That's in May, and that will probably be my summer occupation.

TD: Do you expect work to come out of that?

BN: I would hope so. It's quite an experience. I hope I have time to work — that's the thing. That's why it's hard to say what I'll be doing. It's really difficult to know what kind of change a child will make. I will probably continue with the Kwik Print. I don't have any immediate book ideas. Getting **Breaking the Rules** done was perfect timing as far as I'm concerned. That's finished and the show at Witkin is going to be the month of February (1978). I hope in the summer to keep working on the Kwik Prints and see how things go from then on. I am trying to store up enough of the Kwik Print images to eventually do a four color book, a collection of my work. I don't know if it would be an attempt to critically deal with the imagery, a text, but there might be something like that in it. A mini-retrospective; there will be ten years of work pretty soon.

TD: You have access to it?

BN: Quite a bit of it. I've always made a good slide record of things and you can get fairly good reproduction from a 35mm slide. An awful lot of my work is gone. I have sold quite a bit over the years, traded it and found homes for it, so it's really scattered all over the place. By going through my records I could probably pull together a fairly interesting combination of images.

TD: That's a long range project?

BN: Yes, I don't have any immediate plans for that. I have to recoup some of my expenses from some of these other projects before I can make another investment.

New York City
January 2, 1978

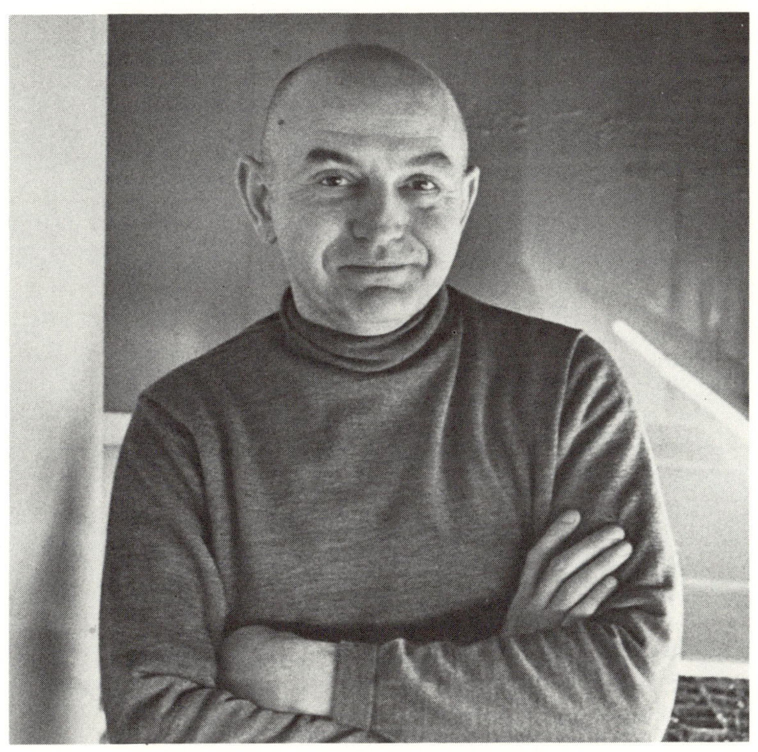

Duane Michals

Interviewer: Could you say something about how your interest in mysticism and religion affects your work?

Duane Michals: It affects my life. It's more important than photography; it's more important than anything. Unfortunately I don't live that way, but I think it's the central question. I would rather ultimately be a dilettante photographer and professional mystic than a dilettante mystic and a professional photographer. I use photography very well. Photography is the way I help explain my experience to myself, but mysticism is what it's all about. Everything else is distraction. This interview is distraction; getting published is a distraction; everything is a distraction, and distractions we use to keep ourselves from facing the central issue, the central question. And the central question is: What am I doing here? Who am I? What is this place? and, What happens when I die? Next to that everything else is fun and games and nonsense.

The interview with Duane Michals took place in the study of his brownstone home in New York City on May 1, 1975. It was tape recorded and appears essentially as it was recorded. The only changes concerned the clarification of a point here, a point there. At the time of our talk, Duane had published two books, **Sequences** and **The Journey of the Spirit After Death** and his work also had appeared in many publications.

Duane Michals, slim, of average height, with disarmingly open good looks, is a bright, articulate, charming man. In a moment or two he has one at ease as he chats easily and rapidly about a variety of concerns. He has a certain disdain for many photographers, and yet is very aware of the work going on in the field, giving the impression of having seen everything that is published. Like a good-natured mischief-maker, he projects an image of the photographer as iconoclastic imp.

Born: McKeesport, Pennsylvania, February 18, 1932.
B.A.Degree: University of Denver, 1952
Attended: Parsons School of Design, 1956.
Books:
    Sequences. Doubleday & Company, Inc. New York, 1970.
    The Journey of the Spirit After Death. Winter House Ltd. New York, 1971.
    Take One and See Mt. Fujiyama. Stefan Mihal (privately published). New York, 1976.
    Real Dreams. Addison House. Danbury, New Hampshire, 1976.
    Homage to Cavafy. Addison House. Danbury, New Hampshire, 1978.
Currently: Photographer, New York City.

Tom Dugan: How did you become a photographer?

Duane Michals: Oh, very simple. I was 29 going on 30, 28, 29 or 30, I forget exactly and, in a way, photography chose me in the sense that here was something I had run into. It was an accident. I realized I liked doing it and circumstances had conspired to present me with opportunities, like I met a guy who had come by who was a friend of a friend who saw my photographs, who was a photographer, and he said, "I have a studio, you can come use my studio on weekends," and he gave me a key, and I started taking pictures of friends. So if he hadn't happened I probably wouldn't have become a photographer. All these little series of events; he was the one who taught me how to use a light meter, he was sort of my guide, I'd question and he'd help me. He was the one who taught me how to print, really, he was the one, and so, if it hadn't been for him, he was a great aid, I just thought when I was that age, look, if you like taking pictures, why don't you? Who's stopping you? I mean, you have to remember no one was stopping me, I was stopping me. So it was very natural. I think the best things come that are very natural to you and it was very natural to me to pursue it. My first goal was, I was making a hundred and a quarter a week and I would like to make a hundred and a quarter taking portraits. Wouldn't that be nice? I knew nothing about business, I knew nothing about being a photographer, I knew nothing about agents and the mechanics of making it as a photographer, but my initial impulse was, wouldn't it be nice if I could make $125 a week doing what I like to do which is to photograph people and that's how I got into the business.

TD: What were you doing before becoming a photographer?

DM: I was a very bad designer. I had great taste, but I wasn't particularly talented and if I had stayed a designer, today I would be very unhappy because I probably would've been a third-rate designer. I was working at Time, Inc. doing all those house organ ads and little junk. *Time-Life, Sports Illustrated,* and that stuff. Most of the time I looked around and realized — I was about 26, 27 — and all these other guys were — I was the youngest one in the office and they were all, say like 35, and they were all fat and living in Connecticut and going to the Caribbean for the 20th time this winter and I said, "Oh, my God, is this it, is that what it's all about, is this what one would want to be?" I thought it was rather revolting. So when I had a chance, I took it. My main ideal was just to make enough money in doing portraits, which I like to do. I never wanted to be a studio, I never wanted to be a business. That's initially how I got into it.

TD: Now when you took portraits at that point, did you take your own kind of portrait and not other people's idealizations of themselves?

DM: Oh, sure.

TD: You were not taking idealizations of the people?

DM: Never. As a matter of fact, initially, I started to do a few jobs just to make money. I would do shootings for people and after about the fourth one, when I realized what people wanted, I just stopped doing it. I couldn't deal with trying to flatter people, make them look younger or make their noses look small or whatever they wanted to look small, small. I never did that. It's amazing I've been able to do as well as I have considering my attitude, but when I do jobs I go very responsible, being a depression child. I feel very responsible to doing jobs, and try to give people what they want. My philosophy is, if you don't want to do it, then don't take their money. Gene Smith to the contrary, I don't think that accepting jobs is where you do your number. I think you do your number through yourself. When I do something for myself nobody tells me what to do. If I do an assignment for somebody I know they have certain things they want, so I will try to satisfy them and take their money for it. If I don't plan on satisfying them, then I shouldn't take their money. It's very simple. I mean *Life* magazine is not out to let me do my number and make me famous at their expense. They have other problems.

TD: Who were some of your early influences?

DM: I've not been influenced by any particular photographer. I've been more influenced by painters. I find most photographers are very boring. A photographer who, if anybody influenced me, would be Atget, in spirit. First, when I did my New York City things, empty rooms, they were pretty much inspired by Atget and they were transitional pictures which led me to sequences.

I love Robert Frank. I think Robert Frank is more important than Walker Evans and Ansel Adams. I think Robert Frank is a monumentally important photographer, the complete photographer. I love him. I think he's just great. I've never taken anything from him. I think that people like Lee Friedlander and Gary Winogrand and legions, Danny Lyon, Bruce Davidson, are all versions of the Robert Frank and/or the Cartier-Bresson school of thought. I think in every generation there's one original point of view. Robert Frank is the original point of view of this last thirty years in this country. Every bike picture, every suburban picture, every car wrapped in plastic, American flag picture, every gasoline picture that kids have milked for the last twenty years, — I just love Robert Frank.

My real influences have been painters. I love, for instance, William Blake. I think William Blake is a genius. Wherever you are, William Blake, I love you. And I like the Renaissance painters. I like Balthus. I like Magritte, of course, I've pretty much gone through Magritte. I take from lots of things. I'm completely open. I take from everything. Photographers are very peripheral, very narrow-minded. They look a lot and that's their cop-out. When people describe photographers they usually say, "My, he has good vision, doesn't he see well." You never hear anyone describe a photographer as having a great mind, or a vivid imagination or what a head. It's always an observer, a spectator, he's always responding, he's the ultimate voyeur. Cartier-Bresson is a total voyeur, always pretending he's a palm tree in a corner of a room. I don't believe it.

TD: How did you begin to do your own work?

DM: You see the danger with most photographers who come to photography, — I did not come the photography route, I did not do the whole thing about being an amateur. I'm not like George Tice who was an amateur and then became a professional. I did not go to photography school, I was not into photography as such. I was just out to take some pictures for myself. I didn't even know there was a George Eastman House; I didn't know any of that kind of shit. I just did what I wanted to do, so that was never on my back to unload. My initial thought was, "Wouldn't it be nice to make a living taking portraits of people because that's what I like to do?" After I did that for awhile I realized that the medium could be used in other ways. Photographers are constipated; they only operate in a very narrow piece of the pie we call being alive. Well, their piece of the pie is the kind you would get in a very expensive restaurant for about five dollars, when there is all this other stuff. A photographer's point of view has to change. I don't care if it changes or not, but it's always — I'm digressing — but it's always the idea of being a spectator, looking for something to take a picture of. My point of view is never that. My point of view is: I am life. That was it. So it came to me working, first doing portraits, and then the room pictures and, things were happening in my private life that were very upsetting, and that's what I wanted to talk about. I didn't want to go to Harlem and photograph black people. I'm a white guy from Pittsburgh. It's not to say it shouldn't be done, but for me to show a lot of black people sitting in rooms aesthetically posed, and then do a $25 art book on it, somehow is disturbing, so I can only talk about my own life, my own experience, and the minute I discovered myself, it was opening a pandora's box because I was totally free. I didn't need a grant to go to Alaska; I didn't need a motor bike to go across country a la Frank. I became the McCoy which is what everybody should realize, that there is a McCoy. They're it.

TD: How long did it take you to make a decent living?

DM: Instantly, I got work instantly. I knew a couple of art directors; I knew one from my contact at *Sports Illustrated*. My first year I went from zero to a hundred. If I had had to wait six months to get a job, I probably would have collapsed. I mean I probably would have been starved out, depressed and dropped it, but I didn't. I made it happen. Kids say to me, "How do I get work?" You do the same thing I do, — that was the era of magazines — you look up a magazine. That's all I knew to do. I'd look up who the art director was and take my portfolio. There are such fantasies among students today about making a living in New York. They all say to me, "How can you be creative living in New York?" I say, "How can you be creative living in Syracuse, how can you be creative sitting in Eastman House in Rochester?" You are it. I live in this oasis, I live very comfortably. Living in New York has nothing to do with it, except there are more jobs available here.

TD: How much commercial work do you do now?

DM: I don't know, I may do one or two jobs a week. I'm not commercially ambitious. I make more money than I ever thought I'd make, which is relatively small compared to Avedon, I'm sure, and Bert Stern and those people. But I'm not interested in making a lot of money. I'm interested in my freedom. I'm interested in doing enough jobs to live comfortably, to be able to buy $25 art books when I want to, not to have to worry about the price of film, and yet I want also to have the freedom to do what I want to do with my life, with my work. It's very easy to get tricked into that route where you open a studio, have three assistants and you're doing a thousand dollars a day, overhead alone. Who needs that? I'm not capable. I'm a real loner, I like being by myself, I like my privacy, I like the freedom to do what I want to do, when I want to do it. If I took an agent I could probably make a lot of money, but I'm not interested in a lot of money, I'm interested in freedom and in finding out what my life's all about. And that's what I've done. Everybody does it, except they don't realize it. I know what I'm doing. Most people do it without knowing what they're doing, so if they find themselves walled into a corner, they built that wall themselves. Somebody once said to me, about successful photography, "He's stuck with that studio and all those models and everything, and what he really wants to do is photograph rabbis on the lower east side." I said, "Bullshit, if he wanted to photograph rabbis, he'd photograph rabbis." We do ultimately what we want to do. I wouldn't be damaged if I were locked in this apartment with my camera. I could take pictures forever. Other people who have to rely on something to photograph would go bananas because there's nothing for them to photograph.

TD: What was your childhood like? Were you part of a peer group or were you a loner?

DM: A loner, because there was only one other kid my age in my neighborhood. We were what was commonly called, in those days, poor. A tacky word, poor. It was tough, tough financially.

TD: Did you realize you were poor at the time?

DM: No, I realized it later. When I was in high school I realized it but, at the time, when I was a kid, I wasn't aware of it. I loved it. I thought it was the best place in the world anybody could possibly live. The inequities of the situation I became aware of later, as I got older, of course. I'm not the world's most insensitive person and I was certainly aware of the haves and have-nots.

TD: What about your education?

DM: When I was in high school I got a Saturday scholarship to the Carnegie Tech. I used to like to paint and draw; I was very precocious, and they had a thing there for neighborhood kids. I got a scholarship to the University of Denver and graduated from there, then went to Parsons for a year after the army; it was a disaster. I wanted to learn how to put together magazines and they were teaching me a lot of shit and nonsense, so I'm a Parson's dropout. I don't know how anybody could spend four years going to photography school, whatever they take. How you can spend more than four months in a photography school is beyond me. That's it.

TD: What personal characteristics do you feel made the choice of photography a logical one?

DM: I don't know. All I know is that some people go through life out of register, like they should be writing poetry, but they're selling shoes. They never become what they should have been, and all I know is that I'm doing what I should be doing because it suits me, it fits me, I'm in rhythm with myself, thus I flow with myself. The minute you find yourself bumping up against your elbows, the minute you're out of step, then you're in trouble, it doesn't work. Most people are like that. Some people happen to fit, I fit. My life fits me.

TD: Did you realize that immediately or did it take a while?

DM: No, no I'm 43. I only know things after the fact. During experiences I'm very aware if things seem right or I'm very aware of whatever. I appreciate everything, I must say. Maybe that's from a legacy of having had no money or being observant how other lives can be led. I realize the great luxuries I have and what I've done, I've made happen, so it's not an accident. Some people are unhappy, they make unhappy choices. I happen to make happy choices for myself. I appreciate everything, I take nothing for granted. I think I'm one of the luckiest people in the world. I really appreciate my life and if I should drop dead tomorrow — I'm very aware of death — I wouldn't want anybody ever to cry for me because I've had it, I mean, I've had it.

TD: How would you describe yourself in terms of your photography?

DM: You mean by what label I would describe myself? I don't know. There's not a label for my category yet. It hasn't been resolved. It will be. I hate labels. I could describe myself by saying what I'm not. I'm not a street photographer; I'm not a spectator; I have an imagination, like everybody else. I just happen to use my imagination. I operate out of my mind. I invent. I'm an adventurer. I invent my photographs. None of my photographs would be in existence without my making them happen. Most photographer's photographs have a life of their own. Whether Cartier-Bresson was there to see that thing happen or whether Frank happened to see that thing happen, it would have occurred without him. None of my photographs would have occurred without me. What you're looking at is my mind and the revelation is that everything is your mind, what you're hearing is in your mind, it's all in your mind. I don't know how you would describe me. I'm getting labeled as a surrealist. I'm interested in metaphysics most of all, beyond anything. I'm interested in reality beyond anything, and photography deals with reality, but I don't know how I would describe myself. How would you describe me?

TD: I think what you said about coming out of your imagination best describes you. About a week ago I was looking at a portfolio of your portraits and I remembered all the portraits I had ever seen by you. I find them very moving and when you alluded to the fact that each one is something that you invented, that wouldn't have happened, that's even true of your portraits.

DM: Cartier-Bresson would make portraits by letting somebody be in their living room sitting around and smoking. He would pretend he's not there; of course they would know he was there. He would just loaf around and shoot all day long catching them picking their nose and whatever. I wouldn't do that. Even in portraits I would take charge. I think portrait photographers have two responsibilities. One to themselves as artists, and one to the sitters, and I think you should never violate the sitters by having them doing something ridiculous like in **Observations.** Lots of Avedon's portraits were outrageous because he used those people in a nasty way, making the Duchess of Windsor look like a prune, or going through a contact sheet, you know you always get those shots where somebody is winking or yawning or twitching or making a funny face, and then picking those out. I think it's a violation of the person. That's really a triumph of style over content. At this point the content happens to be somebody's life. People do get hurt if they look funny in a magazine, so I think it's your responsibility. You should permit them to be what they are, and never violate that. But underneath all of that should be your subtle manipulation of your point of view of the context that they're photographed in. That's why people who operate on photographing against no-seam paper all day long, when they have that harsh reality to deal with, have to then rely on getting the person to do something very quirky and make an interesting picture, whether it's Halsman having them jump in the air against no-seam or Avedon blowing a fan on them and having their hair blow in their face or having them look very mean or very boring, or reading bored as being mean or whatever.

TD: Is isolation necessary for your work?

DM: Yes.

TD: You have been described as a portrait of the photographer as a young monk.

DM: Oh, that's nice. The thing that bothers me about that is somebody in an interview in a paper described me as being a mystic. I was very upset by that because I'm not a mystic. I would give my right arm to be a mystic. Everything has to go, including photography. I wish to God I were a mystic; I'm not. So somebody who knows nothing about mysticism would think that I was a mystic, but, believe me, I'm a dilettante mystic. Oh, boy, if I were a mystic, that's what I'd like. I'm interested in that area, but it's like reading a hundred love stories and then falling in love. Well, I've read about 75 love stories. The difference between reading about them and knowing is the experience.

TD: You just read about it, you don't practice anything?

DM: Oh, yeah, I practice, but that's not the same thing. Yeah, I meditate. I've been meditating for about eight years. Even saying that sounds pretentious because anything I'm going to say in that area is going to sound pretentious, so I won't say anymore.

TD: Do you feel that you function as well as you could?

DM: Yeah, I feel that given my set of needs which are not everybody's needs, they're my needs, I function very well in terms of what my life should be. If I try to function in terms of my brother's needs, I would be very unhappy; if I tried to function in terms of what my mother wanted, and my father, then I'd be very unhappy. Luckily I'm smart enough to function in terms of my own needs. Yes, in that sense I am. I think that's why my work works for me, because I am functioning, integrated, whatever.

TD: And there's nothing in the way of your work?

DM: No, no, in fact, keeping those channels open is very important to me, between myself, my mind, and my photography. If I were not integrated, there would be problems in the way, I'd be constipated again.

TD: Is success important to you?

DM: Yes. I wish I could say it wasn't. You cannot grow up in this culture and pretend it's not important. I think anybody who pretends it's not, is full of bullshit. I don't believe that for five minutes. I think that everybody wants to make it, everybody wants to be well-known, I think all those kids out there who want to become famous, but pretend that what they really want to do is go down and photograph Appalachia. They're full of shit, too, because what they'll do is come back and do another $15 job on those people and they'll still be sitting down there. So I think success is important, but that's not the issue. The issue is not being successful, the issue is knowing how to deal with it and putting it in its right place, so it fits where it should in your life. It's also such a relative term. For instance, if my idea of being successful would mean to be Richard Avedon, and have the studio and make $100,000 and do Revlon commercials or whatever, then I'd be very unhappy because I wouldn't be successful. But I have defined in my own terms, what success is, and the money, and being well-known, that's nice, but that's incidental. Success is joy, the joy of knowing that what you're doing is right and has to do with you, is honest and is clean. Success is to produce one body of work that you know, without anybody else telling you, is good and it has to do with your life and it communicates and there's joy in it. You don't set out to become successful, you practice on your work and if your work is true, you will then be successful.

TD: Yeah, I like that. How does the creative process work for you?

DM: I don't really know and I don't think I want to know. I believe in intuition, I trust my intuition. My intuition knows more than I do. I, myself, will get in the way and inhibit myself. For me, the creative process is keeping myself open to everything that occurs to me in my mind, not be frightened by it, and knowing when it's really good and latching on to it. Well, let me put it this way, we are in flux, we are this whole thing. The sun comes up without my telling it to come up every morning, and birds make their nests without anybody telling them how to make nests, and ideas pop into my head, and my fingernails grow without my telling them to grow, so I'm not so great. I'm in the process. What I do is permit it to happen, I permit the ideas to flow through me and I bring it together.

TD: OK. How do you bring it together?

DM: By making it happen, by conceding or something, finding it curious, not knowing what it means, just finding it curious and interesting and then making it happen itself.

TD: So do you write it down?

DM: I never write it down; it stays in my head.

TD: There's no script? You just bring the elements together?

DM: For me, the easiest part is taking photographs, actually. The hardest thing is wondering about what I wonder about, wondering what I think is important, the observations and making them happen, I mean organizing my mind in such a way that I can make it happen on film, that's the hard part. To me it's not photography, it's not a matter of category, the key word is not being a photographer, or being a painter or whatever. What's important is expression. That covers all that. And how well do I express myself in terms of what I'm to communicate with. That's what counts. Whether you paint it or poet it or play it or sculpt it or photograph it, it doesn't matter. The question is: after all this effort, what is being communicated and how well do I express what I'm feeling in the middle of this curiosity that I'm in?

TD: How much time do you spend on your personal work?

DM: I work at it everyday. I may only take pictures twice a month or once a month, but there's no fat, when I take pictures, there's no waste. Sometimes I see people with cameras and I think, my God, they must shoot everything that moves, hoping by some weird, freak accident they're going to get something important, and there's a great deal of waste. When I actually do — when I say I work at it every day, I'm counting my mind, thinking and being curious and functioning, observing and responding — that's taking pictures as far as I'm concerned. The actual act of taking photographs may be, as I said, only once a month or, when I'm hot, maybe twice a month, or whatever; it depends.

TD: There's no such thing as casual shooting for you?

DM: Never, no. I'm not casual about my work. I'm very serious about it. Like I was home — my father died — and I took some pictures of the family and even then, that, I could not do so casually. No, I'm very serious about it. I would never walk around with a camera looking for something on the street or hoping for some curiosity I could record. Maybe if I'm lucky I'll see somebody with their clothes on fire and take a picture. No, I don't work that way.

TD: When did you first start doing sequences? How did that come about?

DM: About 1966, '65 or '66. I did those empty rooms; there was a painter I liked, a lot of things came together, and I was lucky to latch on to them. That was one of the things. The other thing is, there's a painter I like, Balthus, and he did a street scene, a painting which I've always liked, so I set up my own street scene. That was the first photograph I ever invented. And once I realized that that was possible, a great door opened for me. Where's it written you can't make your own photographs? There are so many of these rules in photography. They're full of shit. I don't know who ever made these rules. They're just nonsense. I can do anything I want and Minor White is not going to say, "Sorry, you don't do that." Or Nathan or Szarkowski. Nobody can tell me what to do. So when I set up that first picture, it was marvelous because I thought, this is great, I can make anything I want happen. So that was part of the process. I don't remember exactly how I arrived at the sequential notion, how I expanded the single frame. I don't really remember that, but the ingredients were: wanting to talk about things in photographs that had to do with my life, and realizing I could invent my own photograph. And those are the two essential ingredients. My vision and my thinking turned inward; I was always introspective, and now I had a vehicle, I could use my introspection and make something happen. It's almost anti-American to be introspective, because here everything is, we're all going to go down to Guatamala and photograph unwed mothers and save them the way we saved Saigon and the way we saved Cambodia. We're going to turn everybody into marvelous little outgoing, like in schools, where if you're anti-social, if you don't fit in, everyone's got to fit in and smile a lot. God forbid you just sit in your room and think about something. People should always use everything of their lives and most people are so unaware of their lives. It's understandable, especially young people, they don't realize that they're it. They're always out there looking for someone to emulate.

TD: Can you talk about your evolution as a photographer? Will you ever stop doing sequences?

DM: I don't know what I'll do. I don't know what I'll do tomorrow. Things are changing for me. I haven't stopped doing single photographs; I've changed the sequences from being cinematic to being more literary. I've pretty much done death in as a subject to date. I must have done about five sequences that deal with it or relate to it, one way or another, and I've done a number of portraits about death, self-portraits and other things about death, so I work through subjects. And now I'm working on eroticism and I've always been interested in personal identity. That keeps coming up in the work. So I do tend to work through certain things. The new work is more literary. I've taken them out of being cinematic, and now they are more illustrations with captions. If you would see all the illustrations for **Alice in Wonderland,** and I never read the book, these are like that. I find that writing expands what I can say a little more. So there are changes.

TD: The self-portrait with guardian angel, is that new?

DM: Yeah, I love the idea.

TD: I do, too. I like the way you combine the words with the picture.

DM: Do you realize the freedom there is? I mean if I want to photograph myself, damn it, I'll do it. Nobody's going to tell me I can't. I mean that's fantastic. You can do anything.

TD: It's becoming more interesting. I started out to be a documentarian, now I find myself moving radically away from that. I've realized what you have realized, that it all comes from within.

DM: Even documentary is coming from within. Interesting thing about documentary photographs, I have a feeling that in another year absolutely every square inch of American life will be photographed by somebody. I mean Friedlander's done parties, Davidson did black people, Lyons did jails. Everybody is cutting out a segment of American life. Somebody will do every gas station. It's so incredible. It will become so desperate, looking for something to photograph, if you don't grab your hunk of subject matter. People are going to start photographing ridiculous things because all the other categories will have been taken. Somebody will do an elbow book because American elbows are . . .

TD: Well, somebody did busts, a book called Profiles.

DM: That's what I'm talking about. Somebody will do a nose book, because if your point of view is always external and all the categories are being taken you really get desperate.

TD: Yeah, you go crazy looking. Do you think the day will come when you won't do commercial work?

DM: I have no idea. I love taking photographs. I don't look down on commercial work. I enjoy taking pictures. I love meeting famous people, I like traveling, it's fun. I'll always take photographs, as far as I can tell; eventually, I hope to be able to live off my private work. The potential in photography is enormous. Private work will become very valuable in time. Twenty years from now, I think, the work will be very valuable.

TD: In your opinion what are some of the important picture books and which, if any, inspired you?

DM: I loved **The Americans** which was the first photography book I ever bought. I bought the French version. When I was working at Time, Inc. I saw it in a French bookstore. I think it's probably the most profound, important photography book. I like any book on Atget, even the bad ones. I love Atget. Those are very important to me. I like August Sander, I've seen a lovely August Sander book. I like Irving Penn's book very much, **Moments Preserved,** I like Irving Penn, I think he's a beautiful photographer. I like Ralph Gibson's books very much; I like **Tulsa** (Larry Clark) very much; I like my own books very much. I like the book form very much, I love books, so I like the book format. I prefer my work to be seen in books rather than in exhibits. I'm not interested in exhibits very much. I hope to do another book with a lot of my new sequences. Trying to think what other ones I've left out. I like Diane's (Arbus, **Diane Arbus**) book very much. I did not like books like **Suburbia** (Bill Owens). I'm very bored with that kind of American documentary book on suburban life. I find them predictable and boring. I think those discoveries were made a long time ago. People have to stop looking at appearances. Don't show me a lady living in a mobile home with a TV set, wearing funny clothes. That's costume. I want to know what goes on in her mind. I want to know what kind of boredom she must reek of sitting there all afternoon, eating TV dinners. I'm not interested in appearances because nothing is to me what it appears to be. And nobody is what they appear to be. I'm interested in what she thinks about. I'm interested in how a person arrives at that point. That's the hard part. The easy part is photographing a curiousity. Curiosities take no insight to photograph. Everybody recognizes curiosities.

TD: Will you do a book of your portraits soon?

DM: I don't know, maybe eventually. I have enough of them. I love doing portraits. I do them all the time. Maybe someday. Everything takes time and I never rush anything.

TD: Do you self-publish your books?

DM: No, I may do one now though. This one I'm thinking of, **(Take One and See Mt. Fujiyama)** I may publish myself. I like the idea of self-publishing, except it's very expensive and you have to have a lot of money. But I would like to do this next one myself. I'm interested in cheap books, too. I'm not interested in $25 books, I'm not interested in $10 books, I'm interested in $3.95 books. I would rather have cheaper printing and less good paper and make the book available at a very inexpensive price. I think when I'm 75 I would like to do a $40 book, but at 43 I would like to do a $4.30 book. I'm interested in communication and availability.

TD: Could you discuss your personal approach to the technical aspects of your work?

DM: I think you should know completely how to take photographs, know everything your camera can do, know what your film can do, know how long you can hand-hold a camera, know how far you can push the film or whatever, then forget about it. I think you should know every trick you can do in the darkroom, then forget about it. The only thing that counts is the photograph. I think if a darkroom technique becomes a thing in itself, then it gets in the way. I don't think that printing is an art. I think printing is a craft. I think photography is an art. I think anybody can learn how to print, to be a technician. Very few people can be artists, so I wouldn't trivialize the word "art", referring to good printers as great artists. A gorgeously printed print of a turd — I don't know why I say turd, it doesn't sound nice — is still a gorgeous print of a turd. Robert Frank gave me a not-so-hot print of one of his pictures. I wouldn't care if that print were rotten and turning purple, I would love that print, because of what that print is, so all these kids running around, someone comes up and says he spent three days in a darkroom printing this, I think he must be a total fool. Either he's a terribly inept printer, or a terribly inept photographer who doesn't know how to expose film properly. I can't imagine what print would ever take that long. It's nonsense. That's all show business. What counts is what the content of the photograph is. It's just like anything else. I think if you're going to be a good writer, you should know how to spell and typewrite, then you forget about it. If you're going to be a good photographer, you should know your craft, then forget about it.

TD: You seem to prefer small prints.

DM: I love them. I love intimate scale.

TD: Do you print your portraits the same size?

DM: I print two sizes: 4 x 5 on 5 x 7 and 5 x 7 on 8 x 10.

TD: You don't go bigger than that?

DM: No. I like small people, small rooms, small dogs, little portions of food, short novels, and short interviews.

TD: When you send prints to a gallery, you don't mount them?

DM: No. I haven't printed in two or three years. I stopped printing about three years ago. I found a printer I like — I use two printers — but one I particularly like. I thought if I ever found a good printer, I'd let him do all the printing and that's what I'm doing. I don't have any hang-ups. I'm not interested in the precious print and I had no hang-ups about letting somebody else print, at all. I know what the photograph's about and if I find somebody who understands what I want in a print, that's terrific.

I take great pride when I can do a very difficult photograph technically well. There's pride in that, but it's not where I live. It's incidental. Photography is a mechanical process; you have to know how to operate technically. Painting isn't mechanical. You can spill paint, and get something. But when you're dealing with machines, it's not in spite of the camera that you take a good picture, it's the nature of the beast.

TD: You don't use the Zone System?

DM: Never. I was in Boston once — I've heard of the Zone System but I don't know what it is — and somebody asked me that question and I said, "I don't really know what the Zone System is," and everybody started to laugh. I really don't and I really don't care to know. I think it's more stuff to get in the way. I have a very "See Dick, see Jane" attitude about photography.

TD: When you do a sequence, how does it unfold and conclude? Do you ever reshoot?

DM: Never. I'm very narrow. I always say I have an attention span of a five year old. I get very excited about something and I shoot it. I've only reshot one thing ever in my life, even if I know it could be done better, because at that point I'm already on another idea that I like even more.

TD: How do the events of your personal life affect your work?

DM: Every way, totally, completely. My father just died and I'm sure two years from now I'll pull something out of all these feelings. Everything in my personal life is used. Memories of childhood, everything.

TD: Do you do any writing?

DM: I'm writing now with the work. I'm writing on the photographs. I like writing. It gives me more chance of failing. Not only as a speller, which I'm terrible at, but as a writer. And that's great. I believe in failures. I believe in noble failures. I'm anti-perfection. I hate the perfect print. I wish there were some way of making good imperfect prints. I like to see vulnerability in work, in people. I think we should stay vulnerable. It hurts to be vulnerable, but I believe it is essential. Now I forgot your question.

TD: I'm intrigued with your ideas on failing.

DM: Oh, yeah, I think growing is essential. If we had realized in this country that it would be more noble for us to fail in Viet Nam in 1970 than to fail totally in 1975, how much more grand we would be as people. I'm all for failures. We don't dare fail in this country. How awful. I love to admit I was fired as a waiter. I was fired; I was a terribly inept waiter. Some people are not cut out to be waiters. I think failure is terrific, especially if you learn from it.

TD: But what if you fail as a photographer?

DM: But I won't.

TD: Yeah, right. There's less risk involved now.

DM: Yeah, that's of value, everything is of value.

TD: Failure is more interesting from where you're sitting than from where I'm sitting.

DM: That's true, but I had to go through that process.

TD: Yeah, but I wonder if you were as philosophical about it at that point.

DM: No. I'm looking back on it. At that point there was an enormous mountain called Failure which I had to climb over. I hadn't proven anything at that point. But I think failure is essential because maybe if you failed at something, you could go on. Maybe you shouldn't be a photographer, maybe if you failed at being a photographer, then it's necessary for you to go on and find what you should really be doing is writing the great American novel.

TD: With whom do you discuss your work?

DM: Nobody. After I shoot it, I might tell one or two friends about something I was working on, but not telling it in the sense of wanting their approval, but telling it because I might think it's so amusing or funny that I'm just bursting to tell somebody about it. But I really don't discuss my work with anyone.

TD: Do you show it to your friends?

DM: After I'm finished.

TD: When you complete a sequence are there perhaps twenty photographs and you cut them down to fifteen?

DM: It's usually pretty much right on the button. There's no fat, it's very tight. I know exactly what I want. I'd say I'm eighty percent right on, most of the time.

TD: Do you do some printing with sandwiches?

DM: Occasionally, not often. As a matter of fact now that I have somebody else doing the printing I try to do everything in the camera, so it's easier for a printer to do. It doesn't demand too much complicated darkroom work. I try to make it all happen in the camera. I'm getting more and more simple in that sense, in terms of printing because I want to keep it all in the camera.

TD: You've just done the two books?

DM: Two and a gallery in Cologne brought out two little books, but they're really pamphlets. They call them books. They did **Things are Queer** and **Chance Meeting** as separate little books. Alskog is bringing out a book on me as part of that series they did on Bert Stern and others. The next group will be myself, Art Kane and a couple of other people. I'll have that one out. Ralph Gibson is doing a book on printing with lots of photographers (**Darkroom**). I'm one of them, and I may like to print my own, do this new book of my own work.

TD: That will be a book of sequences?

DM: Yeah. Also **Sequences** was published in Italy, too. It was called **Sequenze.**

TD: Will you do more books?

DM: I'd like to do more books, but it takes a long time and I'm not in any big rush. When I get a body of work then I'll do another book.

TD: Your last book was in '72?

DM: It's so funny. I've had so many people calling me up trying to find copies of **Sequences** and **Journey of the Spirit.** They're impossible to find. They're completely sold out.

TD: Will you reissue Sequences?

DM: Doubleday wants to. I haven't thought about it. I guess I should call them up. But, to me, that's old news. I'm now interested in what I'm working on. But I do think it's terrific to be sold out. I think books are very important for a photographer. In the future, like now, the new era, there are no magazines anymore to be seen — just books. Books are the way. There are so many dumb books being published on photography. I don't know how they get published, who the market is, who buys them? I have no idea. I don't.

TD: How do you select people for portraits if not on commercial assignment?

DM: I don't do that many portraits that aren't commercial assignments unless it happens to be somebody I like or somebody I find interesting or a particular artist I'm very fond of. I've made an effort to photograph some artists whom I particularly like, like Magritte and Joseph Cornell, or Charles Steinberg. I photographed DeChirico. These are people who meant something to me, so I made an effort to see them. I would like to photograph Francis Bacon if I had the chance, because I love his work very much. And I was in London and with people who knew him, but he was away on a holiday, so I missed him.

TD: Are you satisfied with the books that you've done?

DM: Generally, yes. I would have liked them to have been printed better because the printing was very bad, but it didn't hurt me because my photographs don't depend on good printing. If your photographs had to do with water running over pebbles and they're reproduced so you don't get those shades of gray, you're out of luck because that's what the print's about, those aesthetics. The aesthetics of my photographs do not deal with that kind of information. It really deals with a kind of story-telling information which is not destroyed by bad printing. It's lessened, but it's not wounded. These other photographs would be mortally wounded, mine would just be bruised.

TD: You didn't design or layout the books?

DM: No, but I specified that look because I like books to look like that. Small and a single picture on a page. I'd like to change it though, next book, somewhat; maybe make the photographs larger.

TD: But you'll still use a single photograph per page?

DM: Probably.

TD: I assume you were satisfied with the distribution because they were sold out.

DM: Certainly, I have no complaints. That's the advantage with being involved with a large company like Doubleday because they have more salesmen than other companies have. That's a marvelous kind of mechanical thing.

TD: At what point do you start thinking "book"?

DM: Well, I've always loved books. I'm a bookaholic, if there's such a thing. If I'm ever lost, just go to a bookstore, I'll be there, probably in a corner, covered with dust. But I love books, the way other people like alcohol. I can't stay away from them, so even my portfolio, I issued a portfolio, I did my own book. That's very natural for me to think "book," because I'm so crazy about them. I guess I've always had books on the brain.

TD: Your final form for all your personal work is books?

DM: Yeah, ideally, not too many exhibits, but I can best see in book format. Again because I love books.

TD: Does any gallery handle your work?

DM: I have work now with Light (Gallery).* I recently had work in Witkin (Gallery), but I took it out of there because I didn't like being part of a big stable. Every year Light would ask me to have a show and every year I would say no, but I decided to have a show. They hit me on a very low day. I'm glad. I have no contract with them, and Wilde in Cologne shows my work and Die Brucke in Vienna shows it. They all sell, but I would change galleries if I had a better offer. I don't want to be part of anybody's group. I like to keep my options open.

TD: Do you see any difficulties or drawbacks in doing books? For example, it would take a few years to assemble enough work to do a book. In the interim, do you try to have it published in annuals?

*Michals is now with Janis Gallery.

DM: If somebody calls up and wants to show something. I love to show new themes. I've been very bored in having the same photographs published, so I take every opportunity to have something new published. I always feel very good once something has been published because I know I can always find a copy someplace, so if I lost all my negatives, at least there would be a record someplace of that photograph. I like to be published, particularly new things. Yeah, while I'm working I probably would have some things shown someplace within a two or three year period.

TD: Do you work only in 35mm?

DM: Um hum. I probably should use a larger camera the way I work, but I'm just too lazy.

TD: What has been the response to your sequences, from critics and people in general?

DM: Terrific. I only had one bad review and once I began to read it and I realized it was a negative review, I didn't finish it. I didn't see any point in filling my head with negative thoughts that, when I felt insecure, I would pull out and beat my head against. So, generally, it's been very good. I have absolutely no complaints.

TD: Do you feel people understand your work?

DM: I don't know if they do or not. They respond to it. Whether they respond to it in the way I want them to, or in their own way, doesn't make any difference. The fact is that something is operating. There's movement between myself and another person.

TD: Is it the process that is important to you and not necessarily what happens after the work is completed?

DM: You mean the act of taking the photograph? Not at all. What's important is what happens afterwards. The importance is in the photograph.

TD: Once you do the sequence, for you, what happens to the sequence afterwards, in terms of audience, is that important?

DM: Yeah, it's important, I guess. They have lives of their own. Once something is done it's like throwing a frisbie out. It goes, and then I go to California and meet somebody who says, "You know I saw Paradise Regained and I really dug it." You get to a place and realize these things are like little paper airplanes just shooting out. It's amazing. One of the joys of photography is, you don't understand that 200,000 people saw that. It's staggering to realize the responses. The work has a life of its own. I've had one sequence that's been published five, maybe more, times, and very often, under a different context. Maybe each time the way was valid. It was marvelous.

TD: Are all the sequences the same number of photographs and you have condensed versions of them?

DM: No, no. Once I arrive at the format, it stays.

TD: That's the way it has to be published?

DM: Yeah. Every now and then, without telling me, somebody will publish something. In France they did it, where they cut out a picture. I was very annoyed because, as far as I'm concerned, it's like publishing somebody's poems and, because you didn't have enough space on the page, you knock off a few stanzas to make it fit.

TD: Does positive criticism make you feel good?

DM: Of course, if I recognize it. I'm very bull-headed and, just like anybody who is well into what he's doing, you have to have a developed ego. Anybody who is making any kind of a name for himself in work, I can't bear that kind of humility, I'm so bored with that kind of tacky, cheap humility. "Oh, me!" You know. "Do you really think that that's terrific?" That's such bullshit. Anybody who has a strong point of view also has a very strong ego and, of course, one's ownness is increased from what you agree with. I tend to dismiss criticism, if there is any, that I don't like. I really hate that kind of false humility, especially when it's the kind that people set out to save other people's lives. When a person's altruistic, they're going to do something on the prune pickers and, as a result of some hip New York photographer flying to California or photographing onion pickers outside San Antonio, he gets $700 a day to photograph these kids, comes back and they do a book that not one of these people, picking prunes or whatever, could afford to buy and they're doing something for humanity. They're doing something for themselves.

TD: How have your books affected your reputation?

DM: Books always help. That's how reputations are built. You don't get a reputation by sitting on your hands. Books are marvelous for establishing a reputation. One book could do it. **Sequences** put me on the map. Books are very important. You can't have a reputation without being seen and only can be seen through books or publications.

TD: How has your life changed since the books? Did you do workshops before the books?

DM: I never do workshops. I hate workshops. I give talks. I'll do a one-night stand or maybe stay for a day and a half or something, but I never do workshops. Poverty may drive me into the arms of workshops. I think that the whole workshop thing can become a sort of business, a very facile kind of business where you have a formula. I don't want to be involved. It's not interesting.

My life has stayed pretty much the same. What's happened is that I get invitations to places, have lots of people call me up, get mail from people I've never heard of before and I have people come over here, but essentially, I just keep working the way I worked before. Nothing has really changed.

TD: Have you sold prints as a result?

DM: Sure, I sell more and more, which is nice. I like to make money. It's about time photographers started making some money with their work. I'm so tired of people putting down selling prints as if it were something dirty. It's about time photographers could afford to eat from their own work. Every other field does it. This is the last field, the photographers. What photographer could ever have lived off his work? And how many of them, if they don't teach? I'm one of the very few people who do different jobs. Bruce Davidson does jobs, Lee Friedlander does jobs, but most photographers teach. I think it's marvelous. I hope eventually I can live completely off the work. And I may be able to, when I'm eighty, and eat one meal a day.

TD: Who, if anyone, has been instrumental in your career?

DM: Danny Entin, the guy who lent me his studio, taught me how to use a ligh meter. He's just a marvelous guy — a saint. I still go to see him when I have problems. He's been the most instrumental. I'm very lucky because I'm a good example of somebody who could make a career out of nothing. I never studied with Minor White; I never studied with anybody; I'm completely the product of my own energy and I've never had a major influence; I never loafed with Robert Frank and I never palled around with whomever. I've had lots of help, art directors giving me jobs, people responding to my work, Szarkowski giving me a show at the Modern. That's all help, you can't bunk that, but essentially there was no guiding light, there was no particular person who did anything. I did everything pretty much on my own.

TD: The thing that comes across, to me, about you is that you have a tremendous amount of self-confidence.

DM: I am self-confident, but that's easy at this point.

TD: It wasn't always so?

DM: Well, I'll tell you, the hardest thing in my life was being in the Army. I was a 2nd Lieutenant in armor; I received my commission in quartermaster during the Korean War and I was luckily sent to Germany, and to me, that's the worst, that's the pit, that's the bottom. I hated every minute of it and yet I survived, and I did well, and I've always felt that if I could survive in that situation, I could survive anything. Between the army and cancer, there's really not too much; also I get confidence from my work. From the very beginning I always thought I was terrific, and I think you have to. If you don't think you're terrific, who's going to? It has to start from there, like I'm my favorite photographer. Also it's like the rich get richer and poor get poorer. The more work you get and the more you're seen and the more books you have published, the more work you get, and the more you're seen and the more books you have published. So what you have to do is get the ball rolling and that means getting out there and getting your stuff seen. So it's easy now. I can get almost anything I do, that I like, published, sooner or later, or seen. In the beginning I had to get it moving.

TD: You couldn't at this point, live without commercial work?

DM: I like doing commercial work. I think it's very important for me to do commercial work. I don't do that much. People have the illusion that I do a great deal of it. I don't, but I do enough to live comfortably. I don't want my private work to carry too much of a burden. I don't want to make my money out of that kind of work because then I will have to start producing to make money. I don't want my private work ever to have the responsibility of providing me my income. It sounds very peculiar, but even if I got to the point where I could live without doing any commercial work at all, I would always want to do commercial work. It helps me keep my head straight, it helps me keep myself balanced in terms of the seriousness of my own work; doing jobs are a whole other kind of problem, a whole other kind of exercise. What I feel is a real intrusion into my private sphere, is doing workshops and teaching. It's much more of an intrusion because then I'm really dealing with the core of my thinking and feelings about photography, in a most private way. I'm totally exhausted from doing that sort of thing. Commercial work is exhausting, but it's another kind of solution. It's more of an exercise, it's a nice change of pace. I love to take photographs, that's one of the great pleasures. I enjoy taking photographs.

TD: Could you say something about how your interest in mysticism and religion affects your work?

DM: It affects my life. It's more important than photography; it's more important than anything. Unfortunately I don't live that way, but I think it's the central question. I would rather ultimately be a dilettante photographer and professional mystic than a dilettante mystic and a professional photographer. I use photography very well. Photography is the way I help explain my experience to myself, but mysticism is what it's all about. Everything else is distraction. This interview is distraction; getting published is a distraction; everything is a distraction, and distractions we use to keep ourselves from facing the central issue, the central question. And the central question is: What am I doing here? Who am I? What is this place? and What happens when I die? Next to that everything else is fun and games and nonsense.

TD: And that's what you deal with all the time?

DM: I don't. I'll spend the rest of my life and probably not even then deal with it, but that's the central question for me. The photography business, not business, the cult or the photography machinery — there are words for what I'm trying to say — is not interesting to me. What's interesting to me is my awareness of my life which is just amazing, and my awareness of my death which is even more amazing. So the central question is: What is this place? What's going on here?

TD: When you write on your prints, is it based on dreams and such or is it fictional?

DM: It's just a thought. It's like haiku. It's just an instant. It's like saying: 'The sun came up / I was tired./ A bird sang / I wasn't tired.' It's nothing. I'm not trying to make anything out of it. That's rotten haiku, incidentally, in fact it's not even haiku. I'm just like that.

TD: Are dreams important to your photography?

DM: No. I wish I used dreams more. I'm fascinated with dreams and I only did two sequences on dreams. I'd like to do a lot more. But I'm not there right now, I'm working on other things.

TD: Were you always interested in mysticism?

DM: I was always interested in religion. I was a Catholic and by the time I got out of the army I had pretty much kicked Catholicism completely. I spent my twenties running around getting laid and doing all those things, and in my thirties, once I established my life, got into photography, and got lots of things placed, then the whole thing began to come back. Once I quieted lots of noise out of my life, in the stillness all this important stuff started coming back. So it's always been there, I just put it on the shelf for about ten years, then I took it off the shelf again. I think it's very important.

TD: Basically the way you deal with it is through reading about it and meditating?

DM: I read; I meditate, I would like to do more. There's a big cliche in meditation and mysticism that when the pupil is ready, the teacher will appear. And I think that's quite true. In my work I arrived at sequences because I was doing ideas that I hadn't thought of two years before that. And now I'm doing ideas I hadn't thought of two years ago and I have no idea what I'll be doing two years from now, where my mind will be. It keeps opening.

TD: And you just deal with what you're ready to deal with?

DM: Yeah. The minute you have to force something, it doesn't work. But when I'm there it just flows naturally and I'm quite ready to solve the problem. It's not an effort. When it becomes an effort, when I have to force it, it doesn't work. It really solves itself at that point. When the question is asked, then the answer appears. That sounds corny, but that's a version of what I mean.

TD: What are your plans for books in the future?

DM: I would like to do this new book with new sequences.

TD: Is that what it will be called, New Sequences?

DM: No, no, no. I don't know what it's going to be called. I'm working on a new sequence now called Take One and See Mount Fujiyama which is a very crazy sequence and I thought I might include that in the new book. I might even call the new book **Take One and See Mount Fujiyama,** but I don't know.

**New York City
May 1, 1975**

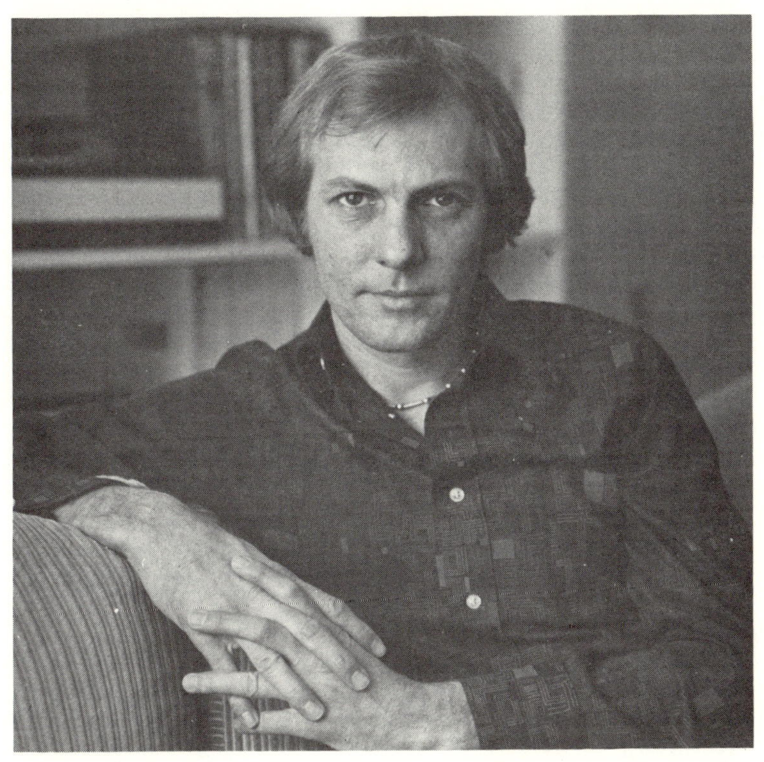

George Tice

Interviewer: Can you discuss the evolution of the process?

George Tice: I'm not that creative a thinker that I have all these unfulfilled ideas. I really wouldn't make it in advertising photography. I don't think advertising is that creative. It's probably the art director's ideas; you follow and complete his thing. For instance, after two years of working on **Urban Landscapes,** there's not a hell of a lot of things I have in mind to do next. One thing is certain, I don't want to get into any big projects. **Paterson** and **Urban Landscapes** are an accumulation of working nine years. I'm just not into that kind of commitment right now. I'm thinking more in terms of designing entire books. I'm not interested in making isolated pictures; I'm more into the whole thing, the typography, the sequencing, the printing, the total thing. **Paterson** evolved out of — it didn't evolve so much. I took a few pictures of rock formations while I was on Garrett Mountain. After awhile I felt I should do it as a series, or a book. I don't understand everything about the process, but something was telling me to do it. There was some motivation; I had to do it, not really knowing why. In fact, I was questioning it quite a bit. It was unlike anything I had ever done. I really didn't know why I was doing it. All I know was, there was a need to do it.

On March 6, 1975, several days after George Tice moved into a new apartment in Carteret, New Jersey, our conversation took place. I knew and was impressed with **Paterson,** which won the Grand Prix du Festival in Arles, France, as the best photography book of the year. During my visit he showed me dummies for **George A. Tice: Photographs 1953-1973** and **Urban Landscapes** which were published shortly thereafter. Tice's achievement in **Urban Landscapes** completely overwhelmed me. To this day, **Urban Landscapes,** like **Paterson,** is not fully appreciated. The interview, tape-recorded, lasted three and a half hours, and two bottles of wine.

George Tice, handsome, tall, well-built, is one of the best organized, hardest working individuals I've ever known. On every visit I've found him printing, doing restoration work, or putting the finishing touches to a print, a portfolio, or a book. A few of the projects he was involved with during my visits includes: a Francis Brugiuere portfolio, and Edward Weston platinum-print portfolio, restoration work on prints by Atget and, on numerous occasions, the making of his book, **Artie Van Blarcum: An Extended Portrait.** In fact, I was visiting George the morning he made the first print, the cover photograph, for that series. It was fascinating to watch that book unfold over a two year period. During subsequent visits, George would show me a few more photographs, then, after a time, transcriptions of interviews which became the text for the book. I consider myself fortunate to have observed George Tice so often, and to the degree of intimacy he allows.

Born: Newark, New Jersey. October 13, 1938.
Attended: Newark Vocational and Technical High School.
Books: 018
   Fields of Peace, with Millen Brand. Doubleday & Company, Inc. New York, 1970.
   Goodbye, River, Goodbye, with George Mendoza. Doubleday & Company, Inc. New York, 1971.
   Paterson. Rutgers University Press. New Brunswick, New Jersey, 1972.
   Seacoast Maine, with Martin Dibner. Doubleday & Company, Inc. New York, 1973.
   George A. Tice: Photograph 1953-1973. Rutgers University Press. New Brunswick, New Jersey, 1975.
   Urban Landscapes. Rutgers University Press. New Brunswick, New Jersey, 1975.
   Artie Van Blarcum: An Extended Portrait. Addison House. Danbury, New Hampshire, 1977.
   Currently: Photographer, Iselin, New Jersey.

Tom Dugan: At one time you made your living from portrait photography, yet in your Paterson book you don't deal with portraits at all.
George Tice: I guess it's because I did that for ten years. Now I've gotten away from it.
   TD: How much commercial work do you do now?
   GT: Very little. The commercial work I do is mostly restoration work.
   TD: You identify strongly with New Jersey.
   GT: I was born here. I live here.
   TD: When you started photographing in Paterson, did you think you'd do a book someday?
   GT: When I was photographing Paterson, people would say, "Why Paterson?" I

spent four years doing that project and I started to question myself, "Why Paterson?" There wasn't a commercial publisher that would touch that book. I didn't know if it would be published or not. I had a book in mind. The picture book is what I'll continue to work out.

TD: Have you ever done any writing?

GT: Not much. I might try using a tape recorder. It's a machine very much like the camera. There's a book that came out about the same time as Davidson's **East 100th Street** called **The Block** by Herb Goro. He used a tape recorder.

TD: How did you become a photographer?

GT: I made a full circle; after 22 or 23 years I'm back where I first started. When I was fourteen I joined the Carteret Camera Club. I had a baby brownie first, then I bought a 35mm Kodak Pony, and began entering competitions. When we moved to Newark I joined a camera club there, too, then transferred to vocational high school and majored in commercial photography. They sent kids there that couldn't make it in regular high school. They weren't very serious students. After six months of vocational school, I was sixteen, so I quit and took a job, in the summer, as a darkroom assistant and I never went back. I worked at that job for only three or four months, when I got into an argument with the printer and quit. After that I held various jobs like stock boy, office boy, and when I turned seventeen I joined the Navy. In the Navy I wanted to get into photography, but I wasn't a high school graduate, so they wouldn't allow me to go to photography school; I was put into Communications. Later some officer managed to get me into the photo lab as a striker which was on-the-job training. I learned quickly and was put on the shooting crew. Everyday I would shoot all kinds of assignments, officers' portraits, accidents, medical photography, anything that came up. That gave me a lot of different experiences in 3½ years. When I came out I went to New York looking for a job as a photographer, but the only thing I was offered were trainee jobs. I wasn't a trainee, I was a photographer. I was always the top photographer, whether I was on a ship or on shore duty. If it was important that a good job was done, I was put on that job, whatever it was. All I was offered were jobs at $40, $50, or $60 a week. I went around for a week and was very humiliated and said to myself, "I'm never going to do this again." I was on unemployment for about a month, then took a job with a portrait studio in Newark for $50. I could have collected $40 a week unemployment, but I was getting bored. I worked there as a printer for about three months and that was enough of that. Next I took a job for $60 a week in a camera shop, selling camera equipment, then I got married again. I was married and divorced first while in the Navy. When I married the second time I knew I had to make some money. I knew I could make more money doing home portraits. I could make $100 a week. I took that as a temporary job and ten years passed. I just kept having more kids and more kids and I was making more and more money, and I was stuck in that job. I would always look in the want ads to see if there was some ideal job in photography. The job I was looking for just didn't exist: Artist-photographer. I found out I had to create this job. All this time, while I was doing this "temporary job," I knew that I couldn't wait for conditions to be ideal to say that I would begin working when this happens or that happens. I would have to do my own work. I worked about 40 hours a week doing home portraits: babies, children, family groups. Then I would work evenings and weekends on my own work. I worked about an eighty-hour week. I got back into the camera club thing and exhibited in salons. I got very into that, exhibiting all over the world in international salons. I built a reputation in that area. I became one of the leading 100 exhibitors of the world. Then I felt that was a deadend. All I had done was accumulate a lot of trophies and medals, maybe a thousand of them. I dropped out of that in '65, moved to California for a while, looked for work there and ended up doing the same thing for less money, but it gave me the chance to do a little photography there. When I came back, instead of working for somebody, I worked on my own, knocking on doors, doing portraits. I did that for a while and the studio induced me to come back. They made me the manager of the studio, so I didn't have to photograph anymore. I was in charge of about twenty photographers. I did that for a few years, then felt I couldn't take it any longer and, at the same time (1969) I was gaining recognition and making some money from my personal work in print sales, magazines, and a few other things, so felt I could make it on my own. I quit my job and just free-lanced. Since that time my personal photography has become my work. I've cut out all commercial work. I won't do anything unless it involves a lot of money or it's something that will coincide with my own photography. If it's something I do as an assignment, then I have to be able to use some of the pictures. Since that time I've been living off my work. Primarily, print sales are my main source of income, along with teaching, book royalties, a few commercial assignments, and some restoration work.

TD: Do you always have to worry about making a living?

GT: Since '69, I've had a certain income from print sales, maybe $15,000 a year.

TD: Is this through Witkin Gallery?

GT: Primarily and, like yesterday, the Schoelkoph Gallery was having a Margaret Bourke-White show and the prints were in bad condition, faded and I reprocessed the whole show. That's something I can always fall back on, restoration work. Very few people know anything about restoration. Without considering myself to be an authority, I am an authority because there are no other authorities. If a problem came up, it was given to me.

TD: How did you get into restoration?

GT: Through Witkin. He would have different problems come up and I'd say, "Well, I'll see what I can do with it." That's been going on for six years.

TD: How did you get into platinum printing?

GT: I saw a show at the Museum of Modern Art that included a few photographs by Frederick Evans in platinum. I thought they were the lushest prints I had ever seen. I started researching. I recall reading at times what different people had to say about platinum printing. Strand, Stieglitz, Emerson. They always spoke of it as the deluxe medium. I felt the same way. They stopped making platinum paper the year before I was born, but why couldn't I make it? It took me about nine months to perfect it. There was nobody to fall back on. It was a matter of just working through trial and research until I finally got it down.

TD: It's definitely a very important happening in terms of your reputation and in earning a living?

GT: Not so much in terms of earning a living; I don't sell that many platinum prints, maybe fifteen or sixteen prints a year. I don't do that much in platinum, just certain, very selective pictures which I choose to print in platinum or palladium. Some people might know of me for that, some people might know of me for **Paterson,** some people might know of me for the book on the Amish **(Fields of Peace),** some people might know of me as a teacher. People know of me for particular things. They might not connect them all together.

TD: Who were some of your earliest influences?

GT: The earliest influences were people in the camera club. I remember in the Carteret Camera Club somebody who made terrific prints. I thought if I could ever get to that stage, that would be super. I remember this one guy whose work I admired, and about ten years ago, while visiting the Cranford Camera Club, I was asked to judge there — here was this guy I held in such high esteem. I was looking at his prints ten years later; they didn't seem like much. I don't know too much about early influences. At some point Weston was an influence, Stieglitz, Weston, and Frederick Evans. But also, I could name Walker Evans, Harry Callahan and Ansel Adams in certain ways. Adams more for technique.

TD: How did you gain a reputation as a master printer? Many photographers have been working as long as you have and they seem to be satisfied to make a good print and not go any further, but you have gone much, much further. Do you feel you have a particular affinity for printing? Is it something that came easy, something that holds a certain fascination for you?

GT: I think it's just being very critical, not having the attitude that that will do, or is good enough. I just try to satisfy myself. A print may be ordered and after printing it, I know that print is satisfactory, quite acceptable, but if I know I can do it a little better, I will destroy the others, go ahead and do it again.

TD: What's your favorite paper?

GT: My favorite paper is Brovira.

TD: What wouldn't you use Brovira for?

GT: I could use it for almost everything. My work falls into little series and each series I print on a different paper. **Paterson,** I printed on a semi-matte paper, rather than a glossy paper, then I gold toned to a bluish color. I feel that the cold blue tones work for most of the pictures in the series.

The Ghost town series (Bodie, California), I print on a warm tone paper like Portiga Rapid because I think that works best for those pictures.

TD: How'd you get into toning?

GT: I tone everything. There are two reasons for toning: 1) image color and 2) permanence. It's getting the precise color that determines the mood and feeling of how people interpret or see the picture. For instance, in this picture, "Oak Tree," I experimented with about twenty different formulas. None of them were precisely what I wanted, some came close, and I ended up double toning it with two different toners to get the exact shade of brown that I wanted, a warm coolness in brown.

TD: What paper is that?

GT: Brovira. I tone it first in Selenium, then in Kodak Brown Toner. There's one on permanent exhibit at the Museum of Modern Art and that's done with Nelson's gold toner. That's how I first toned it.

TD: Why, if you wanted a brownish tone, didn't you start with Portriga?

GT: There are infinite shades of brown, from warm to cool brown.

TD: One thing that is intriquing about photographers is the type of personality that leads one to a career in the medium. When you were growing up did you feel you were outside the crowd or a joiner?

GT: My first 15 years were spent traveling the country in a trailer. My step-father was an itinerant barn painter. We moved about every four to six weeks. I missed a lot of school and was always the new kid at school. This was my mother's background. We were called "travelers", originating 'way back from the time of caravans. We were a mixture of Irish, Scottish and gypsies; we lived in trailer camps. I did feel that I was apart. If you are an artist you look at things a little differently. You might not know you're an artist, but there's something that sets you apart from other people, how you feel about things, how you see things. You know your friends don't see things that way. I decided when I was fourteen that I wanted to be a photographer and I haven't changed my mind on that. I have had to discipline myself, channel my energy into photography. While there are other interests I could have, I feel there is only one thing I can really do well. You can't be a man of all talents. So I put all my eggs into one basket — photography.

TD: How did you come to settle down after traveling for 15 years?

GT: At different times we stopped the traveling life and would take an apartment for as long as a year. I left home when I was seventeen.

TD: Do your people continue to travel?

GT: They have at different times since I've been married.

TD: Do you consider yourself a socially-concerned photographer?

GT: I'm concerned about the things I photograph. When I was photographing the Pennsylvania Germans, I was concerned with documenting what was there, that this was a passing way of life. It is passing. They're moving out of Pennsylvania. The price of land is now so high, it's not practical to farm it. My concern was getting it down — recording it.

TD: Do you consider yourself a documentarian?

GT: In a sense. I'd say I do pictorial documents. You do your thing, and under that guise, you could say I documented Paterson, N.J., but people who have seen the book and have been there, didn't recognize anything. It's very much Paterson. This is the record that is left behind. My photographs are what future generations will look back on, what Paterson, N.J. was, which is only what I chose to document.

TD: In Paterson, **you used an 8 x 10 view camera for the landscapes and a 35mm SLR for the candids, and in printing you use a variety of materials and techniques. Do you consider yourself a Rennaissance Man in photography and was it necessary to master the medium so thoroughly?**

GT: I suppose I never thought about it that way, or at least not lately, but there was a time when I approached a job and felt that even though this wasn't my thing, I could do it. I've touched, in some way, every phase of photography. I was thinking the other night about my experience in aerial photography, making photographic maps, shooting at intervals at different altitudes and going over shooting sequences and taking those pictures and assembling them into a mosaic. All this expertise I have in this area, how do I use that now?

TD: You did that in the Navy?

GT: Yeah, you can't go up to a certain altitude and just photograph down, there are clouds in the way, so you do it at a lower altitude. The wind blows the plane a little and roads don't meet and you're stretching paper and your paper shrinks. You have to process all the paper the same way so it all shrinks the same way. It was a very specialized thing. But to get back to your question, I suppose the answer is yes.

TD: Do you still use 35mm?

GT: Yes, for certain things. What I've been doing for **Urban Landscapes,** is all 8 x 10, but I think I'll use 35 for the next book. There're certain things that you can do with an 8 x 10 that you can't do in 35, and vice versa; a different way of seeing. I think I've had enough of cities and suburbs after finishing this project.

TD: Did you do Fields of Peace **in 35mm?**

GT: 35 and 2¼, about half and half.

TD: At what point did you get into 8 x 10?

GT: 1967.

TD: How did that come about?

GT: I first got a 4 x 5. I guess it was because of (Paul) Caponigro. I had my first show at the Underground Gallery, and he came to the show and felt the work was very close to view camera photography in approach. After all, a 2¼ camera, which I was using mostly, is kind of a compromise between the 35 hand camera and the view camera. Most of my subjects are static, they weren't going to run away. It wasn't the spur of the moment type of thing, they're all very studied and I had time to set a tripod up. He put me in touch with somebody who had a 4 x 5 camera for sale. I bought it and, this was in '65, but I couldn't get used to using it. I had used it in the Navy for certain things, but I couldn't get used to using it creatively. First of all, it was hard to figure out the swings and tilts. I really didn't begin to use it until about two years later. I worked with it one winter doing the ice series, and that's the only thing I did with it. I was making only contact prints, then I got a 4 x 5 enlarger and started enlarging them. After I enlarged them I felt something was lost so I bought an 8 x 10 camera; that was in '67.

TD: You also print your 8 x 10 by projection?

GT: Yeah, now I do. I didn't until I became Steichen's printer. His negatives were 8 x 10 and whenever I would get a job I had to rent a darkroom with an 8 x 10 enlarger. I started getting a lot of jobs and thought I may as well buy an enlarger. I never had any intention of enlarging my own work, but after he died I had this enlarger so I got into making 16 x 20 prints from 8 x 10 negatives. I used to make everything in an 8 x 10 format or smaller. A big print to me was 11 x 14, but the 16 x 20 prints were really superb.

TD: Is isolation necessary for your work? Do you simplify your life, try to keep it uncomplicated?

GT: I think you have to make time for what is most important to you. In fact, my life is very complex. For the first time since I was nineteen years old, I'm living alone. It's a whole different thing that I'm adjusting to, I'm sure I'll change with it, I'll be affected by it. Being married, with a house full of kids, my darkroom was an escape hatch, where I could shut myself off. It's a little different, quietier; I do whatever I want now.

TD: Psychologically, do you consider yourself a well-integrated person, and does it matter?

GT: My life has been full of problems. Maybe mine more so than a lot of people because I've had more responsibility at a younger age, like just the fact that a lot of people call me Daddy. I have five children. That's a lot of responsibility. It was difficult initially because I had no education. I wasn't a high school graduate. Making it was a long range thing. Now I'm as much into my personal life as I am into my artistic life. I had very little personal life for twenty years. I was willing to make all the sacrifices for my photography. I'm no longer willing to do that.

TD: Why?

GT: Because a lot of the goals I have attained. I'm getting more into myself. My work is affected by my personal life, whether I work or I don't work. I don't, as far as photographing, work that hard. I would say if you averaged out the last twenty years that I might photograph one day a month, which isn't a hell of a lot. If you averaged out the last few years when I was working more, maybe I was photographing two days a month. Maybe I would get two or three pictures a month. I'm just after one picture a day. The last picture I took was December 30. I've been going through a separation, finding an apartment, moving, buying furniture and waiting for it to be delivered. It's going on three months since I've made a photograph, but in the meantime, I'm still absorbing things. I wrote four notes the other day of things that flashed into mind, things that I want to photograph. (Reads) "Oil tank on New Jersey Turnpike in Bayonne heading toward the Holland Tunnel; view from where my

Aunt Esther lives in Elizabeth; view of houses and apartment buildings by Weequahic Park in Newark; dairy sign with cowheads on Morris Avenue in Hillside." I've been writing photographs, and it's a creative thing. I consider it preliminary exploring. This is the way I work anyway. I don't necessarily go around with a camera. I go around looking quite a bit.

TD: Is success important to you now or was it at one time?

GT: It's important. Success itself is very important. It's important for me right now that I continue to be successful, otherwise I can't make child support payments, pay the rent, exist. From an ego point of view, it's not as important because I'm less dependent on what other people think of me; I'm really indifferent to what others think of my work — whether they like it or not. I'm really not affected by it. I'd like them to like it, just like you'd like someone to like you as a person, but if they don't like my work, it doesn't matter because I know what I'm doing.

TD: At what point did it no longer matter?

GT: I never really did try to please anybody. I always did what I wanted to do, I was always headstrong. The only thing that was really important was what I felt was important. I discovered that, at some point, while in the camera club. I was accepted as an equal member with people whom I revered.

TD: What kind of feeling is that? Did you know that someday you were going to be there?

GT: I never doubted that. This, for me, (points to his monograph) is a culmination, very much a milestone. This is really what I worked for. I knew that someday there would be this sort of thing: (reads) **"George A. Tice — Photographs 1953-1973."** I didn't know when this something would come about. It might have taken longer than it did. I think things were very slow starting out and I didn't know if it would be in my own lifetime; historically the acceptance of artists is after they're dead or very old. Renoir said he was getting the best beefsteaks when he didn't have any teeth to chew. It's satisfying to still be relatively young and to have achieved a measure of success. But I worked for it. That wouldn't have come about if I didn't put myself in a position for it to happen.

TD: Do you feel any animosity toward anybody, people who didn't give you a chance as you were coming up?

GT: I think I'm able to place myself in photographic history. I know just where I stand as a photographer. I'm rather obscure in a way; I'm not in the Weston, Steiglitz, Steichen category.

TD: Where would you put yourself in the history of photography if you finished today?

GT: These things change. Just because you're in at this particular time doesn't mean you're in for good. There are people who are in and out of art history. I was thinking about St. Christopher recently. He was in for a couple of thousand years and now he's out.

TD: He's no longer on dashboards?

GT: He's no longer a saint. It's really the taste of the people who write books on photography, critics, the people who teach photography, people who buy pictures. People are really just beginning to be discerning in photography.

TD: Do you think it's harder to make it today than it was 20 years ago?

GT: Today it's accepted, today you can make it as an artist. You couldn't make it as an artist when I came into photography. The rewards are much greater today, but the competition is much stiffer.

TD: You were talking about your method of working earlier; you do a lot of

looking for photographs without your camera. How do you do this? By driving around?

GT: Yeah, I drive around and leave my mind open, wait for some kind of impulse, some sort of recognition, then when that happens I follow through.

TD: Do you see the composition at that point or do you wait until you go back with the camera?

GT: I might see it at that point if I stop and consider everything — lighting, when I might take the picture, if it's night, daytime, different seasons. With this new work, I've gotten very much into different kinds of light: artificial, twilight, three-o'clock-in-the-morning kind of light, the different qualities of light, so my range is greater. It's more a 24-hour time rather than just early morning or late afternoon.

TD: Do you do any color work?

GT: No.

TD: Have you ever?

GT: Just on assignments.

TD: You never felt challenged by color?

GT: I don't like the medium. I don't like it as a print medium. As a reproduction medium, it's O.K.; as a color slide medium, it's fine; as a print medium, I don't like it.

TD: Do you use the Zone System?

GT: No.

TD: What are some of the important picture books and have any of them inspired you? For example, in reference to Paterson, **how do you see William Klein's books,** Moscow, Tokyo, Rome, New York; **Paul Strand's books; Robert Frank's** Americans?

GT: I don't know that much about William Klein's books. I recall seeing a couple of his photographs. I don't think I've seen any of the books, except maybe the jackets. Strand's book, **Tir A Murhain,** is a very fine book. You could break it down to a formula: landscapes, interiors, close-up portraits, full-length portraits, nature. I like his approach to picture books. It's thorough. **The Americans** is a classic. I can appreciate it more in recent years than I could when it came out. I remember when it came out. There was a two-man show, Harry Callahan and Robert Frank, at the Museum of Modern Art, in about 1960. I was very enamored of Callahan's but I didn't think too much of Frank's work. But in time . . .

TD: He's gotten better.

GT: I suppose at the time I was trying to improve my technique and Callahan seemed very concise, organized and balanced, whereas Frank's work was haphazard and crude by comparison. But his overall statement — the content of the book, is very impressive. I think it's very important.

TD: Were there any other picture books that meant something to you through the years or do today?

GT: **Let Us Now Praise Famous Men** is also a very important book, but as a collaboration. It's as important because of Agee as it is Walker Evans. The finest photography book that has been made is the Harry Callahan book (El Mochuelo 1964 edition)

TD: How does the creative process work for you?

GT: It has changed. I used to go out and just look and see and photograph. Working with the 8 x 10 isn't that process at all. Shooting is no accident. The accident doesn't enter into my work at all today. It's all there or it's not there. Today I get more ideas than I used to. I used to have to really see something. Now I can have an idea and go out and look for that idea in reality. I think that's more what I meant. Like now I'm very attuned to what I'm looking for and when I see it I recognize it.

TD: Then you go back with your camera or you have your camera with you?
GT: Either way. It could be either way.
TD: Why did you focus in on Paterson?
GT: I've come to the conclusion it doesn't matter where I work.
TD: The book could just as well have been South Orange, New Jersey?
GT: Sure. There will be definite reasons why you choose something, like why you choose to photograph one house and not another house, why one factory and not another factory. There are definite reasons, but the place really doesn't matter. I've learned that in really looking at New Jersey, working all over, in different places. I did choose Paterson because it was isolated, set in a valley, apart from other areas, and even has natural areas — Garrett Mountain, the Passaic Falls, and historically, it's important. Paterson was the great hope of this country. It was important then, but it's no longer important. I think what distinguished it primarily was the natural areas around the city. Newark, Jersey City, Camden are something else. I could have worked anywhere.
TD: How did you get involved in Urban Landscapes? **Is that an outgrowth of** Paterson?
GT: I felt I finished **Paterson** prematurely. There was more that I wanted to do.
TD: That's interesting because I was just going to ask if you did the book today, how would it be different?
GT: **Paterson?** It would be different; the scene would be different. It would be different because I would be doing some of the things that I've done in **Urban Landscapes.** I think the differences between **Urban Landscapes** and **Paterson** are: qualities of light, times of day, and night, and more on the suburbs, not just the city.
TD: You don't think that Paterson **would satisfy you today. You would go right into** Urban Landscapes **and skip** Paterson?
GT: No. I wouldn't say that. No, that's what got me into this. It's all sequential.
TD: Can you discuss the evolution of the process?
GT: I'm not that creative a thinker that I have all these unfulfilled ideas. I really wouldn't make it in advertising photography. I don't think advertising is that creative. It's probably the art director's ideas; you follow and complete his thing. For instance, after two years of working on **Urban Landscapes,** there's not a hell of a lot of things I have in mind to do next. One thing is certain, I don't want to get into any big projects. **Paterson** and **Urban Landscapes** are an accumulation of working nine years. I'm just not into that kind of commitment right now. I'm not interested in making isolated pictures; I'm more into the whole thing, the typography, the sequencing, the printing, the total thing. **Paterson** evolved out of it — it didn't evolve so much. I took a few pictures of rock formations while I was on Garrett Mountain. After awhile I felt I should do it as a series, or a book. I don't understand everything about the process, but something was telling me to do it. There was some motivation; I had to do it, not really knowing why. In fact, I was questioning it quite a bit. It was unlike anything I had ever done. I really didn't know why I was doing it. All I knew was, there was a need to do it.
TD: How did the process conclude? Under a deadline?
GT: In the publishing. The photographs were due April 30. There was a last ditch April photograph in there and that was it.
TD: Were you satisfied or could you have continued?
GT: I was generally satisfied; you're never really satisfied. You can do more if you had to, or do it better.
TD: How did you edit your work as you went along? At what point did you start to

bring the Paterson series together?

GT: I print as I go along. I'd go out and photograph and proof everything I shot. Then I'd either accept or reject it. If I accepted it, I'd make a fine print. I don't try to focus the whole thing in, like beginning and end. When near the end, I think about how it's all going to fit, see if I've done what I set out to do. Then I'd consider what's missing. Like at the end of **Paterson** there wasn't much I'd done on interiors, so I did a few to round it out. This is basically where I'm at with **Urban Landscapes** now. I could turn it in today and say it's finished, but I prefer to work up to the last minute. The ideas that I'm getting now could go into another book. At some point, you have to say you're finished. This book I've tried to perfect more than any of the others.

TD: How do you do the dummy of the book?

GT: Well, I'll show you. In this book (**George A. Tice — Photographs 1953-1973**) I used photostats because there were larger pictures and scaled down smaller pictures, like those two are 6 x 8. **Urban Landscapes** is going to be reproduced actual size 8 x 10, same format as **Paterson,** so here (dummy) I use my 8 x 10 proof prints, which are very rough prints.

TD: And design and layout you're also doing now?

GT: Yeah. Before I was turning it over to a designer. It's not the right way. I'd like to have total control. If I could get on the presses and print this book, I would do it.

TD: Did you feel you were losing control of a particular part of the book and that's why you wanted to get into the typography?

GT: Yes.

TD: Is this a major commitment now? Is this the way you're going to make your statements from now on?

GT: As far as I can see. I feel that making a book is like a director making a film. You can't work on something for several years, then have somebody else visualize, sequence and scale it. It becomes too much their thing.

TD: Do you feel you lost control of your other books?

GT: In other books, I did have a good designer. The same man designed the first three books, Earl Tidwell. **Fields of Peace; Goodbye, River, Goodbye; Seacoast Maine.** The printing was at best only adequate. The best was **Fields of Peace** and what I didn't like about it, I changed in the second edition, which was printed by another publisher. There're maybe eight pictures I eliminated from the first edition and replaced in the second edition and I made a few other changes, things I didn't like. But I think you can always do that, like this monograph was printed in a very small edition, only 2250, so if this sells out and it goes to press again, I won't change much; but there are certain things that I will change. I always try to improve a second printing.

TD: Did you design the monograph?

GT: I worked three months designing it, narrowing my work down to 121 pictures and relating one picture to another.

TD: What book got you into designing?

GT: **Paterson** did. I went from a big publisher, Doubleday, who has an art department, to a small university press, Rutgers, who has no art department or designers. At the time I turned in the work, I didn't care how they did it. I did envision the format of the book; it should be printed with a cold blue ink, because the pictures are bluish, they should be reproduced full size, and the titles should be under the pictures. The only thing I made a decision about was the first picture and the last picture, and they said, "Well, look if anybody is going to design it, you should." I really didn't want that responsibility, but I took it back and I sequenced it.

It took me quite a while to make those decisions, about a week of looking at the pictures until I couldn't look at them anymore. You might get so far into sequencing a book and maybe you can remember the first ten pictures and then try to follow through. It's like trying to memorize a dozen numbers in your head, there's only so far you can go. Trying to keep track of the whole flow of things is quite difficult. With the exception of the type, I designed **Paterson** and it won an award for design among university presses. After that I took a course on book design at Parsons with Ricky Levinson and I learned about type primarily. I knew enough about pictures, primarily about type, taste in type, scale, so I felt competent enough to do the whole thing. This is the first book I had full control of: selecting the paper, the ink, and sitting with the presses while they're running.

TD: How did you switch to Rutgers University Press? Did you first go to Double-day?

GT: Yeah, and they rejected it. They felt it wasn't a commercial book and I knew that before I went to them; they're in business to make money. The university press has a different attitude. There are certain books of value that are not going to make money. For example, Rutgers did a book on vegetation of New Jersey. A book like that, if it sells a thousand copies in five years, is doing OK, but it's still important to the thousand people who buy it. A commercial publisher is only going to think in terms of a minimum five thousand sales. If they can't see a market for five thousand, it has no commercial value.

TD: So when they rejected you, what did you do?

GT: I just felt that Rutgers University Press might have a different attitude, not that I knew a lot about them. They were New Jersey based and might have an interest because my subject matter was New Jersey.

TD: You knew of Rutgers University Press?

GT: I saw an ad for a couple of their books which were on New Jersey. One was a tour guide, places to go in New Jersey, and I knew they had done scholarly books as well. It was William Sloane, who just died, who was responsible for having **Paterson,** my monograph, and **Urban Landscapes** published. It comes down to individuals.

TD: Rutgers immediately accepted the book?

GT: Well, he did, then he had to convice the press council. When a university press does a book, they're spending taxpayers' money. There's a press council, trustees of the university, who decide where the money is spent, so that they don't go into the red. This is a problem when working with a university press, also it helped that Bruce Davidson's book was published by Harvard University Press. Mine was, in a way, a similar kind of book.

TD: How many copies of Paterson **have been sold to date?**

GT: About two thousand.

TD: Were you satisfied with the distribution?

GT: No, no, that's a disadvantage of a small publisher. Doubleday has two salesmen for each state; a small publisher might have two salesmen for the whole country.

TD: Why don't they distribute through Light Impressions or some such distributor?

GT: That's an idea I think they should pursue. I'll talk to them about it.

TD: With whom did you discuss the Paterson series as it was unfolding?

GT: I showed it to Peter Bunnell, who was at the Museum of Modern Art, after I was into it about a year. I showed it to Caponigro; Szarkowski saw it. They were encouraging.

TD: What did Bunnell think of the series?

GT: He didn't feel that strongly about it, but his remarks were favorable. Something generated, more or less, after it was published. I got a lot of reactions from people.

TD: Did he think it was publishable?

GT: I don't know. I showed it to Mike Hoffman and initially, he felt *Aperture* should publish it. I showed him, after a year's work, maybe 25 pictures and when I was almost finished I showed it to him again and he felt very indifferent toward it. He felt I hadn't really captured the spirit of the place, which immediately turned me off to whatever he had to say. There have been a lot of very favorable reviews and letters that I've received. *The New York Times* did five separate reviews. It got a lot of publicity, but with all the acclaim that it's had, it doesn't go hand-in-hand with the sales.

TD: What did Caponigro think of it?

GT: Caponigro is very perceptive. He wanted a few of the prints. He felt it was good for me to do. A lot of people think you should look at things not as ends in themselves, just as steps along the way. "Well, this is good for you to do because in time . . ." I was always confused by that. What I was doing was meaningful without going beyond that. He thought it was good for me to do.

TD: What about Szarkowski?

GT: I'm not sure what he thought along the way, because when talking with him, I don't completely understand him. I can understand him reading him — articles he's written, but talking to him, I don't completely understand him. Afterwards he wrote a couple of very moving things. He wrote me a letter and said people whom I will never know, generations to come, will appreciate this work more than I realize, that it was a very moving work of art.

TD: Who else responded after publication?

GT: Berenice Abbott; Brassai; Walker Evans, I heard from through other people — different critics.

TD: What did Abbott say, for example?

GT: Abbott wrote me that it's a good book. She hopes it receives the recognition it deserves. There are so few fine things done that she hopes it's recognized.

TD: What about Brassai?

GT: Brassai called me his professor in photography and gave me one of his books and autographed it that way.

TD: Which book did he give you?

GT: His monograph and he autographed, "To George Tice, my professor of photography." And (Ralph) Steiner has written several letters to me. I don't know, I'd have to go through the file.

TD: What about Walker Evans?

GT: I only met Walker Evans once. *Art International* did an article on Walker Evans and myself, comparing me to Evans. I heard from a student who met Evans, that he knew of my work and liked **Paterson.**

TD: From the beginning it was pretty clear that you were doing a book on Paterson?

GT: Very near the beginning, after an initial period of photographing.

TD: How many photographs were there in all?

GT: Approximately 120.

TD: And there are 68 in the book?

GT: Sixty-six. There were 120 - 8 x 10 negatives. I used about 60 - 8 x 10 negatives and about six 35mm shots from three or four contact sheets.

TD: Was anything cut out of the book or included in the book that bothered you?

GT: No, they gave me complete freedom. There are a couple of pictures that I excluded from **Paterson** that I put into **Urban Landscapes.**

TD: Why did you exclude them?

GT: I felt they didn't fit.

TD: Did you consider, at any point, using more text in Paterson?

GT: No. I didn't consider writing myself but, at one point, I thought the only way I would get it published was with a text. When I did this work I was not aware of William Carlos Williams major poem "Paterson," but after I was into it I learned of his work. Being conditioned to the idea that picture books could not exist by themselves, as picture books, there had to be a text — that's how **Fields of Peace** came about — I thought to get it published, it had to have a text and thought this might be a good text for it. Two independent works on the same subject. I had written to Williams' publisher, had met his wife, and she approved, but my editor felt that it wasn't necessary.

TD: How did you decide on the structure of the book?

GT: I felt that because I was using an 8 x 10 camera, they should be reproduced the same size, so the camera used determined the structure.

TD: Did you make a conscious decision not to include portraits?

GT: Well, there are portraits, street portraits.

TD: Yes, but how about formal portraits? You didn't see a place for them in the book?

GT: There could have been, but I chose to use people just passing on the street. In this book (**Urban Landscapes**) I'm just using people as stick figures, so there's even less emphasis on people than there is in **Paterson.**

TD: Did you work longer on Paterson **than you had originally intended?**

GT: No, I wouldn't say that. I didn't know how long it would take.

TD: When did you approach a publisher?

GT: When it was 90% finished.

TD: Were you surprised when Doubleday turned it down?

GT: No. I was just giving them the first option on the book. I thought they would turn it down, but since they published my other books, they had first option on the next.

TD: How did you sell the book to Sloane?

GT: I called him up and told him what I had. They hadn't done any picture books before. Most publishers don't have much experience with picture books. Their background is in publishing texts, but he didn't turn it down on the phone; he told me they hadn't done this before, and would look at it. He felt it was very important and should be published. There are things that you can do in a photograph that can transcend writing, the information is there, open to interpretation. You don't have to write three chapters about it, if the audience is perceptive enough to interpret that information.

TD: Would you have considered self-publishing?

GT: Only in the form of a portfolio.

TD: Were there any problems, other than distribution, with the publishers?

GT: They are slower. It took about a year to get the book out. No, no significant problems.

TD: How long did it take to assemble the dummy?

GT: Since I didn't do the type, about a week sequencing.

TD: Specifically what statement were you making about Paterson?

GT: I don't want to be specific. This is what I see and what I want you to see. There has to be a certain amount of room for someone to go his own way with something. You can't tell someone what he's looking at, what he should see, what he should get out of it. It's not that simple; what you aim to do with it, I think, is very clear photographically. But there are not that many people who can read images. Those who can, are very fluent that way; they know what you're doing. But for others who aren't used to doing that, I would prefer to remain somewhat vague, not so precise, about what I'm doing.

TD: You said that criticism, negative or positive, doesn't bother you one way or the other.

GT: I'm affected by it. I feel elated that so-and-so liked my work or singled out some of my pictures, or brought down by the fact that they didn't, but it's not going to change what I'm doing, my way of photographing.

TD: Do you learn anything from it?

GT: Sometimes. There have been some very perceptive reviews, especially of **Paterson.** There have been some very good reviews of it, but not very good in a complimentary way — just perceptive. Some of the things that I simply did, became a little clearer, did make sense. What I couldn't quite say in words, they were able to say in words, what I was doing in pictures.

TD: Has Paterson affected your reputation?

GT: I think with everything you do you enlarge your audience. **Paterson** is still a very obscure book. Yes, it has affected my reputation.

TD: So obviously you haven't made money on the book?

GT: Not a lot of money. I get royalty checks, every six months or so, for a couple of hundred dollars.

TD: What kind of deal did you get from Rutgers?

GT: Standard contract, 10%.

TD: What's the greatest satisfaction from doing such a book?

GT: Just having the thing exist as a book, even if it was just one book. It doesn't matter if it's ten thousand books. Like doing a portfolio, I've done four limited-edition portfolios, limited to 50 copies, and each one had 12 original photographs. Before I do an edition I do one prototype, one trial portfolio. That's very creative and you're very into doing this one thing, then after you do that one thing you say, well, that's it. Now you have to do 50 sets. The other 50 are just labor. The whole creative act was doing the first one.

TD: How much do they sell for?

GT: They vary. They're less when they're issued. The first one I issued at $75. Two are exhausted and two are still available — one has only four or five left — for $200 or $250 which is reasonable.

TD: Who sells them, Witkin?

GT: Primarily, I have a couple of other outlets out of the city, but Witkin, primarily. New York is primary.

TD: Is that a 60-40 thing?

GT: Right.

TD: Who has been instrumental in your career? Who has helped you; recognized you?

GT: I would say the editor who published my first book, Ken Robbins. He first brought my work to the attention of Doubleday when I was exhibiting work in his mother's gallery in East Orange, New Jersey. Witkin has done a lot to promote me and bring my work before the public. Right now it's his sixth anniversary show, he's published a sixth anniversary portfolio of reproductions, and 200 of the portfolios have an original print of mine. He's done a lot for me. I've helped him out, he's helped me out. We work well together. Phyllis Masser was responsible for my having a one-man show at the Metropolitan Museum of Art (New York).

TD: Do you have dealings with other photographers and do you count photographers as your intimates or friends? Whom do you have contact with?

GT: I have a lot of acquaintances in photography. I'm rather aloof as far as friendship goes. I know just about everyone in the New York area. Most photographers are males, most of my friends are females.

TD: How many of the Paterson **series have you printed in platinum?**

GT: About a dozen, maybe less, maybe ten.

TD: When you print in platinum, how many prints do you make?

GT: One.

TD: And you sell it?

GT: When it sells, I make another one usually.

TD: How often do you print?

GT: About two days a week.

TD: Eight hour days?

GT: Maybe six. I'm in the darkroom more often than I'm shooting.

TD: Do you enjoy printing more?

GT: No.

TD: Does it get tedious at all?

GT: It can. I've organized things a little differently now. The whole photography market has changed. There are certain prints that sell. If I do a hundred prints in a book, maybe there're 15 that will sell consistently, maybe there're another 15 that will sell one or two, then there are 60 that never sell. They won't sell because I don't print them. I feel they should be in the book, but I don't choose to exhibit them, or I don't think people will buy them. I tend to print for a show what I think is the best of my work. So if I'm doing something now, I'll make a half dozen prints from a negative if it sells, rather than going into the darkroom and printing that negative on three or four different occasions. I'll try to print it one time, so when I come to print it again a year later or so, when those prints are exhausted, it won't be just work, I'll enjoy printing it.

TD: Are they all archivally processed?

GT: Yes.

TD: How do you process?

GT: The definition of archival processing is full development, using an acetic acid bath, two fixing baths, hypo-clearing bath, toning, gold, selenium or sulfide toning, washing in an archival washer, drying on plastic screens and mounting on all-rag mount board. That's standard procedure for me.

TD: What does the future hold for you now?

GT: The future is probably more of the same. I don't think the future will be drastically different for me. I'll choose a project and I'll do it. It will be a book or a show or a portfolio, or all three.

TD: How did you get into teaching?

GT: In the summer of 1969, I was asked to teach a workshop in Aspen, Colorado, and did. Of course, I had no experience in teaching, but after that, I was asked by Ben Fernandez to give a course at the New School for Social Research (New York City). Right now I only give one course, but I have given different courses in different places. In the summer, I give workshops in different places. It varies. I have been giving a workshop up at Apeiron (Millerton, New York) for about five years now. Last summer, I gave a workshop at Ansel Adams' Yosemite Workshop; this summer I'll give a workshop up in Maine. Plus I do a few weekend workshops.

TD: Do you always teach platinum printing?

GT: No. The emphasis is always on the print. This is the area where I have the most to offer in teaching. The primary reason people choose me is to improve their printing.

TD: Can you teach someone to be a great printer?

GT: I can teach them to be a better printer.

TD: What's the formula for being a great printer? Can anyone be a great printer, if they desire?

GT: No, I don't think so. Can anyone be a great photographer? It takes taste, sensitivity, dedication, commitment, whatever the ingredients are for being a great photographer, I think it's the same that makes one a great printer.

TD: Can you be a great photographer and a fair printer?

GT: Sure. You can be a great photographer and a poor printer; and vice versa.

TD: Do you have to be a good printer if your medium is picture books?

GT: No. You'd have to be a better printer if you're exhibiting. There's a great deal that's lost. If your prints are just fair, then reproduction can be to your advantage. For instance, with Brassai, you look at his monograph, which is printed in gravure, and they're clean; you look at his prints and they are very crassy by comparison. They're ferrotyped glossy, they need spotting. Same with Cartier-Bresson; his prints come off better in reproduction.

TD: Do you anticipate this when you're making prints?

GT: I make the same kind of print whether it's for reproduction or exhibition, which is the best print I can make. I don't make a better print specifically for reproduction.

TD: Can you make a better print from contact or projection?

GT: You don't get the same kind of print. It depends what your criteria is. If you consider the contact print the ultimate then any degree of enlargement is a disintegration of the image. If your print requires control, you have more control dealing with an image that is projected than you do with a contact image, but my prints don't require much control.

TD: Are most of your prints contact prints?

GT: Mostly.

TD: You dodge and burn-in or whatever, when printing by contact?

GT: Yes, but there's very little to do.

TD: How do you meter?

GT: Average.

TD: A reflected light meter?

GT: Um. hmm.

TD: You don't use a spot meter?

GT: No.

TD: Is there anything in your technique that is different from others?

GT: Photographing or printing?

TD: Both.

GT: In photographing, it's different in so much as 90% of the photographers use a 35mm camera, some other use 2¼, 4 x 5, 5 x 7. But it's a very small group of photographers who use an 8 x 10 camera. That isn't any great achievement in itself, but there are few people who are working with that kind of patience. It requires a great deal of discipline.

In printing there are a few people working like myself. There are others whom I consider to be fine, but probably they approach the print differently. They definitely approach the negative differently.

Like Caponigro. I would definitely consider him to be a fine printer. I've known him for ten years or so, and in making a negative, we use different systems. He uses the Zone System, I use an average kind of system. I place more emphasis on control in the print through different grades of papers. Maybe all his things print on the same grade of paper, very few don't. I do know that he prints differently. Some people just control things arbitrarily, they automatically dodge shadows and burn in highlights. My approach is that I only do what I absolutely have to do as far as interfering with the gradations of the negative; I'm only going to interfere if it's going to improve it. If the negative will print just by dropping it in the frame and pressing the button one second, and produces a fine print, well, that's great because I made a fine negative. That's what I aim at, making things print as simply as possible, without a lot of control.

TD: How many sheets of paper before you make a good print?

GT: I usually have my final print by the third print. I make a test print and one trial print.

TD: You just look at the density or take a reading?

GT: No, I judge the contrast grade. I aim for a #2 paper which I usually get. If I don't, it's usually a #1 or a #3. It'll go one way or the other. From eyeballing the negative, I know what the contrast range of that negative is and what grade of paper it should go on.

TD: Why didn't you get into the Zone System? Wouldn't that simplify things for you?

GT: No, it would complicate things for me. I feel it's a very complex system. I've always been poor in mathematics, like beyond adding, subtracting, multiplying and dividing — it's just something I have no talent for whatsoever — I don't function mathematically. If I had a need for it, if I felt that I was not achieving what I wanted, then I would learn and master the system, but I don't have that need.

TD: Do you think if you were starting today you'd study it?

GT: I don't think so, not speaking against it. There are people who need a very super-precise approach to things and a lot of them really get into that thing as an end in itself, to produce so many zones in a picture or something, and they get off on that. They lose track of what they're really doing, and what they're really doing is making pictures. I would prefer to simplify my way. Perhaps it's simple to somebody who has been working in it, but to me it seems a very complex system of exposure and development. Every step requires a great deal of testing and after twenty some years as a photographer, I've done a lot of testing, and I know pretty well the materials that I work with, what they can do, what they can't do.

TD: What film do you use?

GT: Tri-X. I used to use Panatomic-X as well, for different reasons, but today I just use Tri-X, in all formats, from 35mm to 8 x 10.

TD: What cameras do you use?

GT: I have a couple of Pentaxes; I still have a Rollei; I have a little view camera, a 2¼ x 3¼ Plaubel which I shoot roll film with, and I have an 8 x 10 Deardorf.

TD: What about lenses?

GT: For the 8 x 10, I have three Dagor lenses, wide-angle, normal, slightly telephoto. And for 2¼ x 3¼ I have three Schneider lenses, wide-angle, normal and not telephoto, but long focus which provides better coverage than a telephoto. In 35, the same thing; there's nothing extreme. I try to avoid the distortion that wide-angle lenses give you, what it does to space and foreshortening. What it does to space has nothing to do with my photography, that bizarre effect, so I avoid that, I only use moderately wide angle lenses like 35mm. I dislike the telephoto effect too, the compression of things, so I only use moderately long lenses. My telephoto is 135mm, so there's nothing extreme, just one side of normal and the other side of normal, slightly long and slightly wide.

Carteret, New Jersey
March 6, 1975

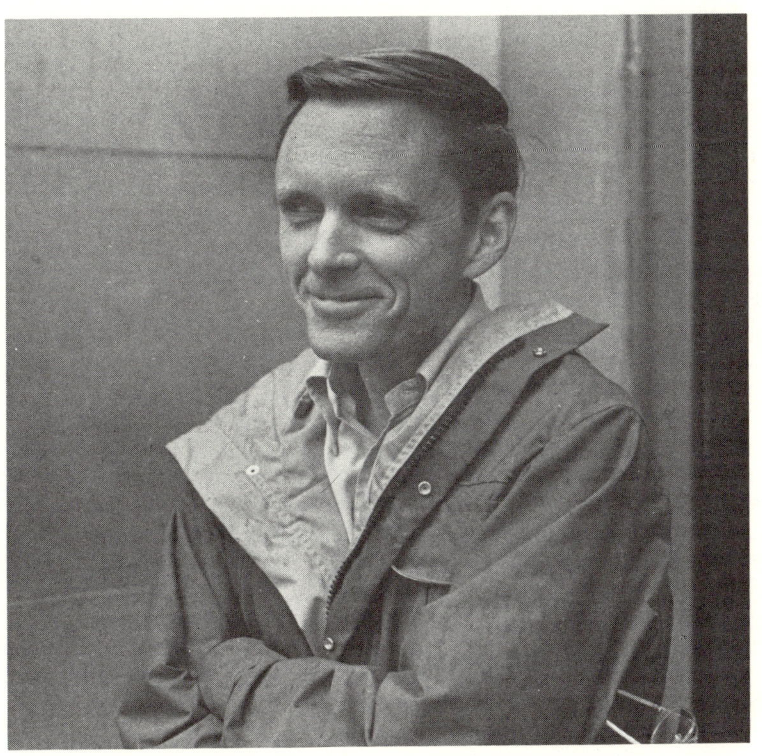

Robert Adams

Interviewer: Basically, is that how you've lived? You haven't done any commercial photography?

Robert Adams: I've done a bit of practically everything, but I found that, for me, the commercial work destroyed the center, the good work. I couldn't feel the same way, even about my equipment, after I'd done some banal assignment. I didn't love the camera the way I had to, to take a good picture. And it took a terrific amount of time to do the commercial assignments. I'd invariably have to dump all the chemicals I used to do serious work in order to run through some stupid 20-shot roll of 35mm. I decided I'd be better off to go back and endure the faculty meetings if it came to that.

When I learned he planned a trip to New York, I phoned Robert Adams at his Longmont, Colorado home and we made arrangements for an interview. I knew his books, **The New West** and **Denver,** and looked forward to meeting the maker of these remarkable documents. The tape recorded conversation, which lasted two hours, took place in the late evening, October 6, 1977, in his room at the Stanhope Hotel on the upper east side of Manhattan. I sent him a copy of the transcription and he reworked it, noting, "At the risk of shocking you, I've done quite a bit of revision.... Some places in the original... I either didn't answer your question or answered it vaguely or redundantly, and in yet other passages I just seemed boring even to myself. So I cut and added." In fact the essence of the interview remains, and certainly the spirit of our talk is unaltered.

Robert Adams presents a person as austere, mysterious and disciplined as his finest landscapes, with a genuine sense of modesty, tinged with a fine edge of sharp humor. Obviously he is a man with a mission, guided by deepest concern and an intense intelligence. Above average height, lean, youthful, clean-cut, he is, if anything, as involved and driven as he appears and, at the same time, careful to be fair and a gracious, friendly host.

Born: East Orange, New Jersey. May 8, 1937.
B.A.: Redlands College, Redlands, California, 1959.
Ph.D.: University of Southern California, Los Angeles, 1965.
Books:
White Churches of the Plains. The Colorado Associated University Press, 1970.
The Architecture and Art of Early Hispanic Colorado. The Colorado Associated Press in cooperation with The State Historical Society of Colorado, 1974.
The New West: Landscapes Along the Colorado Front Range. The Colorado Associated Press, 1974.
Denver: A Photographic Survey of the Metropolitan Area. The Colorado Associated University Press in cooperation with The State Historical Society of Colorado, 1977.
Prairie. Denver Art Museum, 1978.
Currently: Photographer, Longmont, Colorado.

Tom Dugan: How did you get involved with photography?
Robert Adams: It was a mixture of wanting to get out of teaching and wanting to make pictures like the ones that first opened my eyes — pictures like Ansel Adams' "Moonrise," Walker Evans' "Bethlehem, Pennsylvania," and several by Dorothea Lange and Timothy O'Sullivan.
TD: You had no involvement earlier?
RA: No.
TD: Were you visually-oriented?
RA: I'd for a long time sketched and done lino cuts, things like that.
TD: You attended college in southern California?
RA: At a small school, Redlands.
TD: And you were an English major through to a Ph.D.?
RA: Yes. I wanted to be a college teacher. Until I went to my first faculty meeting. (laughs)
TD: Where did you teach?
RA: At Colorado College, a private college of about 1500 students, in Colorado Springs, really a very good school. Probably the main difficulty there came for me in the late 60's when they had to raise their tuition so high that the background of the student body changed. I could look out my office window and see the parking lot filled with Porsches, and realized that the students had more money to fool around with than I did to eat. It was hard to live with.

TD: Were they bright?

RA: Yes, they were good students and the standards were high.

TD: You taught literature?

RA: And a little bit of film history and theory.

TD: Were they parallel interests?

RA: With literature, yes. I'd for years been almost more interested in film than literature. Godard I think even had something to do with shaping my later visual concerns. Or rather Godard's cameraman.

TD: Do you admire any of the documentary filmmakers? The Maysles, Fred Wisemen?

RA: I know a little of the work to which you're referring, but not a lot. The only filmmaker that really stands out for me now — Ozu — is of course long dead, though it is only in the last few years that I've come to know his work. "Tokyo Story" is, I think, on a par with the best of Shakespeare and Rembrandt.

TD: Are there any influences now that you are conscious of?

RA: Weston's and O'Sullivan's work means a lot to me. And Lange's, although only a certain aspect of it is directly relevant to what I'm doing now. And a bunch of painters — Cezanne, Hopper, Whittredge. Beyond that, the most important voice in photography is, to me, John Szarkowski's. **The Photographer's Eye** and **Looking at Photographs** are simply the best things that have been written in our field.

TD: Being out in Colorado, do you see a lot of work?

RA: I see about as much as is probably good for me. I'm not a scholar. The work that interests me the most is work that is close to what I'd like to do.

TD: You have been identified with the Urban Topographers, people like Stephen Shore, Frank Gohlke, Joe Deal, Nick Nixon. How do you feel about that?

RA: The term is too narrow to encompass all our sins. And it suggests a scientific attitude that, in truth, most of us I suspect don't feel.

TD: Are they, nonetheless, the people whose work you look at?

RA: I certainly watch what they're doing, yes. I know Nick perhaps the best of any of them and I admire his pictures very much, especially the ones with people. He's doing something very difficult.

TD: Which other contemporary photographers do you particularly admire?

RA: Mark Tobey once objected that "it's not possible for a painter to be fair to another painter. I have," he said, "something inside me and that's what I'm looking for, no matter how hard I try to be sympathetic to something different." Can I use that as an excuse?

TD: Was there anything in your childhood that led you ultimately to photography?

RA: Not, I think, to photography, but my father's love of the outdoors is, I'm sure, the basis of my concern for the landscape. He was a patient and enthusiastic teacher about streams, animals, trees. It was natural then that through high school and college I did lots of hiking, camping, river running. I worked for the Forest Service, the Park Service.

TD: As a child were you a loner?

RA: I think that anybody with any sense is probably not right in the swim of things. I spent a lot of time alone, although I also have a lot of good memories of playing baseball and the rest. It was a pretty normal childhood, for that time at least.

TD: Where did you grow up?

RA: The first ten years of my life in Madison, New Jersey, a small town not far from the Great Swamp. Then our family moved to Madison, Wisconsin for five years, and then on out to Denver.

TD: Over the past summer I read Gail Sheehy's Passages **in which she stated that adults go through certain stages and undergo a series of crises. Did you change careers in such a time of crisis? She says that 30, 35, 40 are when most people undergo some radical changes in their lives. How old were you when you became a photographer?**

RA: I was 28 when I got my Ph.D. and it was about then that I began to suspect that I ought to change.

TD: Was there a period of years when you were unsure of going one way or the other?

RA: Yes, because the financial implications of the change were so bad. I'm married and, at that time, my wife had only a part-time, non-professional library job. I certainly wasn't qualified to earn an adequate living with anything other than my degree.

TD: How did you ultimately resolve it?

RA: We haven't. We're still living on the edge. My wife ultimately earned a master's degree, which enabled her to get a professional librarian's job, which has been crucial. And I started doing some lecturing and some free lance editing. My parents have helped, and there have been grants.

TD: What grants have you received?

RA: Money to do the book on Hispanic architecture came from a local foundation. Centrally, though, an NEA and a Guggenheim. Those were wonderful.

TD: Basically, is that how you've lived? You haven't done any commercial photography?

RA: I've done a little bit of practically everything, but I found that, for me, the commercial work destroyed the center, the good work. I couldn't feel the same way, even about my equipment, after I'd done some banal assignments. I'd invariably have to dump all the chemicals I used to do serious work in order to run through some stupid 20-shot roll of 35mm. I decided I'd be better off to go back and endure the faculty meetings if it came to that.

TD: So when you photograph you now just do your personal work?

RA: That's right.

TD: Do you sell your prints through Castelli in New York?

RA: Yes.

TD: How did your involvement with them come about?

RA: Through Lewis Baltz. He already was represented by the Gallery and suggested that it could be a profitable thing to investigate.

TD: How did you come to know Lewis Baltz?

RA: He phoned me one day from Los Angeles and suggested I might like to participate in a show out there. I eventually went out for the opening, despite not feeling too well, and he and Mary Ann took A-1 care of me. They're good friends.

TD: Did you know him when he reviewed The New West **for** Art in America?

RA: Yes. And what a welcome review that was.

TD: How well has the book done?

RA: If you mean commercially, the books have all been disasters. The first two, which dealt with historical subjects and are not important photographically, were the only ones to make any money. My arrangement on **White Churches** was for a royalty of 15%. The run was 2500 copies, and I suppose I might have made $1,000 thus far. For the book on Hispanic architecture, the work of locating the subjects and taking the pictures — work rushed through in six weeks — was paid for by the

Boetcher Foundation in Denver, and part of the printing costs were underwritten by the Colorado Council on the Arts. My royalties are 10%, and I've made a thousand or so. For **The New West,** the arrangement is that I'm not to get royalties until there is a second printing. The first printing is in fact nearly sold out now, but there is no likelihood of a second printing because of economics.

TD: Why?

RA: The math is grim for any book selling fewer than five thousand copies. The production costs for **The New West** — just the printing and binding of 1400 copies — were $13,000. The distributor then had to have the book for 35% of its retail price. You can see that just for the book to break even, with no royalty to me and no profit to the publisher, the book would have had to sell for about $30 a copy. Which meant, of course, that it wouldn't sell. So to arrive at a reasonable price the Press had to assume a substantial loss. It was a very courageous thing for them to do. The director of the Press, John Schwartz, an old style bookman notable for both his idealism *and* business acumen, had to make up the deficit on other books. The Press is one of the smallest university presses in the country, and yet they did it, for which I will always be grateful.

TD: They also did your next book, Denver.

RA: The financing of **Denver** was easier because the production costs were underwritten by the NEA. Among other things, that enabled us to bind some inexpensive paperbacks which we could sell within Colorado to a more general audience. Frankly, the National Endowment (for the Arts) has been crucial for me. But I think that is true for many people working today. Where, in fact, would photography in general be without their support? To take just one beautiful example, we'd be without **The American Monument,** Lee Friedlander's book. Some of those pictures have the calm of old tragedy. The book is worth the whole bicentennial and then some.

TD: How do events in your life affect your personal work? Do you photograph every day?

RA: No. When I print, for example, it's about a twelve hour process, and when the last print is through the wash, that's the day. There are also many times when the weather is wrong. Or my spirit is wrong, that happens, too.

TD: Are you project-oriented?

RA: Yes, I find it difficult to do more than one general kind of work at a time.

TD: Are you aware of an evolutionary process in your work?

RA: I've changed several times, though whether that is evolution I'd be a fool to say. The style of what I was doing changed some between **The New West** and **Denver,** and it has again since **Denver.**

TD: In what sense?

RA: I'm photographing land forms at the moment, and they're not, in some senses, as cold as the suburban scenes.

TD: But Lewis Baltz has written that "What distinguishes Adams from most of his photographer contemporaries is the distance, both emotional and intellectual, that he maintains from his subjects."(Art in America—**March/April 1975**).

RA: Well, I hope there is still the distance, because it implies a search for Form beyond social disaster, but I also hope the distance is not passionless. I do know this, the experience of taking them is occasionally an emotional one, like hearing a good song.

TD: Do you foresee a day when you'll be able to make a living without relying on the NEA?

RA: (laughs) I assume the NEA hopes so. And so do I, although it's discouraging sometimes. Frankly, I've come to the conclusion that there is not to be certainty in this business. All I know is, if I'm anything, it is a photographer. If I have to stop photographing, it won't be the end of the world, but I certainly will not be doing what I am supposed to be doing.

TD: How well do you sell through Castelli?

RA: It varies. The arrangement hasn't been going long enough for it to be apparent what is happening, but there are sales, both to museums and to individuals, and they're picking up.

TD: How long have you been with them?

RA: About two years.

TD: Have you done any portfolios?

RA: No, I haven't, but we're talking about it.

TD: How important is success and how do you define that term?

RA: (laughs) Well of course one wants to eat, which is a primary kind of success. And then, beyond behaving decently to others, one wants to try to report on what one sees.

TD: Do you feel neglected thus far?

RA: Oh, no.

TD: You feel you've gotten your due?

RA: Lord, what's one's due? "Use every man after his desert, and who should escape whipping?" Besides, art history is filled with deserving people who never found a sympathetic audience. The odds are bad. One would like, of course, to sell like Ansel Adams. But by and large I feel lucky.

TD: Is isolation necessary for your work?

RA: I think sometimes it helps. It's very easy to spend your time talking about photography, and kid yourself into thinking that talking about it is doing it.

TD: Do you try to keep your life uncomplicated so you can work?

RA: I try, but it's hopeless of course. People are, after all, complicated. And the fact is that photography relies on somewhat involved technology. I finally gave in recently and bought a small nitrogen burst processor to do 4 x 5 film. It's complex, with almost limitless possibilities for breakdowns. But it does give you even development.

TD: How did you get involved with books? How did your first book, White Churches of the Plains, **come about?**

RA: That evolved just as I was beginning to photograph. My wife and I suddenly discovered the great flat land east of where we were living. Colorado is half prairie and half mountains, and we were living right on the dividing line. We'd pile our stuff in the back of the truck and go out for several days. It was great.

TD: Is it primarily a picture book?

RA: The essay is better than most of the pictures. Though I hope the pictures are competent — a few of them I think are even better than that. At any rate, I don't regret doing the book. Many people have enjoyed it, and I've enjoyed the people. The history of the design of **White Churches** is a little sad, however. It was supposed to be a clean, austere book, but it fell into the hands of an imperious designer and production supervisor in Santa Fe. I had a commitment that the book was to involve no bleeds, nothing was to run into the gutter, and so on, but I didn't know enough to distrust her. You have to be rudely suspicious sometimes.

TD: Do you feel that discussion of your work is important? Reviews, showing your work to other people, etc.?

RA: Yes, I read reviews, and I show work to a few people that I respect, but, at some point, in order for it to be my work, I have to make the decisions.

TD: How much attention, via reviews, have your books received?

RA: Well, of course, one would like to get reviewed on the lead page of *The New York Times Book Review.* But that turns out to be the next game after you publish, to get reviewed. Small press books aren't much reviewed, mostly, I suspect, for economic reasons.

TD: Are you satisfied with the distribution of your books?

RA: Distribution is in many ways *the* problem. If it were better, the unit cost could drop and many things would improve. If I said I was completely happy with Light Impressions, I would be lying. But I'm sure what they'd say is that they do all they can for the amount of money that they can earn back from their efforts. The most depressing fact about the book business is that most book stores order by formula, by computer. The manager doesn't sit down with a copy of *Choice* or *Afterimage* and say, "Gee, that sounds interesting, I'll order that." Instead he relies on standing orders with big publishers for, say, fifteen copies of every mystery that a house puts out.

TD: You develop and print as you go along?

RA: Yes.

TD: How structured is your concept from inception?

RA: It evolves.

TD: Was The New West **a book idea from the beginning?**

RA: No, it was not, nor was **Denver.** With respect to the latter, for example, I had the Guggenheim for a year and I knew I wanted to photograph the appearance of Denver, smog and all, so for a year I went and just photographed. I've never taken so many pictures in my life. At the end of the year I printed them up, and then my wife and I went to an unused room in the city library for several weekends and just studied the results. We tried many different kinds of organization before we finally decided on the sequencing we used.

TD: How many pictures were there?

RA: To work from, 300 maybe. Many of those could be culled out quickly. but some couldn't. I've still got some orphans I feel tender about.

TD: When you speak of sustained viewing, how do you view them?

RA: There are frames up around the house, of a standard size, and I mount my work prints, if they're respectable. I don't feel confident about most pictures unless I've looked at them a while. That's partly because the kind of view that I think lasts is one that looks natural and easy, and distinguishing such a picture from a failure can be hard. So I like to look at them when I'm coming in with the groceries, or whatever. I want to catch myself off guard. The trouble is that I remember so clearly the beautiful subject, or my numb hands, or the dark cloth slipping away in the wind. You want so much for the thing to work.

TD: At some point, did you have an interest in architecture?

RA: Yes, I did. I took a year course in architectural drawing in high school, of all places. The course consisted of designing and drawing plans for two houses — heating plans, wiring, everything. I learned a lot, and have kept reading and looking around ever since. When we were in Europe my wife and I spent most of our time in Scandinavia looking at new towns and old churches. And at several unforgettable new churches around Cologne by a man named Rudolf Schwarz. Nobody seems to know of him over here, but I've never experienced buildings like those. Someone said they re-established the orthodox definition of a church as the "container of the uncontainable,'' and they did.

TD: So it seems natural that you photograph what you photograph?

RA: I guess it is, and it's also natural that I find suburban America a pretty distressing place.

TD: Are you hopeful at all?

RA: No, I'm not. It seems to me that as long as the economic system is what it is, very little is going to get better. I live in a town of 35,000 people and we have over 300 realtors. That's 300 people working full time for land development with no restraints, selling houses no matter how ill-built.

TD: At what point do you approach a publisher?

RA: Only after I have a fully developed idea. Never bring in a fragment.

TD: What has The New West **meant in terms of recognition?**

RA: It has been important. A relatively limited number of people see an exhibit. Of course a great many people see an exhibit at the Museum of Modern Art — it has been surprising to me the number of people I've met over the years, even on the West Coast, who happened to have been in New York during the exhibit I shared with Emmet Gowin in '71—but books reach out to an even wider audience. And it's an audience for whom I have a natural inclination. I educated myself as a photographer from books.

TD: So books are a way of getting work out, a calling card?

RA: The primary motivation for doing books is the same as for taking the pictures: to tell the truth about the landscape. Which is not to deny that the tactics of winning an audience are important, but it's easy to forget that the tactics aren't the end.

TD: How did the show at the Museum of Modern Art come about?

RA: I had shown John Szarkowski and Peter Bunnell work once.

TD: How important was that show?

RA: To me, very important. They did a beautiful job. It was a major experience in my life to be able to go and see the work immaculately displayed, carefully sequenced. Among other things, it gave me some confidence that I actually was a photographer, something about which I felt terribly vulnerable. So many people had made sacrifices. It's one thing to muck up yourself — you can even pass that off for heroics — but another to waste other people's sacrifice.

TD: Do you feel your books have made the statement you wanted to make?

RA: Imperfectly. There are some pictures I'd like out, and some others in, but it's done.

TD: What do you think the most difficult aspect in putting a book together is?

RA: Honestly it's all difficult — finding the money, figuring out the typography, sequencing the pictures, doing whatever writing is necessary.

TD: Do you ever go dry for ideas?

RA: Sure, there are times when I don't know what I'm doing. At the end of the Guggenheim year I felt as if I wanted to rest a while.

TD: Once you reject a picture, do you ever resurrect it?

RA: Every once in a while you find something that you've dismissed earlier.

TD: Do you ever go back over your past work?

RA: Yes, there are lessons to be learned.

TD: How often do you send new pictures to the Gallery?

RA: Irregularly.

TD: Do they have a schedule for you to show?

RA: No, though I suspect they would like to have a show every year or two. Unfortunately I just don't work that fast.

TD: How important are the technical considerations to you?

RA: They can be very important. If your film is unevenly developed, for example, you've lost. That's been the worst plague. It took me about a year to learn to develop 120 film evenly. I do it in a rather cumbersome way — in shallow, open tanks — but it's the only way I've ever found to get clear north skies. So, in that sense, technical problems are important. But I'm not interested in darkroom niceties that don't relate to print quality, or permanence. I don't like to experiment. The simpler things get, the better. I just changed from D-76 to D-23 and even the nuisance of making it up makes me edgy. I'd rather be out.

TD: If you could afford it, would you let someone else do it?

RA: The film developing, yes, if they could meet my standards. But not the printing, except maybe the labor of taking prints through the hypo and on out. Printing is basically something the photographer has to do.

TD: Are cameras important?

RA: Yes, you've got to have more or less the right one for the job. As a student of mine said to me once, "If you look at the world through a hole in a cookie, you're going to get crumbs in your eye."

TD: Do you feel right with the 4 x 5 now?

RA: For what I'm doing now, yes, the format and size are right, though the Sinar I've had for about ten years has gotten to me. With tripod and holders it comes to maybe 30 pounds. Hiking up and down mountains with that leaves me good for only an hour or two of seeing. So I've been using a Nagaoka, a little wooden Japanese camera.

TD: Do you ever work in color?

RA: No. I have some interest in color— I can conceive of some things I'd like to do in it— but I cannot see any way that I can afford to have the lab work done that would enable me to control it enough to succeed.

TD: You haven't had portfolios published in magazines like *Popular Photography?*

RA: Pop Photo is a disease. I think it was Ben Shahn who said that one should look at it once, very carefully, and then try never to take pictures like that.

TD: How about *Camera?*

RA: I sent them pictures, but it was like dropping the stuff down a well.

TD: Do you have any plans for another book?

RA: I'd like the new 4 x 5 landscapes to come together as a book, but it would have to be bigger and the reproduction better than in the previous ones. It's not a matter of going precious — the pictures just wouldn't make sense otherwise. All of which means money, and I haven't a guess how to get it.

TD: Are you making bigger prints now that you're working in 4 x 5?

RA: Yes, they're 8 x 10 and sometimes 11 x 14.

TD: Is your work known in Europe and Japan?

RA: That reminds me of Stephen Daedalus dreaming of having books in all the great libraries of the world. (laughs) I've no idea about Japan. (laughs) I think a few people in Europe may have come across some work. It has, at any rate, been shown in Switzerland, England, and Scotland. But I think really that the subject matter that interests me is hard for anyone other than an American to understand and value. You have to know the place firsthand.

TD: What has been the most negative criticism you've received?

RA: The review that hurt the most was the first one, the one in *The New York Times* on the occasion of the show at The Museum of Modern Art. Gene Thornton didn't discuss the pictures, except to dismiss them as cold and sterile. What he did do was attack people whom he thought photographed simply to further their academic careers. Apparently he saw that I had a Ph.D. and assumed that I was an art teacher. He had just been appointed *The Times* photography critic, and people read him.

TD: How do you bounce back from something like that?

RA: Slowly. But friends are the answer, of course.

TD: Is there a tendency not to read reviews?

RA: No, I read them.

TD: What else do you read?

RA: Maybe three or four novels a year. Walker Percy, Jane Austen. It took me about ten years to get over the effects of graduate school, but I really like to read again. I like poetry a lot — Ammons, Graves, Wilbur, Corman. And the essayists — Matthiessen, Hoagland, McPhee, Hellman.

TD: What about magazines?

RA: *Art in America, Exposure, Afterimage, The New York Review of Books, Nation, Commonweal, The New Yorker,* and occasionally quarterlies like *Hudson Review.*

TD: Do you go to movies much?

RA: Not nearly as much as I once did. The seventies are a dreary time with the spectacular exception of "Annie Hall," which I greatly loved. It's wonderful when a director can tell the truth and make you laugh at the same time.

TD: What are your immediate plans for the future?

RA: To survive. (laughs) I've got a little show coming up at the Denver Art Museum, which involves a small book called **Prairie.** And I've just been lucky enough to be included in a pilot project for American Telephone and Telegraph. They're seeing if they can develop a photography project to mark their centennial next year. It's enlightened — we're free to do whatever we want. Maybe the best part of it, from my perspective, is that it will pay enough so I can be out on the road and not be reduced to eating junk food and fighting for the last cheap motel room. Just to be free to work, you can't ask for more than that.

TD: Could you discuss your use of light? Is your favorite a shadowless light?

RA: Stieglitz said it, I think— "Wherever there is light, one can photograph." When you're feeling good, that motto is right. Any kind of light is exciting, if you're not too tired to recognize it.

TD: You don't pursue a certain light?

RA: Only in the sense that landscapes are typified by certain kinds of light. As you know, Denver is now usually covered by smog, so when you're trying to tell the truth about that landscape, you have to try to tell the truth about that atmosphere,

TD: Do you photograph at night much?

RA: I did last summer. It turned out to be hard on the nerves — drunks, suspicious police, beer bottles thrown from passing cars, and hard on the eyes — the glare is bad. But the results can make it worth the trouble.

TD: During the day, how do you work? Do you note scenes and return to photograph, or do you go out searching with your camera?

RA: I note promising areas, but I do a lot of walking. I walked hundreds of miles of city streets that Guggenheim year, for example. A car is good only to get you to the general vicinity. Matisse said somewhere that "in a car, one shouldn't go faster than five kilometers an hour. Otherwise you no longer have a sense of the trees." That's the problem.

**New York City
October 6, 1977**

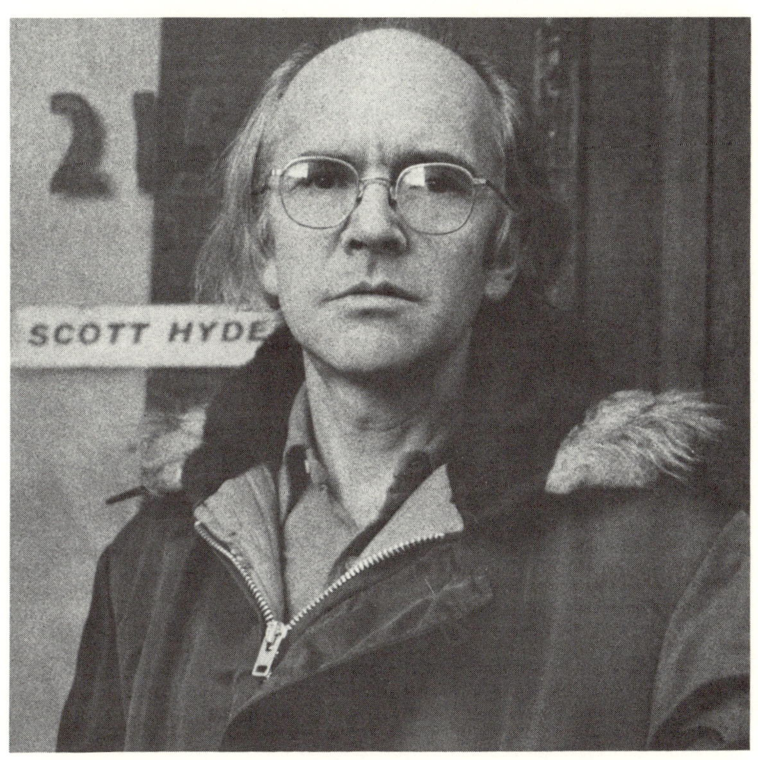

Scott Hyde

Interviewer: Could you discuss the CAPS Book **from idea to finished book?**
Scott Hyde: I've wanted to publish a multiple for a long time. Offset lithoraphy is my medium of first choice, but it's expensive to get on the press with a multi-colored picture. Once on the press, the thing will crank out pictures at such a tremendous rate that the cost per picture is small. It might cost a minimum of several hundred dollars to have a color picture printed, but if you've generated a couple of thousand pictures, the cost is less than a dollar a picture. I've always liked the notion that a picture could be made for less than a dollar. I like bargains; I like things cheap. I'm always saying they don't call me Scott for nothing. I went for grant money to do this; I've gotten several grants over the years. This last one is the only one that resulted in a book. Every other time, I was so poor that I couldn't afford to use the money to publish a book. I did manage to get it together and make that book, but I've been dreaming of doing it for years. The notion of a book is so difficult, so time consuming, and takes so much concentration over such a long period. It is harder than it looks. It's very nice to have it finished and in hand, and the viewer's role is

very much easier than the maker's. The viewer can appreciate a book in a few minutes to a few hours time. The guy who made it has spent hundreds of hours getting the thing together. That sustained work, having nothing to do with making pictures, is the toughest part of doing a book, for me. It's so much more fun to spend your time making a picture than making a book, which is not a picture. It's only the desire to see your work in a cluster, and the possibility that maybe it will be financially rewarding.

Just before Christmas, 1976, I talked with Scott Hyde in his storefront studio in New York's lower east side. I had visited him a number of times to talk and look at work. We would often have coffee and a snack at a small eatery, The Bini-Bon, on 5th Street and 2nd Avenue. I had seen Scott's **CAPS Book** at Lee Witkin's Gallery and Joan Lyons had mentioned it, with a suggestion that I visit Scott. The tape recorded conversation lasted three hours and we have gone over the interview on a number of occasions, mostly for clarification and readability. Initially Scott described his methodology by discussion of a picture not included in the **CAPS Book.** We later decided it would be more interesting if he addressed himself to one of the pictures in his book.

Scott Hyde, tall, lean, intense, exudes a great deal of nervous energy, and seems incapable of sitting still. He's always working on either a commercial assignment or his personal work, and is extremely involved in everything he undertakes. Although he denies an intellectual preoccupation, he derives enormous satisfaction from discussion on a myriad of subjects. If his methodology was not so time-consumingly complex, (if he made silver prints, for example,) his output would be simply prodigious.

Although the **CAPS Book** was originally intended as an unlimited edition, Scott Hyde had declared the edition closed as of June, 1978. He will not reprint these pictures in offset lithography or any other editioning medium. However, he does reserve the right to hand-make unique prints by the Kwik Print or gum bichromate methods. Consequently, the edition is an unnumbered, unsigned, limited edition. Scott is not sure how many copies are in print, but he believes somewhere between two and three hundred. Only about 75 copies remain and are available at $60 per copy.

Born: Montevideo, Minnesota. October 10, 1926.
Attended: Art Center School, Los Angeles, California, 1944-45; Art Students League,
  New York, N.Y., 1947-49; Pratt Graphics Center, New York, N.Y., 1970.
Books:
  CAPS Book. Privately Published, 1975
Currently: Photographer, New York City.

Tom Dugan: How did you get involved in photography?
Scott Hyde: My father was an amateur photographer and I took my first pictures when I was in grade school. It looked like the perfect instrument to capture the likeness of my girlfriend. He taught me vaguely how to print, showed me how to use the enlarger, and I tinkered with it a little. But I didn't get hooked on it until a neighbor across the street, who ran a big portrait studio in Portland, Oregon, hired me to learn darkroom printing. I was 16 or 17, the beginning of World War II, 1942, or 43, and everybody was going. They'd just lost their second printer and thought if they trained a 16 year old, they'd have a guy for two years at least. I learned so slowly,

just hung out with the women who were working in the darkroom, so they fired me. They weren't good teachers, didn't demand that I learn. By then I had a taste for photography, I liked the looks of it, and got a job in a big commercial studio. That gave me my early conditioning towards commercial photography. I was an assistant, helped carry the cases, delivered the pictures, and swept the floor. There were probably twenty employees, the biggest commercial studio in the Pacific Northwest. There was one quite noted photographer there, Ray Atkinson, not known today but, in the 30's and 40's, a well-known name in the photo magazines. He did calendar-type scenics, not as good as Ansel Adams, but he was very popular. It was good experience because he was successful. When I finished high school, I was such a poor student, and disliked school so intensely, I couldn't stand the thought of going on to college, which my parents had anticipated. That summer I was looking through one of my father's photo magazines and saw an ad for The Art Center School in Los Angeles. It's a school similar to the School of Visual Arts (New York), a commercial art-oriented art school. I went to my parents and said, "Here's a school I could imagine going to." They called on the phone instantly. The next day I left for Los Angeles; the term had started the week before. The school was so eager to take in students, being the beginning of the war, and dying on its feet, they let me come down and enroll. I was on my way.

TD: How long did you study there?

SH: I spent that summer and came back to Oregon for my 18th birthday to see whether I would be drafted or not. I was not. It was 1944 and Oregon, being a state full of healthy farm boys, didn't want me. They had all these healthy kids by that point. Earlier in the war they were taking anything that walked, but the services were well filled and could be more selective. Guys with poor vision and flat feet like mine, were being rejected. So I went back to Art Center and took a second semester. The school was still not functioning very well, due to the deprivations of the war and there wasn't much point in taking more than a year's schooling there. Second and third year students were very much on their own and the training was very piecemeal. I lived in Los Angeles until 1947, odd-jobbing.

TD: As a photographer?

SH: Yes, working nights mostly. I worked in nightclub darkrooms. It was a popular thing in those days for girls to run around with Speed Graphics and flash guns and take pictures of the patrons. There were those of us who worked in the basement darkrooms, banging these picutres out in five, ten minutes time. Also I worked nights for about a year in an offset printing plant as a platemaker, and made my first experiments with graphic arts materials, didn't follow up on them, or show them off much, but became familiar with Kodalith film, what it would do, and how swell it was for making solarizations. I had met the editor of *House & Garden* magazine in Los Angeles and when I came to New York I went to work for them, and for various other home furnishing magazines, and have free-lanced ever since.

TD: Did you ever return to school?

SH: When I came to New York I went to the Art Students League, and studied drawing. I always liked to draw, often forget about that, but went five nights a week for a year, just drawing the whole time, in pencil and charcoal. I never got into painting much, not in school anyway. I've done some painting since, and watercolor and pastel; I never liked oils. I also went to Columbia University and took a course in Art Materials for Artists. I always liked to be grounded technically, and thought it would be interesting to study the materials of art, not take art training as such. I figure you have to learn to be an artist on your own, but it's good to know the art materials. Ralph Mayer, who has the best book on art materials, offered a course. I learned all about pigments, vehicles, grounds, oils, waxes, paint, paper, canvas, and other art materials. A fascinating course, though I did discover early on in the course that he was standing in front of the class and reading out of his book. One could read the book and hear everything he had to say; what you couldn't get from the book was to see him work with the materials, the show-and-tell part of the course. At the end of the course we ground some oil paints, made some pastel crayons, worked with some of the materials, and made some of the materials of art.

I took a one-week intensive course from the Leica Technical Center, in the late 50's, that was quite interesting. I bought a Leica in 1950 and found I kept trying to do 8 x 10 pictures with it. I'd look at my contact sheets and say, "Now that one would be nice if I'd done it with a big camera." I wasn't using the camera for what it was intended and also the quality of the pictures wasn't very high. I learned Rodinal in that course, and I've used it ever since. I like it because it's a long scale developer. It's grainy, not a fine grain developer, but it keeps up the film speed and it's soft working.

TD: Do you see a conflict between the commercial work and the serious work?

SH: No, not anymore. I appreciate the commercial work as a means of earning a living. I did in the beginning, used to put it down. When I first came to New York I was a poor commercial worker. I did the work proud with resentment. Having tried to earn money other ways, such as teaching, I now appreciate commercial photography. I don't like teaching, tried to do it for ten years and never could get my head around it, so I have an appreciation for commercial work as a way of earning a livelihood. I think also I've matured and have the feeling that it doesn't much matter what you do. When you're dead and gone, it won't matter what you did. Somebody said yesterday, "Your pictures are the thing that matters, and when you're dead and gone, that will matter." I said, "When I'm dead and gone, the work won't matter to me, so what I do today doesn't matter." I have a much more Zen approach to things. If you do what you do with full concentration, commercial work is the same as artistic work, which is not an attitude I fully live, but something I intellectually believe, and hope to feel someday. I get a lot more enjoyment from doing good commercial work now, than I did, and it gives me actual satisfaction to do a good job. I'm not a capitalist. The purposes to which the work is put don't attract me, or appeal to me. That whole side of commercial exploitation of consumers, of which I am a part, doesn't attract me; but, God, I can't get into that whole moralistic thing. I would like to earn my living selling good pictures, selling the pictures I do on my own assignment, as against somebody else' assignment, but I don't.

TD: Of what influences are you most conscious? Who has influenced you and who influences you now?

SH: I'm probably as much influenced by painters as by photographers, which shows in the work. People see my work and say, "Is this photography?" or "This isn't exactly photography," or "Is this really photography?" The artist who has had the most influence over many years, though I don't spend much energy thinking or working towards his work now, is Paul Klee. It's that flowering creativity, everything he touched turned to Art; Picasso, for the same reason, that flowering creativity. But, of photographers, my favorite is Edward Weston. I don't think he was the most gifted who has ever lived. I think Steichen and Stieglitz were both more gifted as artists. What I admire in Weston is the devotion of his life to photography. Those two guys were always sidetripping. Steichen was once into painting; he was a personality; he was the Commander in the Navy; he was the fashion photographer; and he was the head of the photography department at The Museum of Modern Art. He was always into things other than photography, and the same with Stieglitz, always with the writing. They were power trippers, influential people. The need to be influential kept getting in the way of their photography, whereas Weston didn't seem to need to be influential. He just needed to be an artist. And while it's meaningless, maybe even destructive to replay a life, I wish Stieglitz had devoted himself to photography with the devotion that Weston did. The results might have really been stunning.

TD: Do any of the people working now move you?

SH: They're very fine photographers, though they don't have much influence on me, my work, my development anymore. When you get off into your own thing so much...(pause).

TD: Do you see contemporary photographers devoting their lives to their art the way Weston did?

SH: Yes. They can do it more meaningfully now. You get a guy like Ralph Gibson who can orient his life totally as an artist in the craft of photography; though he does, of course, do the workshops. He may enjoy the feedback of workshops. Syl Labrot likes to teach, doesn't have to teach, but likes to because of the feedback and the relationship to students. Paul Klee liked to teach because he felt it clarified his ideas about what he was doing. On the other hand, when I read Paul Klee's writing about teaching, it's so incredibly abstract. What he was doing was analyzing his own work after the fact of the work, and my feeling is that when you get so analytical about work after it's done, you're not imparting anything to the student about how to do it. It's merely analysis after the fact. Klee didn't do these analytical things when he was making the pictures.

TD: What do you remember about your childhood and did anything in your childhood lead you to photography? Do you see a relationship?

SH: Yes. When I was young I got interested in chemistry and my parents encouraged my interest, thought that would be a nice activity. At the same time I liked drawing and painting, was always quite visually-oriented. Photography is a natural combination of technologic and visual interests, and it appealed to me. I have an incident in my childhood which I credit with starting or influencing my fascination with color. One day my sister and I were hanging around the house. It was Saturday, or summertime, and my father was home. We were bored, went to him and said, "What will we do, give us something to do." He thought for a minute, then set us up in the backyard with an old wooden bench. He went down into the basement, took these empty bottles, and filled them with red, yellow, and blue food coloring dye in water and said, "Here, if you take a little of this one, a little of that one, you get green." The two of us spent this entirely enchanted afternoon mixing these little dabs of color into glasses and then playing them like a zylophone when we got bored with that. We made a water zylophone. I can still see it all, the sunlight, the old bench, the rows of bottles of colored water. I think that had an influence, a persistent dream-like fascination with colors.

TD: Did you consider your childhood a happy one?

SH: No. My father was a petty tyrant. He was a bully, a tyrant, in a petty way. It was out of concern, I think, but he had a very Victorian way. I feel like I was tyrannized by him and grew up nervous and anxious. My father, who had been a dentist, contracted rheumatoid arthritis, and had to give up dentistry right in the middle of the depression. The family was reduced to living on my mother's work as a clerk in a bank. We moved from Minnesota to Oregon, where his family was, for his health, though Oregon wasn't much healthier for arthritics, it was better than Minnesota. It was very hard times and my parents' anxieties came out in a super fussiness over my sister's and my behavior. My sister and I were kind of played off against each other a little bit. She was a year older and they'd point to her as the example of good behavior, so we grew up disliking each other somewhat. It took years to evolve a good relationship with her.

My father was inventive and playful. He told me years later — he eventually became an optician — he couldn't practice dentistry because he couldn't stand for long periods—that his work supported him in his hobbies: photography, growing roses, and later orchids, stamps and coins. He was a play-oriented man, but it was always spare time play. He was playful with his hands, liked making funny things. He did give me that, playfulness with hands. I used to make model airplanes and boats for which I got a lot of credit.

TD: Were you a part of your peer group or more of a loner?

SH: I was more a loner. The kids' interests, in the immediate neighborhood, didn't parallel mine; they were more interested in athletics. My father, being an arthritic and somewhat crippled, had never given me a role model in terms of action and physical activities. I never grew up doing any of those things well. I didn't really get a good peer friend until I was in high school. I tinkered around with various musical instruments, played drums and got a friend, a very fine piano player. We formed a band, and then I had a good peer relationship.

TD: How do events of your life affect your personal work?

SH: I think I'm beginning to mature to the extent that I have less need for recognition from my work. Events in my life don't have much effect on the type of picture, the technique, the subject matter, or the work in that way. Events in my life do have an effect on my relationship to the work. I feel I'm maturing in my personal life and outlook towards life in general, and it gives me a more mature attitude towards the work, and that's in the direction of less need for recognition. Most artists, I think, get into art, not only liking to do that art and make pictures, but because they need the recognition. I can remember, as a young child, being angry and frustrated, put down by somebody, an adult or other children, and having the feeling I'd show them all someday. I think that's a driving spirit, or was for me, for many years, so I generalize and presume that other artists have that feeling. It's good to get over the need to prove oneself to peers, contemporaries or anybody. The sheer joy of being on the earth and seeing it all unfold is a more sustaining thing than momentary recognition. Recognition is a little warming of the ego. You get a picture in a photo magazine, it warms your ego for a few minutes, but you pay for it. The cost comes when you get a disappointment of that kind. You apply to a magazine with your pictures and they don't take them. Then you have a rejection on your hands and you deal with the negative side of the recognition. That's a blow to the ego. If you can live your life without your ego, and give yourself the right to not care whether you succeed or don't succeed, you're in better shape.

TD: Do you forsee a time when you won't have to do commercial work? Does that appeal to you?

SH: Yes, enormously. It's occurred to me, in recent years, as a hypothetical situation, that if you would give me my choice of recognition or money for my work, I would take the money, at this point, where once I would have taken the recognition. If I could make enough money at doing personal work, it would permit me to do nothing but personal work. As it is now, I put in enormously long weeks of work. I average 60, 70 hours of work a week, between personal and commercial work. To earn a reasonably comfortable life style takes a lot of time because I'm not very efficient at it. The reason I'm not efficient at it is my attention is divided between personal and commercial work. I could be a successful commercial photographer if I wasn't also an artist, and the net result, of course, is that I'm not doing either that well. I'm not devoting myself to my art when 40 or more hours a week is spent at commercial work. As it stands now, more of my time is spent earning money than doing creative work. In commercial work, if you're not actually working at making money, then you're hustling jobs and promoting business. I haven't pursued, very energetically, sales of my personal work. A lot more could be done. By working as I do, in offset lithography, and making a picture which is readily available, in terms of price, to a wide audience — my pictures go for five to twenty dollars or a little more for a few of them — but such a low return per picture needs a wide audience, and it's a different audience from the serious photography collector, by and large. In fact, the "serious" photography collector is not interested in my work because of the ephemeral nature of the medium I use. Libraries and museums are not afraid of it, but it does fall outside that "serious" collectors' medium, which depends on a certain uniqueness to be valuable.

TD: Are you in any other gallery besides the Witkin?

SH: No. It's not that I have an exclusive arrangement with Lee (Witkin), he doesn't demand an exclusive arrangement of anyone. No one's ever asked.

TD: Do you feel isolation is necessary in your personal work?

SH: There are stages in the development of pictures where I think it's vital. At the moment when pictures occur to me, it's almost invariably when I'm in a state of isolation. I'm by myself in the country or the studio, and usually in a state of heightened, nonverbal activity. I'm thinking pictures, or I'm kind of high, my eyes and image-making functions are working much more energetically than my verbal, or so-called thinking functions. That can only happen when you're not with other people. When you're with other people, you tend to think in words, and communicate in words. By and large, my pictures occur as visual constructs in my mind, which either derive from what I'm looking at, as when I'm out in the world, in nature, in the woods, see a scene, and mentally translate it onto paper; or sometimes, in the studio, a picture will occur to me as a visual projection, a possible way of making a picture, and again it's always a projection onto paper, a translation from the original scene. I've no interest in going out into the world of nature, pointing my camera at a scene, and recording it. It's the thing that Ansel Adams used to stress about looking at the scene and projecting it in your mind as a finished print. Previsualization was his term, except I do it in my graphic processes and colors rather than in a continuous tone scale of grays.

TD: Are you doing this with a picture you've already taken?

SH: It can happen while looking at a contact sheet. I can see a picture where the inspiration to take the original was only a mild impulse. I can sit and look at a contact sheet and suddenly say, "Hey, I could do this, that, and that, perform these operations on this negative and make this finished picture." At which point I'll also project whether I'll want to do it as a gum bichromate, a variant gum bichromate, an offset lithograph, or a silkscreen. Each of those media make for different kinds of pictures and deal best with different kinds of imagery.

TD: Do you work in different media at certain times?

SH: There was a time that happened. Now, having made myself familiar with three or four processes that I like, I'll look at a given picture and project the quality of the image, the colors, the scale, and buzz through, in my mind, all the different processes and pick one. They behave differently. The gum bichromate and the variant gum bichromate processes I don't often think of as the final, finished, best method to render a picture. I like multiple print processes, so generally it comes down to silkscreen or offset lithography.

TD: Where do your ideas come from? How does the creative process work for you? Is it merely hard work or do you believe there's such a thing as the creative process?

SH: No, I don't think it's a function of work or effort, if we equate work with effort. It's the opposite. It's a permissive happening, really creative work, as against work wherein we unconsciously imitate something we've admired of our own or somebody else's, which is to say the kind of pictures we ourselves, or no one we know has ever made, occurs, if you think of it in terms of computer functions, in a kind of random process. I might look at a scene that has never appealed to me before or that I never photographed, and spin my computer, run it past all the different processes that I work in, and all the colors I can think of, and maybe some of them will come together, and I'll say, "Hey, I can do the thing in orange and blue, and get a black shadow tone and so on, and how would that look?" You look at that picture for a while, and spin the wheels again. All that happens on a less than conscious level, of course. If you go out and try to do that thing which I just described, then it becomes an intellectual process again. Part of that maturing I was talking about earlier is permissiveness in terms of the unconscious and subconscious, not to be afraid to permit the unconscious and subconscious to function, and even perhaps to practice not talking to oneself. Most of us in the civilized world spend most of our waking hours talking to ourselves. There's this constant dialogue going on inside, and we're beginning to learn through the influence of things like various forms of Buddhism that have come into the West, that there are other ways of permitting your mind to function. The Carlos Castaneda conversations with Don Juan books have been a big influence on me in opening up the possibilities that there are other than logical processes going on inside of us, and we can open ourselves up to these nonlogical parts of ourselves to our own enormous benefit, especially artists. Many people do this as a matter of course, become so enchanted with this side of themselves, go crazy, and can't function in the real, everyday world. They stay out in that nonlogical, intuitive area all the time, but a balance of logical and nonlogical functions can be very helpful to an artist. Ram Dass says, "The good bodhisatva always remembers his zip code number."

TD: We generally speak of people as sane or insane. How about the state of mind that is unsane, that can go back and forth between both states. I've known people who have been diagnosed as insane, and many times, the way they operate, I also operate at times. The difference is I don't recognize anybody having the authority to label me. Perhaps artists, more than anyone else, should recognize the insane side as simply an aspect of their natures.

SH: Right, absolutely. Robert Rauschenberg, when he was in the Navy, in the 2nd World War, worked in a mental hospital, and came to the realization that what we all need is a combination of those functions. His feeling was that it's helpful to understand the nonsane, unsane, insane side of ourselves. He's another artist who can permit that contact with his unconscious to come out in his work. People are frequently terrified of the notion of permitting their unconscious, or insane side, to surface.

TD: With whom do you discuss your work?

SH: I don't do it much, but I'm not nervous about talking about my work early on, in ideas. Syl Labrot and I talk sometimes. We've known each other for over ten years.

We became acquainted during the Heliography (Gallery) days, and we exchange notions about where we're at, or where we might be going next. Probably more with my wife than anybody else because I see her more and I tend to be a loner. I don't have many acquaintances. I just don't have time for it, so I discuss it very little, for lack of time. I don't hang out anymore. I don't go to parties; we don't even entertain or go out much, which is the time that sort of thing tends to happen. I don't have a policy against it.

TD: When you complete work do you just bring it up to Lee Witkin?

SH: I tend to do work in fits and starts. Generally, when an occasion for exhibiting comes up, the work comes together. In between shows, somebody occasionally will request something for a publication. I always think it's fun to do something new, rather than dig through the box and say, "Let's see what I've got that they can publish?" When an invitation to show comes along, it obliges me to focus my mind strongly on what I'm doing right now and do some of that. I kind of play it by ear, what I'm doing next. In between periods, I'll work along at whatever might seem most interesting at the time. My pictures take so long from inception, from the time I shoot the film until I have the final edition in hand, that at any given moment, I have a couple of dozen pictures in mid-process. I'll pick one up, drop another one, or start a new one and carry it along to a point. Then they go into various bins, envelopes and stacks around here, as the spirit moves me.

The most enjoyable work period I ever had was when I was working in Carl Sesto's printing plant, doing the **CAPS Book.** I was getting up every morning early, stumbling out of bed, and over to the light table, and worked on pictures until late at night, when Carl would shut the lights, and we'd all go to bed. That went on for about three weeks and was extraordinarily enjoyable.

TD: You don't seem to be the type who would care to go back and reprint old work. Is that so?

SH: Yes, it's true. One of the problems I got into with my **CAPS Book** was, when the grant came through, and I decided to publish the book, I said to myself, "Don't start experimenting. Take those pictures which you've carried to a good state of completion and you like, and are done, and are successful"—I mean by successful that they'll print without severe problems—"and go with those. Don't start experimenting on Carl's press because you'll tie the whole thing up and nothing will ever get finished." But I couldn't resist. I had a notion about several of those pictures. There's one, a sunset, which doesn't have any image, in effect. It's all done with the press. The image is a solid block on the plate; you print it once red, once yellow, once blue, manipulate the fountain on the press to lighten and darken areas of the picture, and make a synthetic sunset. It's so hard to resist the temptation to make new pictures. While you know the book, in terms of acceptance, would be more successful, it's just no fun. How many times does somebody turn a press over to me? Yes, I don't like to print old pictures. There're always so many new ones backed up, in my head, on contact sheets, so many new ones. It's one of the distressing things, not severely distressing, it's a good feeling, too, that at any given moment, I have about 50 pictures I'd like to make, and can't. Any one of them will take from 10 to 100 lab hours, and I just don't have that many. I can generate pictures, think them up, and start them faster than I can finish them.

Oh, listen, let me get into something which is kind of interesting when we were talking about sanity, insanity. I once, in about 1950, a long time ago, had a thoroughgoing schizophrenic breakdown, just as kooky as I could be, and had to be hospitalized briefly. It was a thrilling experience in that I came out of it with this certain feeling that there's no need to dry up creatively. The unconscious mind is so full of images, notions, directions and things an artist can use, that there's no fear at all of running out of things to say as an artist. All you need is to get in tune with the unconscious, without going crazy. It's taken all the years since to learn how. One can go on learning to do that through one's whole life, more and more. You never stop being a student in that area.

TD: Could you take a picture and describe your methodology from idea through to completion?

SH: Let's take the last picture in the **CAPS Book,** a view of grasses growing out of a pond. This was made with a very ancient box camera—not that that was any aid to the picture, it could have been made with any camera. The picture was previsualized about the way you see it. I couldn't decide the exact colors I ended up using, but I visualized them pretty much. The problem was: bright green grass emerging from dark water. How could I render it in the least number of ink layers, transparent ink at that? I worked from a single negative. First, I made one printer that prints a block of solid pale blue overall. Then a yellow printer which also prints solid overall, except for a few "holes" where there are spots of blue sky reflecting in the water; this had to be done with hand-work. I made a litho positive to size and opaqued out everything, except those little spots which come up blue. This positive is contact printed onto litho film for the yellow printing negative, which prints yellow overall, making it all green, except for a few spots of blue. The image which really carries the picture is printed in a kind of red-brown. This has some blank highlight areas which permit the green and blue to show through, making the green grass and blue sky reflections. That was a hard color to get. This was a picture I promised myself I wouldn't make at Carl's. I hadn't worked out the colors completely; I hadn't even proofed it successfully. I was just so eager to see it that we used it. I made Carl stop and wash the press twice because the red color was coming up all wrong. We had a kind of plum color at one point, which hit on top of the green and got a dead gray, just a flat-out middle-tone gray, horrible looking. We moved around the color wheel towards red-orange, and knocked that down to a red-brown color. It's still not the perfect color. I could tinker with it some more. I would like a 4th printing negative, maybe a black printer, or a deeper red, which would print only shadow tones, then you would see the tree trunks reflected in the pond, and some of the deeper shadows. That would enhance the depth of the picture dramatically.

TD: What is the focus in your work? Do you work in series? Do you see the single picture or a series as the final form?

SH: Largely, they're single pictures, though I have sets of pictures as themes. I get fascinated with clouds, or water, and ripples on the water, but, essentially, they're separate pictures. I don't, even in my book, exploit the book form as a narrative, or sequence, at all. The pictures are totally separate, one from the other. It is a valid and valuable style to exploit the picture book as a narrative, in the way Ralph Gibson has shown us. Of course, people have done it before and since Ralph, but Ralph does it so stunningly, in that marvelous aspect of art work which falls between still photography and cinema. I don't do that. Mine are separate stills, really separate. Each picture has its own set of separate problems. I've been doing some semi-conceptual works in the area of taking a single image and working variations from it, reversing all the tonalities, making a picture of the original scene as positive, and then flop the negative. That's one of the things I got into in the **CAPS Book.** There're two pictures adjacent of a water surface, in which all the tonalities are reversed, the highlights of one become the shadows in the second one, and so on. That again was a qualified failure, and I should have worked it out. Perhaps not one of the best picture sets in the book.

TD: Many photographers are issuing portfolios as a means of generating income. Does the idea of a portfolio appeal to you?

SH: I spend so long on any one picture that by the time I'm done, my mind is ready to do something totally different, and portfolios, by and large, have a coherence. My **CAPS Book** is, in effect, a portfolio, in that it's a book that can be dismembered into portfolio form, but the only continuity among the pictures is the medium it's printed in. Pictures don't relate.

TD: What equipment and materials do you use? I know you're fascinated by materials and equipment.

SH: I'll say at the beginning that a serious artist has to guard himself against an over-fascination with materials and processes. They are interesting, but it becomes tinkering when you permit the materials to dominate. The only interesting thing about different processes and materials is: what'll they do for my vision? Having different materials at my command gives me the advantage of making a given picture and being able to choose among several to find the most appropriate means of rendering the picture. Almost all the stuff is done with a 35mm camera, while walking around, looking at the world outside the door, and right now, almost all of it is in nature. I had a period when I was developing these methods of work, where I did a lot of cityscapes and imagery of people. Just at the moment, and I presume it's more or less temporary, I'm into a very heavy nature thing. Maybe it's living in the lower east side, which is the quintessence of city living. It's given me a fascination with the world of nature. Maybe if I lived in nature I'd go back to city pictures. I work mostly in 35mm because it's easy to garner the images that way. I believe in shooting a lot of pictures. I go out and shoot and shoot, and working as slowly as I do, I shoot enormously more pictures than will ever get printed. I make contact sheets, but most of my contact sheets never have one of the images printed. I don't know what the percentage is, but a very tiny number. It keeps my trigger finger loose to keep shooting. The smallest impulse will cause me to take a picture. That's one of the lessons of 35mm and Cartier-Bresson. We no longer have to agonize over every shutter click, as we did when we worked with big cameras and tripods. The advantage, for me, of 35mm, too, is that it gives me a grainy negative which I can render onto Kodalith and get a semblance of tonality, using the Tri-X grain. If I have too fine grain an image, then I can't use the grain of the original negative to render the effect of tonality. For some reason, I'm opposed to the halftone screen. Since I think largely in terms of printing press for the final rendering of my picture, I have to render it onto the printing plate in some way, which means a gravelly, grainy Kodalith image or a halftone screen. I use the halftone screen sometimes, if necessary. In my **CAPS Book** there are some, one or more of the pictures have a halftone tint on part or all the picture.

I just bought an ancient Canon to replace my ancient Leica, which finally wore out. The Canon body takes my screw-mount Leica lenses. Almost everything is done with a 50mm lens. I have a 28mm lens which I bought from Gene Smith, when he was selling off equipment one time. I shoot Tri-X. Most of the pictures are straight black and white, though lately I've come to do more and more three-color process photography in the camera. I take three pictures on Tri-X, one after the other of the same scene, each through one of the trichrome filters, deep red, deep green and deep blue. If the red image is printed in cyan, the green image in magenta and the blue in yellow, I have a full color picture. I do them in the camera, even hand-held, which introduces little differences between the images. Sometimes I even move the camera laterally an inch or so between exposures to introduce a stereo effect in the images. If the subject is moving, the wind is blowing the leaves, or the ripples on the water, then you get other differences among the three images, all effects I like. I do some work with various box cameras, primitive cameras. I don't know why exactly I got started with that, partly the fascination with the roots of the medium, in the sense that other hand-artists, noted painters or sculptors, will go back to drawing for periods of time. It takes them back to the simplest, most primitive level of work. We have this notion that the box camera will do certain kinds of pictures just as well as any other camera, and it's partly to find out what those kinds of pictures are that I play with a box camera. The other thing that is fascinating is if you work with color film, because a box camera has a simple, one-element lens, you get color fringing. I like anything that lends extra color to the pictures. I've exploited that, both by shooting color film and shooting trichrome pictures. There's some misregister between the various images, due to the lenses not being corrected for color film. Technically, it's a mistake, but it makes nice color fringes around things.

TD: Could you address yourself to selling your work. Is your work selling better as time goes by? Are you gaining an audience?

SH: No, that isn't the way it works for an artist. Your work sells along with your recognition in the media. Artists, like me, who don't do much to stay visible, go up and down in their recognizability. It's becoming apparent to me that it's part of your function as an artist. If you want recognition, then you must make yourself recognizable. You must do those things which get you recognized. The chances of gaining recognition and, therefore, good sales, are small, if you sit and wait for it to happen or wait for somebody else to do it.

TD: Could you discuss the CAPS Book **from idea to finished book?**

SH: I've wanted to publish a multiple for a long time. Offset lithography is my medium of first choice, but it's expensive to get on the press with a multi-colored picture. Once on the press, the thing will crank out pictures at such a tremendous rate that the cost per picture is small. It might cost a minimum of several hundred dollars to have a color picture printed, but if you've generated a couple of thousand pictures, the cost is less than a dollar a picture. I've always liked the notion that a picture could be made for less than a dollar. I like bargains; I like things cheap. I'm always saying they don't call me Scott for nothing. I went for grant money to do this; I've gotten several grants over the years. This last one is the only one that resulted in a book. Every other time, I was so poor that I couldn't afford to use the money to publish a book. I did manage to get it together and make that book, but I've been dreaming of doing it for years. The notion of a book is so difficult, so time-consuming, and takes so much concentration over such a long period. It is harder than it looks. It's very nice to have it finished and in hand, and the viewer's role is very much easier than the maker's. The viewer can appreciate a book in a few minutes to a few hours time. The guy who made it has spent hundreds of hours getting the thing together. That sustained work, having nothing to do with making pictures, is the toughest part of doing a book, for me. It's so much more fun to spend your time making a picture than making a book, which is not a picture. It's only the desire to see your work in a cluster, and the possibility that maybe it will be financially rewarding.

TD: Could you get into the physical problems of making the book a reality, selecting the pictures, deciding on Carl Sesto, and the actual printing of the book?

SH: I kept my eyes out for years for a printer that I thought I could work with. I bumped into Nathan Lyons and he was carrying Carl Sesto's MFA thesis, from The Visual Studies Workshop, a superb series of prints, 10 or 12 black and whites of rocks and ice on the shore of the lake in Rochester, printed in duotone on the workshop's flat-bed, hand-operated, Vandecook offset proofing press. They were so stunning that I said, "This is the guy who could print my book." Carl had set up shop in the Boston area. After a lot of scratching around I found Carl and he was happy to do it. I made a date with him for the summer of '75. When I got up there they were doing Michael Becotte's book, **Space Capsule,** and were having enormous problems getting just the right effects and were a little bogged down and two, three weeks behind schedule, which was driving everybody crazy. It turned out to be fortunate for me because, while I had my pictures in mind, I knew I wanted a 10 page book, and in my interview with Carl, had decided on the paper, the size of the run, the size of the book, those technical questions. There would be 10 pictures on 12 pages, the front and back pages are blank, except for a little text. I brought 12 proof prints and sets of negatives to make the final decision. There were several I was in doubt about being able to pull off or deal with, and finally narrowed it down to the 10 I used. I did all the stripping, which is the process wherein the litho negatives are taped into big orange sheets of plastic as masking for the moment they will be exposed onto the offset plates. I could have had Carl and Chuck Gershwin, who worked with him, do it, but I was fascinated to do it myself, eager in that way that we artists like to control everything. I wanted to make sure it was all done exactly the way I wanted it, so I had them teach me how to do all the operations. There were over 30 plates, and over 30 big flats, plastic sheets bearing the negatives involved in the book. I was enjoying it enormously, very fussy, perfectionistic sort of work, done with T-squares, rulers and razor blades. Chuck Gershwin was my main teacher throughout that process because he was working alongside me on the regular house jobs. He ended up giving me most of my instruction while Carl and Michael Becotte were sweating out Michael's book on the press. Finally they finished Michael's book, at about the time I was ready to go on the press and, in fact, it worked out quite smoothly. When we got on the press, it was a very hot week in July, and we had severe press problems caused by the extreme heat. The shop was not air conditioned, but we went ahead anyway. Finally we did get a technician in to help us. He figured our problems were due to thinning of the ink in the excessive heat, so by pounding a little powder magnesium into the ink, we thickened it up and solved our most severe problems, after ruining enormous quantities of paper. This somewhat shortened the run on the book. After the book is printed, you count the number of each page and if page 3 is the smallest number of pages, that's the size of the edition. If you have 250 copies of page 3, you have 250 books, no matter how many copies of page 4 you have. I ended up with considerable overrun on some pages and between 200 and 300 copies of the book. At that point, from a strictly legal standpoint, I suppose I could have forced Carl to go back on the press and reprint the short pages, but none of us was quite up to that. Even I wasn't up to that, so we let the edition go at that. We'll print the extra ones if we ever go to another edition. The book is not intended as a limited edition and might someday go to additional editions, but that would only be in the event that it became enormously more popular an object than it is today. I can't imagine it at all, going back and printing that thing over.

TD: How many copies had you projected to print?

SH: 500. There are between 200 and 300. We didn't even number them.

TD: How did you decide to call it the CAPS Book?

SH: I was trying to think of a title when I realized it had one. I was already calling it my **CAPS Book,** so I thought, "What the hell, that could be the name as well as any."

TD: How did you select the images for the book?

SH: That was very much a horse trading procedure. At the time, I could have made all new pictures or used all old pictures or a combination as I, in fact, did. It was partly a choice of colors. I didn't want to restrict myself to those pictures which are made in process red, yellow and blue, the standard printing ink colors. It would be too limiting for me. I like very much to work with brown, purple, orange and nonprocess colors. On the other hand, I couldn't have an unlimited number of colors. I couldn't come up with 10 pictures, each in three colors, all different, and have 30 colors of ink. It's too time consuming to change inks that often. I was trading off, hoping to hit between 8 and 10 colors for 10 pictures. That became a limiting factor on my choices, too. I couldn't have too many widely divergent colors. It was horse trading of that kind, plus putting up a picture, finished and known to be easy. I can tell, having done these things as long as I have, which pictures will be fairly easy to print, and which might cause problems. I can be wrong. Some can be easy that I thought difficult and vice versa. When it came to tradeoffs between certain pictures known to be easy as against pictures which weren't entirely complete or worked out in my mind, I would go for pictures which weren't quite complete. They were so much more interesting. We worked out the problems with qualified success, qualified failure. There are about three pictures in the book which were relatively experimental, from the standpoint of the press in that the final selection of ink color hadn't been chosen, or that depended on exploiting the mechanics of the printing press to generate the image. Those became quite experimental and risky, but, on balance, I don't regret having experimented. I learned so much. I learned not to do those pictures over again, or it can't be done on a press of that size. The one of the sunset sky should really have been done poster size, for instance, where you could really control the flow of ink over a wide stretch. To try to do it on a 10 inch long image didn't allow the degree of control that a three foot long image would. The experiments were worth it, though they made the book less successful as a finished object.

TD: Did you ever have aspirations towards becoming the classic photojournalist, or *Life* magazine photographer?

SH: No. I felt very unsure during the years I was developing as a photographer. When I came to New York in 1947, the photographers I admired most were Edward Weston and Walker Evans. I worked with a 4 x 5 view camera on a tripod for several years after I came to New York. Then I worked a little with a Rolleiflex, the camera got a little smaller, then I learned to use that Leica. Actually I had a period where I worked with color film, in the middle 50's. I'd always loved color since I was a child, but I deliberately developed myself slowly as a photographer, didn't go with my fascination with color because I wanted a firm grounding in black and white and straight photography. I knew the minute I started with color I'd probably drop black and white. When I did I used standard color materials, 4 x 5 Ektachrome primarily. I worked with what I believe are called virtual images, synthetic images, where there was no object in front of the camera, but I worked with the light itself. I would work in a darkened room, with no lens, just a chunk of glass where the lens would have been. I experimented around to make little point-source lights, not a spot light, but a little pin point of light, as small as you can get it, and beam it into the broken glass and get a diffraction of white light across the film, splattered, rainbow effects, and spectrum effects, and work with in and out of focus, simple lenses, anamorphic lenses, with various color and light phenomena. These would make multi-colored, abstract images. Very little of that stuff was published. Four of them appeared in a show Steichen organized for The Museum of Modern Art, in the late '50's early 60's, called "A Sense of Abstraction." I found it kind of empty. I had a dream one night. I saw an image which was a combination of one of my color images and a theater stage, a very beautiful Australian dark opal and black effects with flashes of color, and simultaneously a stage, and another which was very light and pearly, beautifully clear, pastel colors and very high key lighting, and again, a stage; but both stages were empty. I took this later on—at the time the significance didn't strike me—to mean that I was saying to myself that I was becoming dissatisfied with this kind of imagery. It was so devoid of life, so totally abstract. Photography has this peerless ability to depict and resonate with a real life that I was totally leaving out in my use of the medium, and missing. It was at that point that I began to work with images from reality.

The particular method that I use, shooting in black and white and printing the images together, in colors, or taking three disparate black and white pictures, and printing each in a different color, one on top of the other, came to me as a sudden, very distinct insight. I can still remember it very clearly. I was walking in the woods, along this trail, and had my old Leica with me. The woods were very beautiful, and I kept lifting the camera up and sighting, wanting to shoot, but having the feeling that it was useless. The quality of beauty that I was getting would never come through this little camera, on black and white film. The camera was so small and I was seeing 8 x 10 color. I knew it was useless to attempt to capture the quality that I was feeling. It occurred to me that maybe if I were to take several pictures and print them together I would get the sense of the walk in the woods. I was charmed with the sense of walking in the woods. No one picture could get the sense of a walk in the woods. I thought maybe a montage, and I had never made a montage before. I'd seen Harry Callahan's and Jerry Uelsmann's and my favorite photographer at that time, Val Telberg's. It wasn't in my nature, the minute I saw something that intrigued me, to go out and try it, but to let it perk. Apparently this interest in montage had been perking in the back of my mind without my being much aware of it. I thought that would be a way to get a sense of a walk in the woods, a montage of several views. About 15 minutes later I got very excited with this notion. If I printed each one in a different color, I would get, not only the nice combinations of color, but would be able to separate the three pictures visually. By looking at the picture and making your eyes see only red, or only blue, and so on, you could have a hope of visually separating the images, at least to some extent, whereas three black and white images printed on top of each other tend to blend much more thoroughly. The combinations of colors, plus the notion that you might even be able to separate them was interesting.

TD: How long ago did that take place?

SH: About 1958. Even after I had the notion, it was a couple of years before I made the first one, even knowing it was what I wanted to do, was working towards. I wanted the proper medium for doing it.

TD: How long has the CAPS Book **been out and what has been the reaction thus far?**

SH: It came out in midsummer '75. Lee Witkin gave a nice little book party, and sold three copies, two to a good friend of mine, and I don't know who bought the third one. I would say it dropped into the mainstream of art with barely a ripple. There was a little spate of sales, Light Impressions tells me, shortly after it came out. It's never had a major review or even a minor review. Light Impressions says nice things about it in their catalogue. It didn't sell out quickly and they still have copies. After about a year, I realized it was selling very slowly and decided to raise the price, in reverse of the usual method of remaindering such things, from $30 to $50. What difference does it make? It isn't going to affect the sales. When it does finally sell, it'll go for $50, rather than $30. If the operation had been on a larger scale, I could have asked a smaller price. When one starts a project of this kind, one agonizes over the final price of the book. You don't know at the start how expensive it's going to end up, though in terms of promotion it's helpful to give the price with the first notice that the book is coming out. You try to estimate the final price. If your distributor is about to publish a catalogue, you have to give him a price. I settled on $30, which seemed a little high at moments, and at other moments didn't. I had considered prices ranging from $10 to $30; I never considered more. I put it at the higher figure, which is fortunate, considering that the run was short. The decision to raise the price to $50 is somewhat willful on my part, and based on the scarcity principle. I have occasionally put myself in opposition to that, but I like the book and value it highly. I consider it a portfolio of 10 original prints, and even at $50, you're getting original prints at $5 a piece. They happen to be unsigned, unlimited and unnumbered, but original nonetheless. I feel I'm still confronting that situation by offering at a moderate price, an unsigned work of art. And the collector who buys it is also defying the system. It's not the rule. I'm not stingy with my signature either. If anybody wants me to sign anything, I sign it immediately and don't raise the price for its having been signed. That whole notion of the signature having value is really eccentric, considered in the light of aesthetics. Pictures have value, signatures don't have value as art, but in practice they do. I still say it's eccentric.

TD: Do you feel the book has done anything for your reputation among your fellow artists?

SH: Not that I can notice. I've had a few individuals say they liked it. I don't think it's done much for my reputation. I don't think it's my best work, either. It's older things that have been published; it's semi-successful experiments, and doesn't represent me well in that it's not my 10 best, by a long ways, but it was a valuable experience as an art action, an event in my career.

TD: Will you do another book?

SH: I have no plans to. I expect sometime it will happen again. I didn't become enamored of the process, procedure and notion of bookmaking out of this experience. Maybe if the books had sold out in the first three months, it would incline me to want to make the effort again. Since there was relatively little response, and as the whole procedure of cranking out a book is so laborious, and there's not even financial remuneration at the end, I'm not that intrigued with it. Because I make my pictures one at a time, and don't exploit the medium for its narrative or sequential possibilities, I don't need it for my kind of picture making.

TD: Is there any particular way you edit your work?

SH: I try not to do any editing at the picture taking stage. I try to permit myself to photograph anything and everything that appeals to me. Like most photographers, I used to go around looking for good pictures, and not take bad pictures, but that can be a defeating process, and is certainly not necessary with a 35mm camera, where the cost and effort of shooting a picture is so minimal. Why should one refuse to take anything that appeals, whatever? Editing, the very term, implies picking something, rejecting something, pushing back something, so that something else can come forward. I don't think I do that, in a way, at any point. I look over a contact sheet and a certain picture will intrigue me. A picture will jump forward, or several pictures on the sheet will occur to me as possible for further development, then I have the hard decision of which of those several I'll go with. I usually develop film and make contact sheets in batches. The stuff will pile up around here for six months sometimes, or more. I have pictures that are several years old and the exposed, undeveloped film is in jars in the freezer. When I get a little free time, I'll get that stuff out and develop it. I'm so backed up on pictures that I don't need to develop that film to search for pictures to print. I feel wealthy in pictures. I will sometimes do 6 or 8 rolls in one day or 15 or 20 rolls over two days of developing. My developing is a little protracted in that I fog the film. I expose the film in the darkroom to a low level of raw light. The advantage that this gives is it flattens the image, it lowers the contrast. It also builds up the shadow exposure density level. Since I render almost all my pictures on to litho film, I get an enormous jump in contrast at that step. If I begin with a normal negative, the result is extraordinarily contrasty. I shoot Tri-X at an E.I. between 125 and 400. I just guess at it. I used to rate it at 125, and grossly underdevelop. I would dilute the Rodinal 150:1, which is far beyond their maximum dilution. They recommend dilutions of 25:1, up to 100:1. I would dilute 150:1 and, even then, shorten development to 10 or 12 minutes, which is below the recommended. This would result in a low contrast negative, but I would have to use an E.I. of 125 to get any shadow detail. Then I realized if I flashed to fog the film, I could use the normal ASA of 400, and a more nearly normal development time, and at the same time, build up shadow density. I have a little dim light on the ceiling and stretch the film out, across the tabletop, and blink the light for 1/5 of a second. It's not that dim, I guess. Then I'd put the film on the reel. I go through it all quite carefully. I can't afford any scratches, or uneven development. Those effects are all exaggerated by the rendering onto Kodalith, and can't be corrected in printing. I'll develop about 8 rolls, 10 rolls in a day, before I get tired of it, and I'll look at those contact sheets, and I'll find maybe 10 or 15 pictures that intrigue me. I'll mark those with a little x and put the whole thing away. The pictures that haunt me as I'm falling asleep at night, or hanging around, or relooking at the contact sheets, over and over, are the ones that'll end up getting further work. Yes, that's how I edit. The pictures that are on my mind as I fall asleep at night are the ones that get printed.

TD: Do you have dealings with other photographers?

SH: Not much.

TD: Do you read newspapers or magazines, or watch TV?

SH: I'm more a TV addict than anything, but as I work long hours, I don't even spend much time with the TV, but that's my single largest medium exposure.

TD: Do you read much?

SH: Not much.

TD: Are there any picture books you admire?

SH: I like Syl's (Labrot—**Pleasure Beach**); I like all Ralph's (Gibson—**The Somnambulist; Deja-Vu; Days at Sea**). There are so many fine picture books now. I like Michael Becotte's **Space Capsule,** and the funny, kinky magazines and newspapers that are coming out now are kind of marvelous. *Fotofile* and *Flash,* a newspaper, just pictures, no text, just crazy, zany pictures. I like Peter Hujar's **Portraits in Life and Death.**

**New York City
December 18, 1978**

A. D. Coleman

Interviewer: Do you feel the visual book has been exploited or do you think we're still in the infancy of the movement?

Allan Coleman: I don't think it has been drained dry by any means. There are a lot of books coming out that probably should not be done as expensively or in as large an edition as they're being done in, or maybe not done at all. But there are an increasing number of very fine books coming out. Books which are suggesting a lot of ways of opening up the medium of the photographic book as such through different kinds of experiments in printing — I'm thinking here particularly about **Pleasure Beach** by Syl Labrot — or in which the photographer is exploring the possibility of making an extended statement of some kind, whether it's combining words and images in a way that someone like Gaylord Herron does, or whether it's doing it entirely with images, in the way that Ralph Gibson does in his books. In fact, it's a much more suitable vehicle for the imagery than the original print form because the original print form carries with it certain kinds of assumptions which are, in many ways, antithetical to the ideal situation in which you might experience the work, and be most receptive to it....

On a cold, snowbound St. Valentine's day, February 14, 1978, I interviewed Allan Coleman in his home on Staten Island, N.Y. When I arrived, Allan had just put his son to bed and we sat for an hour over coffee before beginning our conversation. The interview, which was tape recorded, was conducted in front of his living room fireplace and continued well into the night. Allan speaks from a unique position. He is, first and foremost, a critic, but additionally, a bookmaker and publisher as he privately printed two of the three books he has done. He is a man committed to the book as the most viable medium for the dissemination of photography.

Tom Dugan: What is the role of the critic in reference to the picture book?

Allan Coleman: In the case of the material that's self-published, or published by small presses, whether they're small university presses or small independent presses or presses that don't have well-established distribution systems, I think that the critic's role is a very essential role because, in many cases, the books simply will not come to the attention of the audience, of the market for them, without a critical intermediary. I know that when I first started writing for the *Village Voice*, in 1968, there was virtually no place where photography books were being regularly reviewed, at least no place in New York and not really in any other publication that I knew of. And I tried very much to make that column and the column I was writing for *The New York Times* also, a place where, in one way or another, in one context or another, as much of what was coming out as possible would be discussed or referred to or incorporated in some way. But, sometime around 1971, 1972, not very long before I stopped writing for the *Voice* and *The Times*, the amount of material coming out had become so voluminous that after a certain period of craziness and one-armed paperhanger behavior in relationship to it, I realized it was no longer possible for any single critic to cover all the books which were coming out. That in itself is a concurrent problem. There's a shortage of places and vehicles in which to talk about the books. There is an increasing amount of material coming out, much of it — although the actual reproduction quality and the bookmaking quality is very high — I don't think the imagery is of extraordinary importance, and I'm not sure that it deserves the permanence of book form, or the permanence of book form in an expensive, difficult-to-market, large edition. It's a difficult problem the critic is always dealing with as this material comes in: How significant is the work? How hard is it going to be for the work to reach its audience without your particular review of it? Is the work really strong and durable? How big is the actual market for the work as opposed to the size of the edition? I see a lot of work coming out that will not sell anywhere near the number of copies which are printed. It doesn't mean they're bad books, it just means that the person who made them may have overestimated the audience. It's a very complex situation. What we really need is a sort of *New York Review of Photography Books,* some kind of publication that concentrates specifically on the literature of photography in the sense of the books. And also something that hasn't happened, and it's a problem I'm trying to work on in my head because I'd like to help solve it, is there has not yet been what I think is the essential breakthrough past the photography audience to the general public for visual books generally, and photography books specifically. A book like **The Cosmic Bicycle** by Satty might sell ten, twelve thousand copies. A book that just came out on record album jackets will probably sell 25 — 30 thousand copies. As far as I understand the nature of the market for those books, it's what I would assume would be the market for a lot of the best photographic books. They're primarily young people, visually attuned, people who came through certain kinds of experiences in the sixties which opened them up, both drug experiences and creative experiences which opened them up to certain kinds of psychedelic fantasy imagery, to certain kinds of bizzare photography, but who won't, for some reason, come across Duane Michals' **Take One and See Mount Fujiyama,** just as a random example, or won't come across Ralph Gibson's trilogy. And the main reason that they won't come across it, is that it won't ever be presented to them in a context with those other books. It won't be presented to them in *Rolling Stone* (magazine); it won't be presented to them in whatever other magazines they might be reading. And I don't know why. I don't know what the access route is to get those books to that market. I think that that's the key. If photography books are to become really viable as products, without meaning as "merchandise," if they're to be able to be self-sustaining as a produced artifact, they've got to go beyond the market in photography. In photography there are now hundreds and hundreds of books competing against each other for a fairly limited amount of money, if you're talking about the audience of people who are knowledgeable in photography. There's got to come a point where, not that they've got to be sold in supermarkets, but where you've got to be able to walk into Scribner's bookstore and some other bookstores outside of Greenwich Village (but in New York City) and find a display of 20 to 30 visual books, at a reasonable price, that people are going to pick up and take home with them. I don't know how to make that connection. I've been looking for it for a long time.

TD: If visual books were dealt with as seriously by *The New York Times\and The New York Review of Books* **as poetry is dealt with, whereby visual books were discussed as though a book is read as fiction or poetry is read, and is not simply a collection of disparate images, I think there would be an audience. It doesn't seem to me to have proven out that photographers are interested in other photographers'**

work or buy other photographers' work. I think that's a common fallacy and assumption that people selling books perpetuate. I don't think photographers are the audience.

AC: That's partly true. However I found, writing for the *Times* and the *Village Voice*, what I thought was commentary that dealt with books beyond just the fact that they were collections of images, but tried to actually deal with them as books, as organized, coherent statements, when they were, at any rate; people would call and tell me they were delighted with the wonderful review and, as a result of the review, they got three orders for the books. I was never able to establish any kind of meaningful correlation between a review that I gave a book, either positive or negative, and its sales on any significant level. Photography books are underadvertised; we haven't, as a general rule, within photography, really done much in terms of publicizing photographic books, other than through the specifically photographic press. You don't see people going on television; you don't see people going on the talk shows with their books. We haven't really found ways yet of really talking effectively about images, and about photographic books, to an audience that doesn't have the book in front of them. It's a real problem. I was recently on a very early morning show on WBAI talking about **The Grotesque in Photography** and, at a certain point, we had a lot of time, so we decided there were probably a lot of people out there and we should try and describe the images. This is an incredible task, in that context — conversation — not even a written context. We were trying to describe what a Jerry Uelsmann photograph appears like to someone who might never have encountered a Jerry Uelsmann. It's a very bizarre experience. My experience with that book peculiarly is that it's had no advertising at all. It's had no advertising because apparently it is common practice in trade publishing of paperback books, unless it's something that's assumed is going to be a best seller, where there will be a push behind it, that it's cast out upon the water, cold. Your investment in it up through production and distribution is all you sink into it. You throw it out there; it sinks or swims. It finds its own space on the shelf, as they say, or it doesn't. If it sinks, so be it. They don't throw good money after bad. If it surfaces and survives for long enough, then maybe they will start putting some publicity push behind it. The book has had no reviews* that I know of except one totally negative review in the *Village Voice*, a full-page hostile pan, but full-page in the *Village Voice*, nonetheless less, which couldn't hurt, in some ways. Nevertheless, I presume just on the basis of its cover, probably predominantly, because that's what would make someone go to it who didn't know that it existed — nobody has any reason to know this book exists is what I'm saying, except for its presence; which manifests itself by a cover which is a fairly dramatic cover in this case. Then whatever impact the images have — they've sold over one-fourth of their first paperback printing and about a third of their hardbound printing, in maybe four months, which I find very exciting. It means the book sells to people who probably didn't know it existed before they hit it on the book shelf, which is good. I set out to make a book which would sell. There were going to be fifteen thousand copies printed, and it was not my fantasy that it should be remaindered at Marboro (bookstore) for ten years. I would like to get those copies out there *now*. It's been interesting to watch the process from that end and to realize that the only review it received has been the negative review, and yet it's selling well. So there's no correlation there either, to any kind of critical response to the book. I feel very ambivalent about it. What seems to be selling this book — aside

*This interview took place February 14, 1978. Mr. Coleman has informed me that there have been a number of reviews since.

from its contents which I'm sure people look through before they buy — is its cover which attracts them to it, and the fact that there's an excellent distribution system behind it. What I've heard from people I know around the country is that they've seen it in bookstores all over. Those seem to be the key factors. Shelf exposure, something eye-catching about the cover, and solid distribution. It's quite conceivable to me that the book could be panned by every reviewer who sees it, and yet sell very well. I certainly never assumed that the positive reviews that I wrote ever made or broke a book or a photographer. Sometimes I'd see things that I'd said in reviews excerpted in advertising for books. I don't know what affect that had, if any.

TD: Why do you think that someone like Hilton Kramer, who fairly regularly reviews photographic exhibitions, doesn't regularly review books?

AC: I don't think most reviewers take them seriously unless it's a retrospective monograph where they can approach a summing up of someone's career. They're still involved in dealing with photography in terms of original prints, rather than as a means of communicating photographically. Duane Michal's work does not need original prints as a form. He could communicate just as effectively through books in terms of what he's saying now. I think that's true of Ralph Gibson, and a whole lot of other people. That hasn't been recognized by a lot of critics, including a lot of photography critics, who are very much tied still, in one way or another, to the original print. It's certainly true of Gene Thornton, let's say. He's very involved on the one hand with a certain kind of mass-reproduced imagery in his writing, fashion imagery, but he doesn't seem to be particularly interested in photographic books, which are a much more viable way of communicating images and disseminating images, with the exception of images which rely very heavily on the experiencing of the original print. Most of the critics don't seem to come to that point of understanding photography books, so they'll wait for the show.

TD: People now seem to be collecting visual books by such artists as Lynd Ward, Frans Masereel, Rockwell Kent and others and yet that audience does not seem to be tapped for photographic books.

AC: I agree with you, and again I go back to what I was saying before, I don't know the reason. I don't know why that connection has not been made. It hasn't been made with the older people involved in visual books who seem to place photography books in a separate category and it hasn't been done with the younger group who are very involved with other kinds of visual books, not so much with Lynd Ward, but with Zap comics, let's say. That's a kind of visual book which I take very seriously. Once again, they won't think of it in the same vein. Maybe if there was a tradition in America of the kind of photographically illustrated narrative comic book that you have in Latin American culture... I don't know if you've seen those at all, but they're a lot of "true romances" and instead of being drawn cartoon-style, theyll be acted out with actors and a scenario, and little balloons giving the dialogue, and they'll be photo narratives. They'll be very banal, very cliched and the photography will not be particularly interesting, but at least you have people there who are habituated to picking up a photo narrative, a book in essence, even though it's usually magazine form, and reading through it and responding to it as an experience in photography. We don't have anything like that in this culture. We do that with literal photojournalistic material to some extent in magazines and so on, but there's no place where we sit down with a book of photographs for fun.

TD: With the exception of the wedding album or the family album.

AC: Yeah.

TD: Something that sums up this predicament is: George Tice has had three books

published by Rutgers University Press, Paterson, Urban Landscapes **and his monograph,** George A. Tice 1953-1973; **and the monograph is, by far, the best seller among them. People will buy the greatest hits, so to speak, but not the concept books, where the work is in its original form, in effect. I find that a curious way of looking at somebody's work. If I had a choice between his monograph and** Urban Landscapes, **for example, I certainly would take the latter because I like to see the way an artist works as opposed to what he thinks are his best images over a period of years.**

AC: Something here that I think is very important, and I think this is true as much inside photography still as it is among the general public, is that there is an attachment or a fixation on the single image rather than on the extended series, or the sequence or the suite of imagery, again with the exception of photojournalism, where we're accustomed to the idea that there might be a body of work done around an idea or theme or situation. In what we think of as art photography or serious photography, there's the assumption that a book is just a collection of single images. If you talk about the way a book is edited, or sequenced, you're usually talking about the fact that there's a round shape on this page and a round shape on that page, and that's sequencing. The idea that the book itself, or a sequence of photographs itself, is a thing... You can make a sequence into something that is greater than the sum of its parts, and it's important to experience images in a particular order, in a particular rhythm, and it's important to sit with it at a certain tempo, slower than that which we are usually used to approaching photographs maybe, to get into the idea of spending an evening with a book of photographs. Experience them at a slow enough rhythm that you could actually get involved in the space between the images, as well as in the images themselves. This is still a foreign thought, even to most people in photography. Most photographers flip through books the same way you see people at the racks in the book stores. A one-second flip, thumb through, and they won't go from beginning to end necessarily. They'll open at the middle. They won't assume that there's a sequence, that it's a significant sequence. They'll assume that the single images should communicate a thought. I think if you're going to pick up a Duane Michals book and look at it that way, it's going to seem ridiculous; if you're going to pick up a Ralph Gibson book and look at it that way, although Ralph's imagery functions as single imagery also, but that's not the point of **The Somnambulist,** that's not the point of what he was doing in that trilogy, you're going to miss it. It's not just that there are ten hot images in **Days at Sea.** It's like looking for the hot parts in **Lady Chatterley's Lover;** that's not what you read it for, or it's not the only thing you read it for.

TD: At least Duane Michals is literal in his sequencing, so you're kind of forced to follow his concept, but with Ralph Gibson it's less obvious. The audience is illiterate in terms of reading visual books. That is the major problem in gaining an audience because the audience is not aware of this fact, therefore they're not curious about visual books in that sense. They don't think of them as something they have to bring themselves to, and sit, and read and spend an evening, as you said.

AD: This is a problem because an increasing number of books that come out are, in fact, extended statements. They are intended as unified books and intended to be dealt with as a unit of work, whether things are just thematically joined or they're more literally sequenced or serial in nature. We've got to re-educate ourselves within photography to sitting down with that kind of book, and not the "greatest hits" kind of book which used to be the tradition. We've got to find some kind of way, and I don't know what it is, of attuning an audience outside of photography to the fact that this is a kind of experience you have when you deal with photographs and books. Some of those books are things you have to spend time with. You have to consider the relationships between the images. You don't sit there and say, "I like this page and I don't like that page," any more than you would do that with a novel. Presumably you either don't read it at all or you throw it aside after the first couple of pages, or you read it through.

TD: That's what I see the function of the critic to be — to educate his audience, tell the audience how to read a book of photographs. It appears to be such a simple thing that it's overlooked. And it's quite a complex thing. Do you feel the visual book has been exploited or do you think we're still in the infancy of the movement?

AC: I don't think it has been drained dry by any means. There are a lot of books coming out that probably should not be done as expensively or in as large an edition as they're being done in, or maybe not done at all. But there are an increasing number of very fine books coming out. Books which are suggesting a lot of ways of opening up the medium of the photographic book as such through different kinds of experiments in printing — I'm thinking here particularly about **Pleasure Beach** by Syl Labrot — or in which the photographer is exploring the possibility of making an extended statement of some kind, whether it's combining words and images in the way that someone like Gaylord Herron does, or whether it's doing it entirely with images, in the way that Ralph Gibson does in his books. In fact, it's a much more suitable vehicle for the imagery than the original print form because the original print form carries with it certain kinds of assumptions which are, in many ways, antithetical to the ideal situation in which you might experience the work, and be most receptive to it. Original print form necessitates museum or gallery display, unless you're going to assume that someone should be able to buy a sequence of prints, which would be beautiful, but few people can do that. So the best way for someone to experience a sequence, an extended statement, is certainly to be able to experience it over and over again. And to have that kind of repeated experience in any kind of sane way in this culture means you have to have the material accessible to you in your own home. Very few people can find time to go back, and back, to a gallery or a museum during whatever the short run of the work being there. Even if they go back every day they would only experience that work during that one particular phase of their lives and would not have the option of coming back to it a year later, if the impulse moved them. That's another thing that having the work in book form gives you. The lack of intimacy in a one-to-one relationship to the work in museum and gallery context, where you're surrounded by other people, has always been a distraction to me and a problem in regard to being able to slow my rhythm down to the rhythm of the work. You're involved in the rhythm of the public life around you. You're put in a situation where, in one way or another, you're going to be somewhat self-conscious in a way that you wouldn't be at home. I mean you can't look at work nude; you can't look at work just before or after making love; you can't look at the work just before you go to sleep. There are a lot of contexts the work is excluded from in that original print form that it's not excluded from in book form. That's a very important way to be able to experience work. There is some work where you really cannot get the full experience of the imagery except through direct contact with the prints, largely because the person has been committed to the print as the primary vehicle for the work. A prime example of that might be Weston, where no matter how much you may respond to his images simply as images, until you've had the chance to feel the quality of his prints by actual contact with them, you're just not aware of the depth of his sensuality, and his sensual response to the world. But I find an increasing number of photographers who are beginning to think of the print as a matrix for the reproduction, rather than as the end in itself. Once you do that you no longer accept reproductions as inadequate facsimilies of your work, but you can actually start conceptualizing the reproduction as the ideal multiple form for your work to take, with prints being almost a tangential, or irrelevant aspect of your work. There are a lot of images, and I don't think it's in any way denigrating to them to say this, that do not need duotone, for which duotone is superfluous, which don't even need any kind of double-run, but which would provide all their information, all their structure, all their form, and even all their significant tonalities in a good single-run halftone. The little book that I did, **Confirmation,** for example. It would never have occurred to me to go for a fancier reproduction quality. It was just straight single-run halftone. I would have liked a slightly warmer halftone than I got. If I reprint I'll go after a slightly better quality, but those images are in that book for informational purposes. They're not in there to be considered as fine prints. What's important is certain kinds of information. That's all they're there for. I wouldn't go to Rapoport with a project like that. That's become like Mecca for photographers: Whatever you do should be done by Rapoport. Maybe it shouldn't be. Maybe you should explore whoever your local printer is, or learn how to print yourself, which a number of people are doing, or look at some of the other possible printing processes, and go through a very coherent evaluation of your project in terms of what you can afford, what you think the maximum audience for this is going to be, on any kind of realistic level. What kind of reproduction will best serve the images, what kind of reproduction is superfluous, what kind of reproduction is inadequate? Does it need hardcover, what kind of binding is available, how much of it can you do yourself, how much do you have to farm out? Do it in a way where you're not trying to make a posher book than the next guy. Maybe it shouldn't be. Maybe we need more cheap books. One thing I really like about **Confirmation** was that I could, more or less, cover my costs by selling it for $3.50 a copy. I was able to give away half the edition and still make essentially what I paid out for the book. When you go over five bucks, you're doing a specific something to people's pocketbooks; when you go over ten bucks, you're doing a specific thing to people's pocketbooks; and I know, quite aside from photography, that I will make certain decisions about spending more than ten dollars for a book, and I'll make certain decisions about spending more than fifteen dollars for a book, and I'll rarely spend more than twenty dollars for a new book. I love books. I've got a house full of books, but I'll wait for them to come on sale at Marboro's. I don't see a whole lot of books that are worth twenty dollars of the cash that I go out and earn, and I can't afford most of the few that I do see that are worth that much. I think people are tending to be unrealistic that way, tending to want to make such a superb book as a product, as an example of the bookmaker's craft. A lot of times you've got to look at your images and say, "What do these images need? What does this book need? If I brought this out and people could buy it for five dollars, might I not sell eight thousand copies more, or two thousand copies more than I'm going to sell if I bring it out priced at fourteen dollars? What's the range in between there and what compromises would I make? What's acceptable and what isn't?"

TD: Do you think most photographers are unrealistic in their expectations?

AC: I think the books cost a lot of money. To ask somebody to spend as much as a record would cost them, or as much as a movie for two would cost them, is not unrealistic, in terms of a smallish book, at any rate. If you're going to ask them to spend upwards of ten dollars on a book, certainly if you're going to ask them to spend upward of fifteen dollars, you had damn well better be giving them a book that, just in their initial approach to it, when they first see it, and hold it and feel it, is going to make them feel that this is something they're going to go back to time and time again.

TD: When Joan Lyons did Abby Rogers to Her Granddaughter, **about a year and a half ago, she printed five hundred copies and felt it would be a market research test to see how many books she could sell. I think that's an intriguing idea. Maybe photographers should involve themselves more in finding out who their audience is. Maybe doing 250 copies of** Confirmation, **as you did, was a realistic number.**

AC: I thought it was. I'm surprised that there are actually, aside from around a hundred people that I gave copies to, maybe a hundred and fifty people out there, who I didn't give copies to, who were interested enough in it, for whatever their reasons, that they would buy it. I think that was wonderful. When I go back to press, I'll probably do a larger edition, maybe four hundred, maybe even five hundred (maximum) copies. If I do that, I would be very surprised if I run out of copies before ten years from now. When I did that book I did it with the feeling that the material specifically belonged in book form. It was organic and I felt like it should have its own identity, and book form seemed like the right thing. At the same time, I realized that there might not be a whole lot of people who would be interested in this particular kind of little book, which intersects adolescence, romanticism, jazz, pilgrimage and the myth of the artist as a self-destructive hero. That was a very personal statement, and there might not be a very wide audience for it, in photography or outside of photography. I just wanted to make that book, and two hundred and fifty was not going to cost me any more than one hundred and fifty, in any meaningful way. I'm much happier going back to press with it — having found that there actually might be more people out there wanting it — than I would be if I had printed two thousand of it, on the assumption that there should be an audience out there for two thousand copies, and finding myself with 1800 copies now in my closet, and with whatever additional bills would have been involved with that already paid out. Why? Going back to press on that is not going to cost me a whole lot. Nothing has gone up significantly since then.

TD: It's an interesting idea. Photographers seem repeatedly to print more books than they can effectively move and yet they cling adamantly to the idea that there should be that number of people out there for their work. Maybe there should be, but there isn't and it may be a more viable solution to just do the number that they can sell quickly, without having any expectations beyond what is there.

AC: Sure. It's true. You run into some specific economic problems when you get involved in fancy bookmaking, duotone printing and hard binding where it's unfeasible to do a thousand copies. The cost is such that you might as well go to four or five thousand copies. At that point, if you're only going to do a thousand, the price you've got to charge for it is so impossibly high that you won't sell any of them. It's a complicated situation. I think a lot of it has to do with that impulse to make the great book, not just in terms of the imagery, or the coherence, but the reproduction has to be fantastic, and so on. It's wonderful; those books are lovely. But there are closets full of them all over America now. It's getting to the point where virtually everybody is publishing or self-publishing a book; in most cases, it seems to me, they're going to have to eat their books.

TD: That's true even of the good ones. How does an artist go about getting his book reviewed?

AC: The way it mostly happens with me, and I presume generally, people send me copies of the books. For quite a while, when I was writing for the *Voice* and *The*

Times, I tried to review, (and even do more than review; really deal at length with) virtually everything that came across my desk. Toward the end of that period, '72 — '73, that became impossible, just because of the volume that was coming through, and at that point, I left both those forums for that kind of writing, and haven't devoted consistent attention to books since. Recently I've started a column at *Camera 35* which will deal with more than a few dozen books a year out of what is bound to be hundreds that will appear. I'm going to try to concentrate on things that I think are important, but are not being reviewed elsewhere. I'm going to be trying there to bring them to an audience which is a photography audience, but goes beyond the art photography audience. I would love, and have proposed to *Rolling Stone* on several occasions, to have a column devoted to photography with the concentration on photographic books, and have been told by them that "its time has not yet come." I would assume that that's mostly how it happens with everybody, which may be naive.

TD: What is interesting to me is that books such as Syl Labrot's Pleasure Beach, **Gaylord Herron's** Vagabond **and Ralph Gibson's trilogy all came out within a fairly short period of time when you think of the relatively important books within the context of the history of photography. That's a real good indication of what the future will hold.**

AC: Sure. And, by and large, even the books that we think of as the good books of the past in photography, it wasn't the books that had the impact back then, in most cases. There was the work getting out in some other form. There might be a few things that we could cite, but at this point we're looking back at the history of the photographic book and saying to ourselves, "this has been a very important vehicle for the medium." But at the time, I don't think people were dealing with that kind of awareness, few people were. Wright Morris' books were very important, his trilogy: **The Inhabitants, The Home Place** and then, much later, **God's Country and My People. The Inhabitants** and **The Home Place** were very important books, very seminal books. They were totally overlooked at the time. Nobody paid any attention to them.

TD: The Americans **is another example.**

AC: Same thing. A very important book. Ten years after it was made it had revolutionized the medium, but at the time, was remaindered. **Let Us Now Praise Famous Men** (Walker Evans and James Agee) sold three hundred copies. A classic case. They were seminal books, not just as anthologies of images, but seminal books and yet, at the time, no recognition. I think people are very actively, at this point, exploring the photographic book as a medium for the first time. And I think there's a growing audience for that. It's still small and we tend to overestimate it and unless something clicks in the mass consciousness — and it wouldn't have to be a big click. If it were mentioned in the *Midnight Reporter* that Jackie Onassis always looked at a visual book before she went to sleep, that would be probably enough to spring the three to four thousand people who we need from the general audience into buying photographic books on a regular basis... All the serious critics in photography have got to start paying more attention to books and have got to be much more brutal about what is not significant, even though in many cases, and this is painful to me, you know you're dealing with something that somebody sunk their own personal money into, and in many ways, put their own personal lives on the line for, not just their work, where somebody has an economic investment in his own work and you know he spent ten thousand dollars and four months of his time seeing that thing through Rapoport (Printing Corporation) and you look at it and say, "This book is really not worth that energy and that money." That's excruciating. In that regard I'd much rather deal with the commercial publishers where I don't feel that I'm affecting someone's own economics directly by panning a book. But we're going to have to be more brutal because the audience is floundering. The audience is out there faced with this smorgasbord of photographic books which they can't, in most cases, come in direct contact with, unless they happen to be able to get into the Witkin (Gallery) or some place like that. The prices are pretty high and very few really get reviewed more than once or twice. Most of them get a mention in *Afterimage's* Received and Noted section. I really do feel that we need to start, in some forum or in a number of forums, concentrating on the photographic book as a vehicle for photography, as maybe the most appropriate vehicle in our time, certainly as a vehicle whose roots are in the nature of photography itself. For instance, the halftone process and the reproducibility of the images. We have got to start sorting through this stuff. There are mountains and mountains of material coming out, and until we're able to be clearer about what makes a significant photographic book; what the significant photographic books are, it's unrealistic to expect a mass audience, without a background in photography, to be able to walk into a bookstore and make a selection. On what basis do we expect people to buy books? People don't buy books in any other medium that way, that casually. They buy a novel generally because it's received some kind of positive review, unless they're readers of a genre. We've got to find ways of exposing people to these books other than simply the bookstore counter. Maybe television is an answer; maybe people should be going to talk shows and taking ten minutes to take people through their pictures.

TD: I remember David Douglas Duncan doing that years ago on at least two occasions. He did that with Self-Portrait: U.S.A.; **he actually had a spot on the 1968 campaign coverage. Also he had a half-hour show devoted to** War Without Heroes **when that came out. He's a master at marketing his books. How did you get on the talk show with** The Grotesque in Photography?

AC: I know somebody working for the station who had done an interview with me on photography about a year ago and I simply called up and said, "Would you be interested? I know you're running an early morning talk show. I'll come on as a guest." I sent a copy of the book to Casey Allen and said the same thing, "Would you be interested in having this on your TV show on Channel 31?" He said "Sure." I have no idea who these shows reach and probably never will, and have no idea as to what effect, if any, they had on sales. My own feeling, after my experience with this book — and with some other books I've got in the works — is that you sell the book yourself. Even the publishers, by and large, do not sell the book as effectively as the person who does the book. Certainly anything self-published you sell yourself. This is a psychological and professional conflict that a lot of photographers are encountering because, for a long time, in "art photography" or "serious photography," again outside of photojournalism, there's been the tacit assumption that (without meaning it in the sexist way) it was a gentlemen's profession. That is, you didn't ever have to get involved in selling yourself, or merchandising. In fact, if you did, you were in some way cheapening the work and yourself enormously. If you're going to make a book, you're a manufacturer, without getting horribly bourgeois, and since you're a manufacturer, if you're going to assume that people are going to beat a path to your door to buy your product, in a market that's flooded with products, you're a damn fool. Why be a product maker in that case? If you want to sell, you're going to have to go out and sell it and that's going to involve being a merchant, and if you don't like it, don't do it. If you're going to do it, do it — to the hilt. You're going to have to hit dozens of little bookstores and persuade the owners, who see dozens of people coming in with all kinds of books, that they should put your book on display. You're going to have to deal with the fact that there are outlets and routes of access for publicity about these books and you're going to have to find out what they are. You may have to go on talk shows, you may have to give lectures. You may have to do any number of things. Go stand in supermarkets and sell them. Among other things, people outside of photography will start buying photography books when people in photography start coming to them with photography books to sell. The big problem is that photography books are sold primarily, and marketed, to the photography audience. It's like preaching to the converted. It's everybody trying to get a limited amount of money to stretch over an increasingly unlimited number of books. It's not going to happen. Just to support the books you've got to go outside of photography. Well, *do it*.

TD: How important is the book for an artist and would you like more artists to do books?

AC: You have to go back to what you were saying before about why you were writing poetry. You're not a poet, you're not terribly interested in poetry, but you found yourself writing poetry. **(Earlier in the evening, prior to the taping of this interview, over coffee, I had mentioned that I had written a series of poems over a three-month period while in a particularly difficult time in my life and was puzzled as to why I chose that particular medium to express my anguish. TD).** I don't simply advocate doing books. It is fun to make a book. I feel that from the experience of making a commercial book; I feel that from the experience of making a couple of privately produced books. This is an enjoyable experience. It's just as enjoyable to make 250 copies or 50 copies, on the private level, as it is to make 2000 copies. The only reason to make an edition beyond your immediate circle of friends and acquaintances, and relatives you might want to give Christmas presents to, is that there is a market. Make a realistic assessment as to what the market is. It's a very exciting medium to explore, but there are economics involved that you've got to take into account. The real reason to make a book is because you have something that requires book form for its fullest expression. I'm not talking about size of edition. Other than that, it's pointless. It's a kind of careerist move, in a lot of cases, which has certain practical value. It looks good on your resume, and people don't know when they pick up your resume that your parents funded it, and your closet is filled with them, and nobody liked it. That's not a reason to do it. You can still publish a book that way without making 2000 copies. You can make 20 copies in original print form and put the same press name on it and copyright it. Part of what I want to say is: don't make a product for the market unless you feel this thing has to be made, intrinsically to you. It's important that it be made because the work requires it. And without a realistic look at the market, it's pointless. Make books all you want, but don't feel that you've got to make commercially viable books unless you've really got a notion of what commercial viability means. Oddly enough, in this field, although at some point I think it will be different, at this point, the critical response is not a key thing at all in terms of what happens to it. I cannot think of a book which has been made or broken by the criticism in terms of photography books.

TD: Where do you place the picture book in the history of the illustrated book and do you think it is thought of in those terms?

AC: I don't think it is generally. The only person I've really heard speak of it at any real length in those terms is Nathan Lyons. Certainly at any point, from now on, when people start to talk about or to write about the illustrated book as a phenomenon in book cultures, they're going to have to start taking into account the photographic book as a kind of entity in itself. In fact, since photography was invented, there have been more books illustrated with photographs published than in all the other forms of illustrated books combined, prior to that time, maybe even through the present. It's become the most overwhelmingly used means of illustrating books, and in a sense, almost every other form of illustration seems archaic. When we're talking about the illustrated book now I think we're talking predominantly about the photographically illustrated book. It's an inevitable phenomenon. In a way, it's more inevitable than prints as a vehicle for the dissemination of "serious" photographic imagery due to the kinds of limitations we spoke of before, and especially because it makes possible the truly massive dissemination and the rapid dissemination of images and of the ideas and feelings contained in the images. It's, to me, a very natural evolutionary step that photographers — especially right at a point where the classic silver print is probably on the decline due to the diminishing supply of silver — should be moving away from original print form, or at least from that absolute dependence on original print form, and back into the idea of the photograph as a multiple, and as an accessible multiple, rather than a very, very high-priced precious-object multiple. The first photographic prints that were manufactured were not manufactured as one-of-a-kind unique prints, they were mass manufactured in the thousands and people bought them either in book form, as original prints prior to the halftone, or bought them individually and pasted them into books. Maybe it will be seen as an aberration, in the future, that for a period of sixty to seventy years, photography went in the direction of the unique, hand-made, original, signed print as the predominant vehicle for expression, and only after a particular kind of print material disappeared from the market did photographers then return to the original form of photographic image dissemination which is through books or through large-scale multiples of the images.

Staten Island, N.Y.
February 14, 1978

David Godine

Interviewer: Would you encourage a photographer to work towards doing a book?

David Godine: Only if they're able to conceive and grapple with the problems of photographs as books, and not photographs as portfolios. Most of the people we see think we're publishing a wall of photographs, and we're not. We're publishing a book. We're publishing conjugate spreads. That's what a book is, where one photograph, or one-half of a leaf plays against the other half of the leaf, where sequencing, scaling and subject are terribly important, and, I argue, that's very different than going around a gallery and looking at a hundred photographs on the wall.

On March 9, 1978, I interviewed David Godine at the Yale Club in New York City. David Godine is president of David Godine, Publisher in Boston, Massachusetts and a man deeply involved in producing beautifully-produced books. He assumes full responsibility for the choices he makes. The list of books he publishes reveals, to a significant degree, his interests and avocations. He gives the impression of a man motivated by passion for what he does. David Godine publications reflect the sensibilities of the man David Godine.

Tom Dugan: How did you begin publishing photographic titles?

David Godine: We started for precisely the same reasons that I publish anything: I like it. I like photographs and I like particular kinds of photographs. I'm not interested in the broad range of photography any more than I am in poetry or fiction. I have people I care for and I think should be published and I have other people who leave me, more or less, cold. I was always interested in the history of photography because it seemed to me to be not written about extensively, the prototypes of how photography developed, and because it paralleled printing. The greatest printed books were in the first fifty years; as far as I'm concerned the greatest photographs, both in terms of the photographic quality and the technology, more interestingly, came in the first fifty years. I came at it from those two directions.

TD: Do you see yourself as a publisher of historical monographs?

DG: No, not in photography anyway. Every year we've done a new photographer. We've done Rosey Purcell's first book, which was Polaroids; we did Kip Kumler's book; we did Steven Guyon Wilson's book; this year we're doing Olivia Parker's book. We also publish, I thing importantly, criticism. This year we're going to come out with a translation of Gisele Freund's classic book, **Society and Photography,** which is a study of the interrelationship between mass communications in the media and how people perceive reality, or how reality can be shaped by what we read and see in the newspapers. And next spring we're publishing a collection of Janet Malcolm's essays which appeared in *The New Yorker* (magazine) about photography. They interest me because they're on the other side of the spectrum of John

Szarkowski whose opinions I've become increasingly suspicious of, and whose taste I generally disagree with, although, as a human being, I'm very fond of him.

TD: To me the crucial issue is: Why can't photographers get published? Why does or did Ralph Gibson have to self-publish; George Tice and Robert Adams had to go to university presses; Eikoh Hosoe is yet to be published in this country, except in a children's book; and a whole range of photographers still can't be published, or aren't being published?

DG: I don't think it's their fault, first of all. I think most of them have probably tried. I think it's the fault of both the way publishing is set up today, which I don't think they really understand, and the fault of the system, which is very rigid and somewhat archaic. Publishing, to take the first issue, is really set up not the way it was for ten, fifteen or twenty years, or indeed the way it is in my company, which is one human sensibility making decisions about what it likes, and what it wants to bring before the public. It's more of a corporate decision today; it's a decision which frequently entails not one man's mind, but a committee; and the committee, in general, is more geared to commercial best sellers, and books which have break-through potential, and which have subsidiary rights potential than it is to producing a fine art reproductive monograph on an individual photographer. That's number one. The sensitivities of the people involved in the industry are not what they were ten or fifteen years ago, and photography is certainly not high on their list of profit centers. Second is the expense of publishing a photographic book. You're dealing with what is essentially an inferior medium, namely offset, compared to collograph, or collotype, or gravure, or woodburytype, or anything that involves continuous tone reproduction; and to do offset correctly, which is the only way to do it, you have to do 300 line screen duotones. At least we haven't figured out any way to avoid that, and that is a very expensive process. It requires two negatives; it requires very good paper to print on, and it requires a very careful and good printing outfit, of which we have, maybe four in this country to work with. So whereas the commercial publisher could publish three books of fiction, each with a "breakthrough" potential, he could only get one book of photography out of that same amount of dollars, which would have very little potential. The key thing is to remember that publishers lose money publishing books. They don't make any money publishing books; they make money on their subsidiary rights. And the third factor, if you take factor number one as the people who are going to be receptive to this in the industry, the problems and expense of the medium through which you're conveying your material, namely offset, as your second difficulty; the third difficulty is the distribution system which is clearly not geared to handle photographic books other than specialized and very hopeful outlets like Lionel's (Light Impressions). But with the exception of those people who have perceived this need, the average book-store, and the average distributor, looks upon a book of photography as the whale grounded in Nantucket. It's a curiosity which flops around the beach for a certain length of time, and then is usually shoved back into the publisher's lap. Those are three very real difficulties why commercial publishers don't grasp, with amorous intensity, books from photographers.

TD: Do you think that the public will accept photography?

DG: Now that's a different question. The public may accept it, just as the public accepts, let's say, pornography. That doesn't mean that the publisher will publish it. There are many things which the public accepts, which publishers won't touch. The public certainly accepts it more than publishers push it, but they seem to be two different issues.

TD: What books do you think are seminal books in the literature of photography?

DG: That's a tough question because they've appeared at very intermittent intervals. Certainly **The Pencil of Nature** (William Henry Fox Talbot) was one. I think Beaumont Newhall was a seminal figure. Szarkowski's book **Looking at Photographs** is a great book. There are certain privately printed books, **Pleasure Beach** (Syl Labrot). **The American Monument** (Lee Friedlander) of the Eakins Press in terms of the technology that was applied to that, the intelligence; that Friedlander book is a monumental book, in all senses of the word. Then there were books in which somehow the blending of the photograph with the text really worked. The prime example of that would be **Let Us Now Praise Famous Men** (Walker Evans and James Agee). Not the subsequent editions, but the first edition. And, for instance, the photographs that were taken for **Walden** (Henry David Thoreau) were terrific. That was a Limited Editions Club book by Edward Steichen. But that interrelationship between photography and literature has always been an uneasy alliance. **Victorian Photographs of Famous Men and Fair Women** by Julia Margaret Cameron, but that was a limited edition. Most of the books in the early twentieth century were limited editions. It's only really in the 50's, 60's and 70's that you've had commercially available books on or of particular photographers.

TD: Would you encourage a photographer to work toward doing a book?

DG: Only if they're able to conceive and grapple with the problems of photographs as books, and not photographs as portfolios. Most of the people we see think that we're publishing a wall of photographs, and we're not. We're publishing a book. We're publishing conjugate spreads. That's what a book is, where one photograph, or one-half of a leaf plays against the other half of the leaf, where sequencing, scaling and subject are terribly important, and I argue, that's very different than going around a gallery and looking at a hundred photographs on the wall. When I see a photographer I like I frequently am in the position to say, "These are wonderful photographs, but you don't have a book. Now start thinking of it as a book." That's something most of them don't do. The masterpieces in my mind were European. If you look at the early books, published in Paris, of Brassai and Kertesz, you really have a feeling of somebody with great intelligence and sensitivity putting together a sequence of images. They're just spectacular — some of those early books.

TD: If a photographer was interested in privately publishing, what kind of a run should he do?

DG: Boy, I think that's an act of sacrifice, and perhaps suicidal idiocy that I would not advocate in the first place. If he were to come to the position that the only way he could distribute his work is to publish it himself, I would advise him to rely very heavily on direct mail to sell it. I would sell as many copies as I humanly could in advance.

TD: What do you mean by direct mail?

DG: Doing a brochure. Announcing the price of the book, giving some illustrations, what the book looked like, and writing wonderful selling copy — copy that would make people say, "This is an important book." If I did direct mail for **Pleasure Beach** (SYL Labrot), I would have sold out the edition in perhaps 24 hours, maybe 12. It's a great book, but nobody knows it's a great book until they actually see it, fondle it, and hold it. There are things you could say about that book which should be said and which indeed are true, which would have made it a natural book for direct mail. For a small publisher, dealing with the few bookstores that will carry their work is a hassle, which I don't advise for anyone. I doubt if Lionel (Suntop — Light Impressions) would advise it. Dealing with a good distributor, like Lionel, I would advise, even though Lionel I'm sure takes a pretty steep slice, but at least he has the contacts — he does direct mail, he covers the bases. Another thing is the production and design of the book. Every photographer I've ever met thinks he's God's gift to design and production. Most of them don't know a damn thing about it, and they should get somebody who is in the business of designing and producing photographic books, and have it done subject to their approval, but they shouldn't get into doing it themselves. **Pleasure Beach** was a great exception to that, but it was not a conventionally designed book. It was brilliant, in fact, because it *wasn't* a conventionally designed book. The printing is not the difficulty. It's the design, the sequencing, the sizing, etc.

TD: Don't you think a lot of books were ruined by their designers?

DG: Yes, but I think an equal number have been ruined by photographers.

TD: What size edition would you advise?

DG: Anyone who prints more than 5000 of a photographic book today, unless it is of a major, major figure, is taking a serious risk. Even with a major figure like Avedon or Penn, I think publishers have problems. In fact I *know* publishers have problems. And this was a great mistake that many of the commercial houses made a few years back, which is why they're so scared today. They went in and started printing editions of ten thousand and twenty thousand copies. It's insanity because there aren't that many people who are going to plunk out $8.95 for a softcover, or $20.00 for a hardcover of a photographic book. Photographers don't buy them, by and large. The libraries are a little bit afraid of them because they get torn up or ripped off, which they do. The average house, if it's got coffee table book money, is going to spend it on *The Wild Game of Africa*, or *Great Houses of New England*. It's not going to spend it on the monograph of Robert Heinecken.

TD: Don't you feel that that's one of the problems with photographic publishing: too many monographs, and not enough picture books are published?

DG: The basic problem is not enough good *criticism* is published, so there has not been established a corpus of critical apparatus which gives people a frame of reference about photography which they have say, about literature, which they have about news because you have a newspaper as a frame of reference, or you have the TV as a frame of reference. When you get into photographic books, what's your frame of reference? Your eye is your frame of reference, and it's a very unselective source. Most people see these books very unselectively. They have no way to distinguish, and they're very afraid to say, "I will buy what I like." That's the fallback position that terrifies people the most, particularly if they can't quote a source. "Well, I like it because Susan Sontag likes it. I like this position because Scotty Reston likes it." Americans, by and large, are not mentally pioneering as a culture, and that's why the "avant garde" books have real trouble. That's why Ralph Gibson has trouble. It's not the Garry Winogrands of the world who have trouble. He's the easiest kind of photographer to relate to, but Jerry Uelsmann will have trouble. And what he's done, he's done for fifteen years now.

TD: What I don't understand is, why publishers are not more daring in what they publish. I don't understand why monographs are published so much, as opposed to those pieces that are conceived as books. Would you address yourself to that? I don't think there are too many people in publishing who know enough about photography to have any kind of influence.

DG: I think you're probably right. A monograph, to me, isn't a dirty word. We did monographs on (Frank) Sutcliffe, (P.H.) Emerson and (Roger) Fenton, and they're perfectly well-produced monographs on those three important, 19th century photographers. But if you define monographs as a random collection of photographs culled from the photographer's last ten years' work, that is no way to publish a book. You're quite right. Unless the photographer has such an enormous reputation, which almost none of them do, that people will just buy the book because it's a new book by Mr. X.

TD: Even Ansel Adams makes some attempt to make it a book like Photographs of the Southwest **or some such.**

DG: Sure. And I think to be successful, the message of the photographer has to be clear, just the way that the message of a fiction writer, or a poet has to be clear. He has to be saying something, and he has to be saying it in such a way that people can relate to it, to some degree identify with it, talk to their friends about it. It's a discovery — as when you read a good book of fiction you say, "This is terrific. I'm going to tell my friends about this." And that has to present a coherent point of view, which is uniquely yours, it's not someone else's, it's not derivative. And that's what excites me about a few of the photographers I see, not all of them, needless to say, but *some* of those who come in, and you can see these people are doing something different. They have something different to say. They have a new slant on things. That's when a publisher gets excited. But, of course, the majority of the photographs, particularly the "photojournalistic school", does not have that slant. The other problem is: you can't do a photographic book the way you can do a book of poetry or fiction. There you're dealing with letters as metaphor, so whether you print the letters well, or whether you don't print them so well; whether you use a cheap piece of paper, or a good piece of paper; whether you prefer to bind the book, or sew the book, is all irrelevant to the metaphorical content which is presented by 26 letters. But in photography publishing, you're reproducing a unique, continuous-tone object, and you're dealing with a medium which is inherently inferior. There's no way anyone can convince me that offset, as a method, compares to what was available to us fifty years ago. That's number one. You've got to do it right, to do it at all. And that's a drawback because it's not true of fiction, it's not true of poetry. There you can do it right, and you can do it cheaply. In photography, the only way to do it right is to spend a lot of money, and money is scarce these days. Number two is: you don't have, either in the public or in the review media, anything like a critical awareness of what photographers are trying to do today; how it differs from what they were trying to do ten or fifteen years ago. The photographers, by and large, aren't terribly articulate. You can go out and interview Gibson, and get a good interview, but you can't do that with a lot of photographers. If you're a novelist, it's expected that you'll be terrific entertainment, and you are. People have been brought up with prose. They've read it — they read it everyday. Whereas photographs, they're not taught to judge and evaluate. I think that's the major problem in the sales. The books aren't reviewed and unless a book is reviewed, the main source of a publisher's sales, the main steady source which is libraries, is not going to buy the book. Librarians, by and large, won't go to the bathroom unless they read a review telling them it's OK. And they're certainly not going to spend twenty dollars on a monograph, or even an important book unless they read at least three sources that it's a good book, it's OK, you can spend your money on it. They are, historically, a very timid lot.

TD: I take it you're not optimistic?

DG: No, I'm not optimistic about the place of the book in American culture, but that's been a problem for two hundred years. I don't think it's going to be anything that I'm going to solve. As long as there are publishers, and there always will be publishers, or photographers, who care about putting their pictures between covers, we're going to have photographic books published. Also the technology of offset has really come a long way, as much as I downplay it. If you look at what's being done today by Rapoport or Meriden, or Thomas Todd, compared to what was done ten, fifteen or twenty years ago, you realize that we've made quantum leaps in our ability to reproduce photographs; but it's becoming more expensive, and that's what worries me. You've got to have a minimum of ten thousand dollars today to do a good photographic book in a commercially viable quantity.

TD: Being five thousand copies?

DG: Being five thousand, yeah, and that's bringing it in at two dollars a book, which I advise people is very, very difficult to do.

TD: You don't think that some photographers could get away with cheaper offset?

DG: Yes, sure I do, but they're not the photographers I'm interested in, by and large, but some definitely could. That book by Giselle Freund which really is a book on the place of the newspaper, and of the periodical, like *Time* and *Newsweek*, and our perceptions of social problems, certainly doesn't require first rate reproduction, because the way the originals were originally reproduced was second rate, but if we're doing a book of Olivia Parker, or Kip Kumler, then we really do have to worry about that problem. Yes, it depends.

New York City
March 9, 1978

Sid Rapoport

Interviewer: Is that the difference between Stonetone and duotone, the inks?
Sid Rapoport: It's one of the differences. The Stonetone Process depends very much on a whole different procedure. It's the original film, the screens, the nonscreen image, the method in the making of the plates, the inks and the procedure on the press. It's a whole system, rather than one thing by itself. The Stonetone negative, which is a secondary negative, is not a conventional screened negative; it has a very sharp demarcation in the last five steps of the tonal scale, and is a distorted negative, but when it comes in register with the master negative, the conventional halftone negative, it creates an illusion of depth, of highlights, of feeling, that the original silver image has, whereas a conventional duotone has a flatness to it. Our formulation of inks plays a vital part in our reproduction, a vital part.

When the printing of a photographic book is discussed, the first name to invariably surface is that of Sid Rapoport. He's a legend in his own time. Beginning with the American edition of Robert Frank's **The Americans** in 1969, Sid has printed the work of virtually every major and minor photographer in the United States and the list would read like a Who's Who of American Photography. When I visited him he had, a few days before, finished Richard Avedon's new book, **Avedon On Fashion,** and showed me a magnum of Dom Perignon champagne with a tag on which Avedon had written, "To the Greatest, from the Greatest." I interviewed Sid Rapoport on June 16, 1978 in his office at the Rapoport Printing Corporation on Hudson Street in downtown New York City. The plant was buzzing with the typical hectic business routine of such an establishment. Several times Sid was asked for an opinion on a job and responded with a calm, calculated assurance. He's a man proud of his contribution to the photographic book and is largely responsible for establishing a standard of excellence by which all quality photographic books are judged.

Tom Dugan: How did you come to print photographic books? What is your relationship to the photographer and what is his responsibility to you?
Sid Rapoport: It was a culmination of several years of experiments. We had a new technique developed for the reproduction of photographs, which we were using at that time, for the pharmaceutical industry, which was very heavy into advertising; and when that business fell off considerably, we had to look for another avenue for our product. The photography book was a natural. We were able, at all times, to come up with, at first exceptional quality duotones using the fine screen, and then the development of the stonetone process. The first book we printed was Robert Frank's **The Americans.** Unfortunately, they wanted a copy of an already existing book that was printed in the gravure process in France, and we printed it very much with the same feeling of gravure, using the dull matt inks and coming off with a very formidable book. Since then we've found that the results are much better if we don't try to imitate gravure, but in essence, stand on our own feet. We get more out of it,

and we have much better translation of the photograph using our very specialized inks. Subsequent books to that — possibly the next two books, were also attempts at gravure imitation—and then along came **Light 7**, which was an *Aperture* book from Minor White, M.I.T. Press, and that was printed with all the brilliance, and all the clarity, and all the highlights, using our formulated inks. We've improved our technique since, and yet when I look back at the books we printed in that period, and compare with today, those books still stand up very well. They have a very distinct look. This goes back about ten years now. The number of books which we've printed, where the first year it may have been two titles, and the next year four titles, by 1970 we may have printed five titles. We're now probably printing as many as thirty or forty titles a year. Practically every known photographer has come through the shop in one way or the other. Vintage prints of Julia Cameron, Frederick Evans, Fox Talbot, this whole group of Jackson, Bell and Muybridge; we've literally worked with every conceivable known photographer. Vroman's Southwest, the period of 1900-1905; we've just finished the China book for *Aperture;* which is 1860-1905 albumen prints; Stieglitz's **Camera** (magazine) which are all gravures; we've reproduced (Edward) Curtis' work as well as a whole group of new photographers that entered the field. Ralph Gibson. We've worked along consistently, so I think we've developed an instinctive flair for intuitiveness in relation to a print. Whereas our final product hasn't changed so much, what has changed is that we've been able to speed up the technology. We've been able to automate the procedure more than what we had in the past.

TD: Did Robert Frank come here when you were doing his book?

SR: Yes, Robert Frank was here. We followed right up with Danny Lyon's **The Destruction of Lower Manhattan** and they both were here. It was the beginning of how to develop a relationship with a photographer. In many ways you learn to see through the photographer's eyes. We've had some cases in which we've had very, very difficult experiences with photographers who are looking for an exactitude which the process in itself can do, but the law of economics is such that the inflationary costs of producing a book today relies so much on being able to make the plates without any extra expenses, without having to take any extra time in the pressroom, and coming up with a 99% result. It's just when a photographer is looking for 105%, I say 105% because they're looking for something that's better than their print — then we run into difficulty. We run into what I may say is trying to do the impossible, and often enough we do it. But it turns me off in the sense that it's unprofitable. We take great pride in the books we do, and we'll work along with some of the more illustrious names, and go to these extremes, going one further on our own, and make a plate over. As our costs keep rising, we have to keep in mind that the public will not pay the additional cost on that book. We have just finished a superb book called, **Avedon on Fashion,** which will retail at $50, and it's a sizeable run and it is the state of the art. I never appreciated Richard Avedon as a photographer until I was able to see his work from the early fifties right through his *Harper's Bazaar* and *Vogue* days. It's an exciting book, but the exactitude of translation and the problems represented were enormous. It took us six weeks to print the book. How many people can afford to pay that kind of money for a book? It's the kind of thing we're faced with. There's a thing happening in the book publishing industry today which is very critical, and it has to do with the inflationary price of paper, binding, labor, combined with the mass production methods such as web printing. Doing books in large runs has not been successful. I'm not too familiar with the marketing of the Time-Life series or their success. That product is not up to the par of an organization like *Aperture*, which has a very high standard. One thing I can say for *Aperture*, they're very hard buyers and, at the same time, very demanding in their quality, and will not compromise. To get the best, the difference in price is not much. A book that costs us two dollars to manufacture, just the printing end of it, will probably retail in the area of $35 or $40 which is really ridiculous, and the difference in price of getting that book printed, second-rate, that two dollar book can probably be printed for 75¢ or 60¢; so the difference between a magnificently printed book and an ordinary printed book is maybe $1.25. That's the sum we're talking about — and yet that escalates up into the final range enormously. If a publisher has to pay $2 for just the printing of a book with the binding, the paper, and the editorial material, he has a cost of manufacturing a book somewhere in the neighborhood of $7, and that book has to retail for somewhere in the area of $45 or $50. It's one of the flaws in our whole book printing system that the very heart of the book, the printing, is probably the lowest single cost factor. Paper usually costs more than the printing, and binding costs more than the printing of the book. It's a case of the tail wagging the dog. And we're getting a lot of substandard photography books for that difference. We're getting a lot of works that are reproduced where the artist is not getting a fair deal. His work is not translated as it should be. We're unfortunate in the sense that we are in the heart of Manhattan, New York City. Our overhead is considerably more than a Vermont printer would be, and we have to contend with certain manning complements which are set forth by the union, and our price is governed in that sense. I've done everything I can to fight the inflationary cycle by updating equipment, by automating the process, by taking every conceivable step of systemization that could be done, and yet the spiraling costs still continue. Now the so-called prestige publisher is beginning to back away, in essence, to sacrifice a certain amount of quality in meeting a marketing price. Some of the museums won't do it; they'll still insist on a fairly good facsimile reproduction. *Aperture* made an effort at having books printed in another method, and the results just weren't there. You do not get impact, translation, or the overall consistency of page, after page, after page, of a book that's been printed here.

TD: Do you believe it's necessary for all photographers to have that quality of reproduction?

SR: No, it isn't. The first thing a publisher and a photographer have to ask: do they want to pay more for that book? In many cases, a photographer would do so, and the money comes out of his own pocket. It's come down to: if a photographer is a big name (Irving Penn, Richard Avedon, Ansel Adams, Eugene Smith, Jerry Uelsmann, Paul Caponigro), any one of the great names will not compromise and they have the clout to say, "I won't accept a substandard printing of my work." A new photographer has no choice; he has to go along with the publisher. In some of our cases, invariably, the better known names will have it in their contracts with the publisher that it has to be printed here. It's helpful to us. Book printing is very time consuming; it's a labor of love by the people working here. It is not a profitable enterprise to produce a photography book that is absolutely demanding. The time and hours that go into it are enormous.

TD: What's the smallest run you would do?

SR: We would do any quantity, it makes no difference. It's just that a short run is prohibitively expensive. We've had runs as short as five hundred, but when you consider your plate costs plus your make-ready time, you can print a thousand for practically the same price as the five hundred. Your run-on rate is where the difference lies. A publisher who can market profitably, and can afford our work, will try to escalate the run at a given point and try to get it past 17,000, 20,000, 25,000 copies. Then the price per book unit comes down. Some of the books we've printed have run into big numbers as far as reprints. Some of them have had seven, eight, or nine printings. **Diane Arbus** is probably on the 11th printing right now. Some of the reprints are 50,000, 60,000 or 70,000 and really belong on a web press to save that money. A web press would bring it in at maybe 50¢ a book less, and yet the publisher is insisting on an exact duplicate, therefore they can't go to the web. The thing that is disappearing from the book market is that deluxe book. Many of these superb books were on remainder lists and were all snapped up. These books can never be printed again. Those superb gravure books that were printed years ago in Switzerland — the cost of doing a book like that is so prohibitive that probably none will ever be done again. A book like Irving Penn's **Moments Preserved,** a whole series of books that were printed in the 1930's and late 1940's. The devaluation of the dollar has had a drastic effect on the publication of the book. It's had a devastating effect on the sheet-fed gravure industry of Europe. Many an artist used to demand that their book be printed by sheet-fed gravure, now it's out of the question. It just can't be done. A lot of that business has been gravitating toward our shop; it's interesting. I know our results are closer — you can't use the word "better", because gravure has a certain feeling of its own — and a more realistic translation of the photograph than gravure. We have a choice of a wider variety of stocks. We don't have to compromise on the dull mattness of the gravure ink. We can have a luminosity to it, where gravure has to be varnished if they want a luminosity. We don't like to varnish our work; we're very much against it. We get our brilliance from our inks.

TD: Is that the difference between Stonetone and duotone, the inks?

SR: It's one of the differences. The Stonetone process depends very much on a whole different procedure. It's the original film, the screens, the nonscreen image, the method in the making of the plates, the inks, and the procedure on the press. It's a whole system, rather than one thing by itself. The Stonetone negative, which is a secondary negative, is not a conventional screened negative; it has a very sharp demarcation in the last five steps of the tonal scale, and is a distorted negative, but when it comes in register with the master negative, the conventional halftone negative, it creates an illusion of depth, of highlights, of feeling, that the original silver image has, whereas a conventional duotone has a flatness to it. Our formulation of inks plays a vital part in our reproduction — a vital part.

TD: If a photographer wanted you to use random dot instead of the conventional halftone screen, would you do that?

SR: When you say a random dot, Stonetone I refer to as a random grain. We have a patent on the random grain, which is what the Stonetone process is. It would be difficult to do both images using the random grain. It's much better to combine the two, to use a 200, 250 or a 300 line screen, and then the random grain. The random grain is much finer than the screen. It's maybe the equivalent of 400, 500, 600 line; it's extremely fine. It's almost like the grain of the film. We have refined the Stonetone screen. It is in essence a nonscreened, screened image, and we've refined it to the point where we could use it in four-color reproduction by itself, without the conventional screen, and that would be called random grain. I don't see any advantage in it, and it is more difficult and costly to do, than using it properly with a conventional screen. In our color work, we did one book about five or six years ago, called **This Living Reef,** by Douglas Faulkner; it's our one great splash into color. I feel it's probably the greatest book ever printed in color. There are none available. The publisher had a fracus and remaindered the entire thing. It's a crime. The work and effort that went into the printing of that book is beyond anything that has ever been tried before. That is a random grain mixture of color. Half of it is random grain, half of it is conventional screen, and it's combined together in such a way that it's ingenious. It has a depth and a richness of color that is superb. We're getting into that area now where time and labor is so costly that we can't afford to do anything that way any more. We can't afford six-color printing. It's only for the institution that is demanding the ultimate, or something financed by the state, or a grant, where somebody wants to achieve a real facsimile effect, can we begin to entertain the idea of those types of separations. The Douglas Faulkner book is a 200, 250 line master screen, along with a supplementary random screen of every color. Yet the price that it was done for at that time was so reasonable. To try to do it today, with our labor costs up 50% since then, just wouldn't work. We're relying completely on the age of electronics in color separation, and the one thing that amazingly, instead of going up, goes down, is the cost of color separations.

TD: Do you do many books in color?

SR: We have one coming up very shortly — a Polaroid SX-70 book from Lustrum Press. We've done several museum books. Actually color is not, surprisingly, that much more expensive to reproduce than black and white. Just an offhand figure, we're talking about $100 per page more for printing in color.

TD: What percentage of the final cost is that?

SR: It depends on the number of pages in the book. The paper remains constant, the binding remains constant, but it means that the price of the printing may be doubled, so the percentage of the actual book is not much. It may be a difference of only 10-15% more for the actual book. The constants are there — paper and binding. Most of our books run on multicolored presses even though we're just running the two blacks. The difference in presswork is not that high, it's just the difference in platemaking and separation costs.

TD: Do you have favorite books?

SR: Over the years you develop a certain number of favorites. It's odd that the books which I really felt would be great winners were not. When I first printed the (Diane) Arbus book, I didn't see how in the world that would be one of the great sellers, but it is. I printed a book of David Plowden's called **Bridges,** which I had great admiration for because of the text and the real beauty of the photographs, and the time, effort, and love that went into making that book — and it never went into a second printing. It's a magnificent book. Another book I had a great feeling for was a book I printed for Susan Hall and Bob Adelman called **Down Home.** At that time I felt it was the state of the art, and it still is.

TD: That book was remaindered.

SR: Well, it was actually printed to be remaindered, which is an odd thing. It's an excellent book. It was one of my favorites. **Walker Evans,** which we did for The Museum of Modern Art, did have a second printing, and has always been a favorite of mine. **Looking at Photographs** (John Szarkowski) has been a favorite of mine. There really isn't any such thing as favorites because some I shy away from because I know the work and difficulty of doing it. They're all favorites, in a certain sense, some in particular, and it's just odd that the ones which I picked as winners did not do well. I liked that David Plowden book very much. I'm very disappointed in that; I've never even seen it in a book shop.

TD: Do you prefer documentary photography to art photography?

SR: Documentary photography can certainly be art photography. Plowden's book, **Bridges,** is art, and it has a delightful text to go with it. Nancy Serkin's book on

Colonial New England is a book of the same nature, which I'm very fond of. I didn't appreciate the way the book was bound; I think the binder did a poor job. The book is all made up of spreads, and the backbone is so tight that the book doesn't open up flat, and suffers. But the book was never really marketed, and it's a beautiful, beautiful book. I've had any number of favorites, and they have not been successful. They represent a great labor of love and production, in which the artist is involved, the pressroom is involved, and the final book is quite something. A lot depends on the publisher, and how he markets it.

TD: Do you admire books by other printers? Thomas Todd or Meriden?

SR: Not really, no. I admire them for a certain degree of professionalism, and look at them in that sense. Many times, without knowing the name of the printer, there are editions that I've really looked at, and I've liked the whole feeling. Many times I'll have the feeling just a little bit of a heavy hand has been used — the delicacy is gone. Maybe it's an unfounded criticism on my part. You can never really judge. You look at a book and your eye adjusts to it immediately, and it looks good. It's only when you have something that you can compare it with side by side, page by page, that you realize the difference. The eye is not that great an instrument. It's tricked and fooled very easily. It's only in comparison, or knowing the work itself, or having an intuitive feeling for it, that you develop the instincts as to what the achievement is. Some of the books that I've seen Meriden produce I have a very pleasant feeling about, others not at all. There is definitely an intuitive grasp of what happens from the time you make the film, to making the plates, to putting it on the press, and it's that combined system that really makes the book.

TD: Do you have favorite photographers over the years?

SR: Not really, in that sense. I've reached the point where I know almost all of them, and to say I have favorite ones would be a little unfair. I enjoy working with Avedon immensely because of his, of all things, enthusiasm; his boundless energy. I've enjoyed working with Ansel Adams, who has a language all his own in describing what he's looking for in a print's reproduction. I enjoyed working with Paul Strand, who also had a language all his own. In working with these people, it rubs off. I imagined myself a photographer years ago; I am a photographer basically, although ever since I started printing photography books, I probably haven't picked up a camera.

New York City
June 16, 1978

Other books published by Light Impressions Corporation
and available exclusively through them:

HANDBOOK FOR CONTEMPORARY PHOTOGRAPHY, *Arnold Gassan*
THE GUM BICHROMATE BOOK, *David Scopick*
PHOTOGRAPHY: CURRENT PERSPECTIVES, *Ed., Jerome Leibling*
PERCEPTION AND PHOTOGRAPHY, *Richard D. Zakia*

Upcoming Fall 1979:

THE ALBUMEN & SALTED PAPER BOOK, *James Reilly*
PERCEPTUAL QUOTES FOR PHOTOGRAPHERS, *Richard D. Zakia*

Write for free catalog:

LIGHT IMPRESSIONS CORPORATION
Box 3012
Rochester, New York 14614